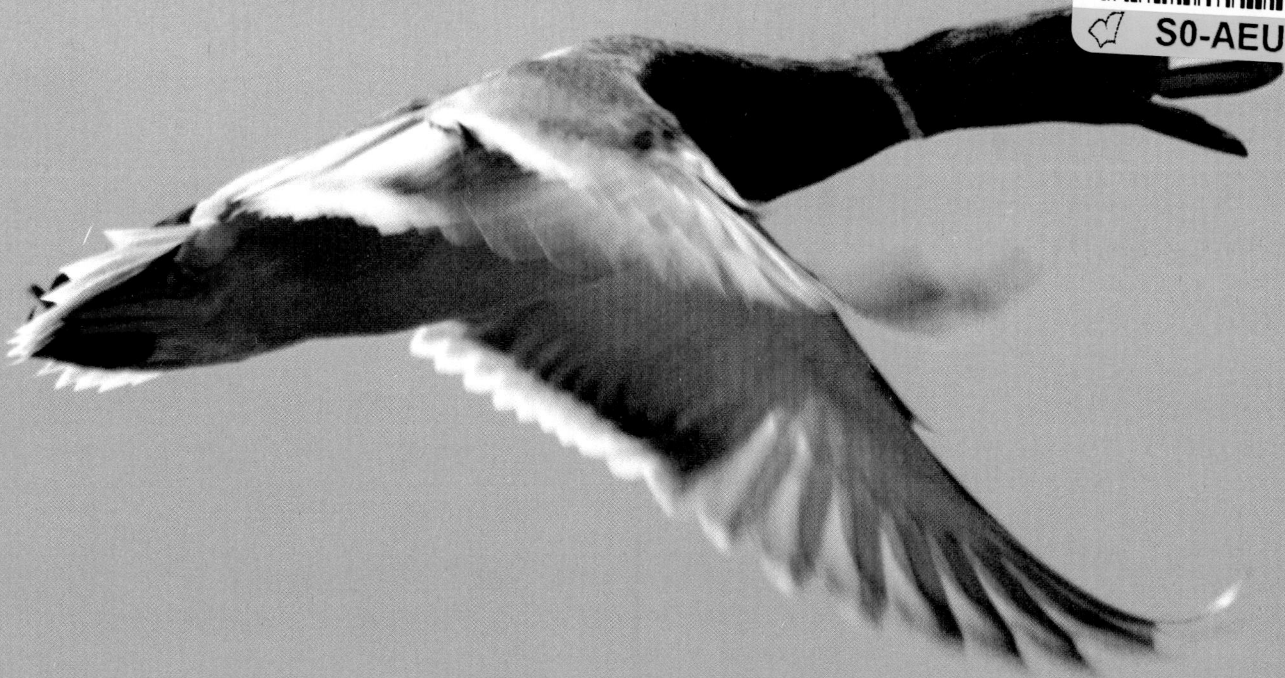

Drakes

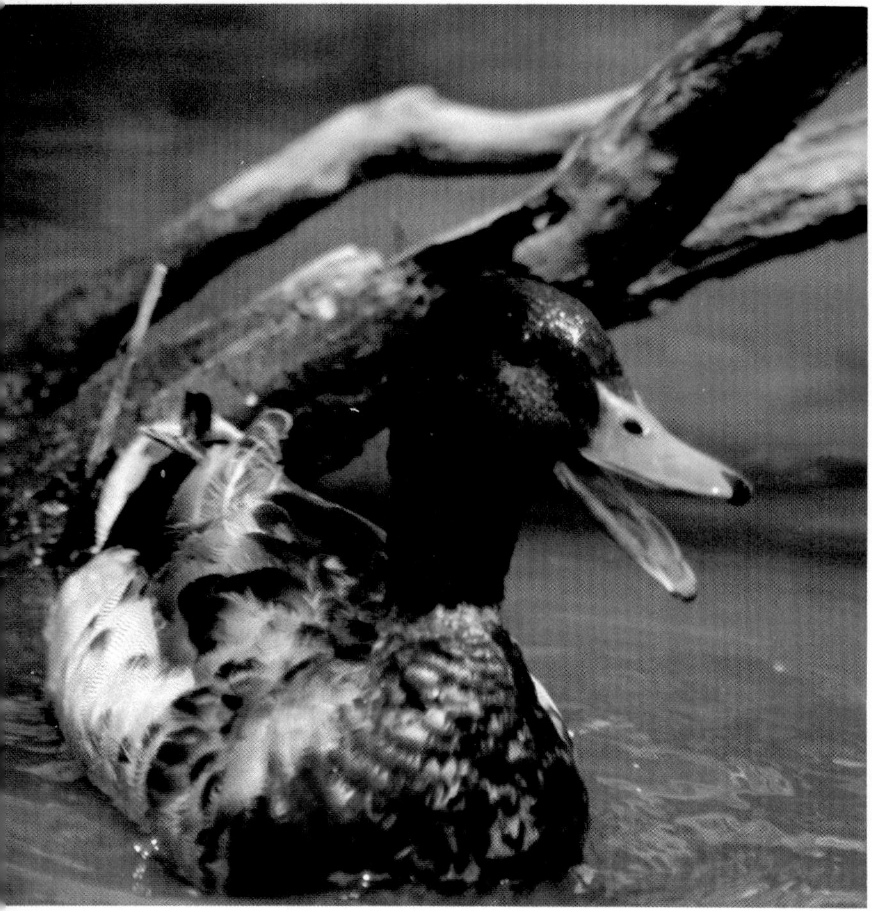

Library of Congress Catalog Card Number: 87-62513
ISBN: 0-88740-116-3

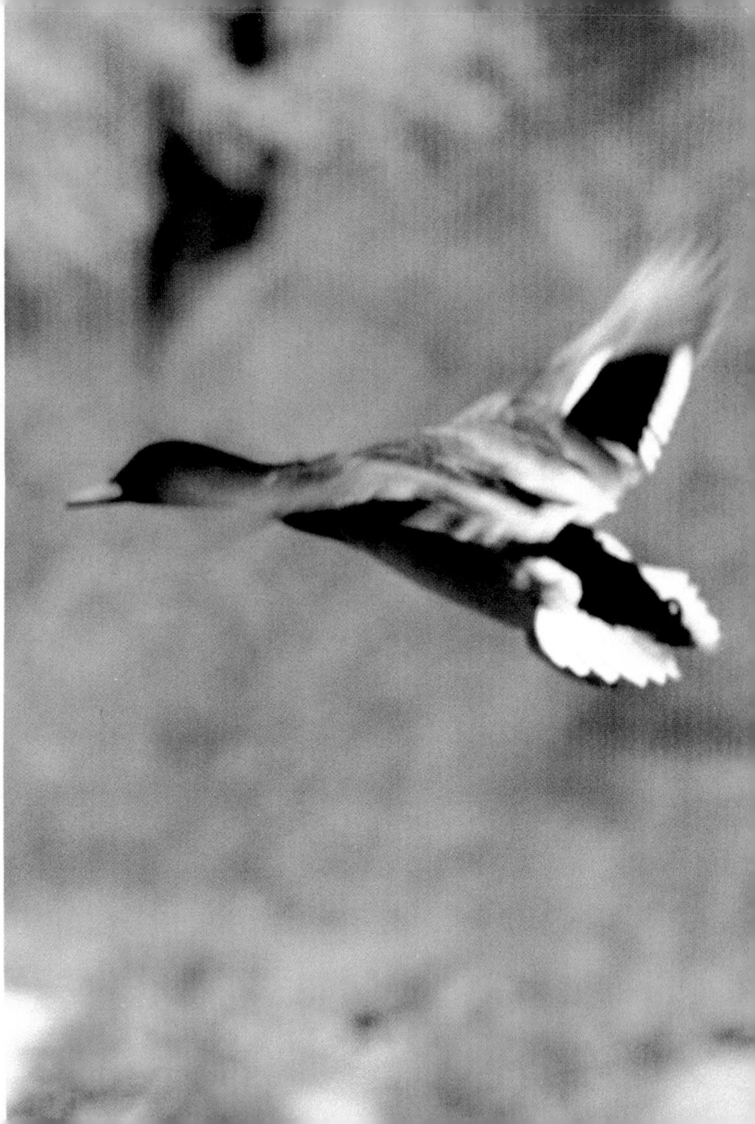

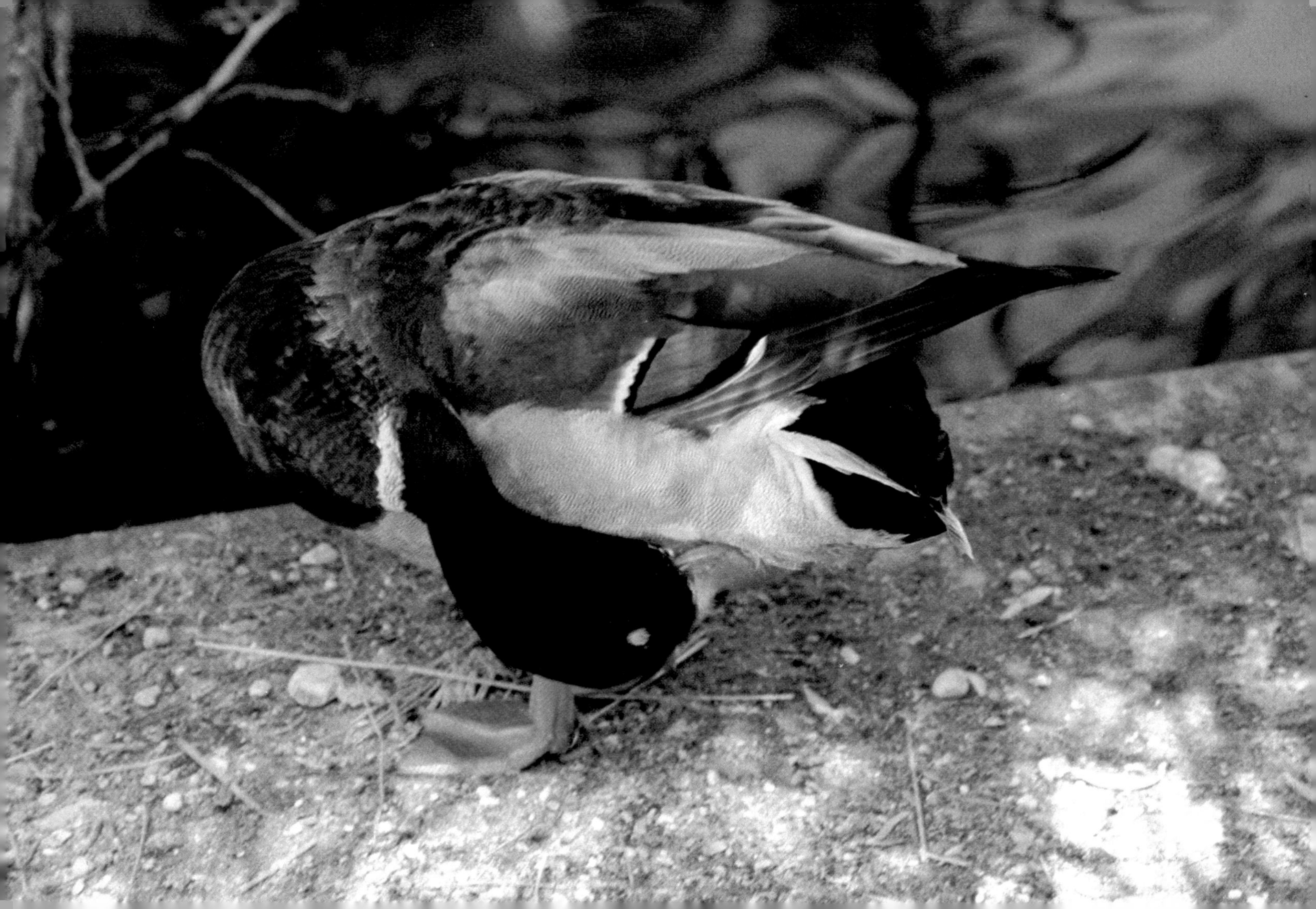

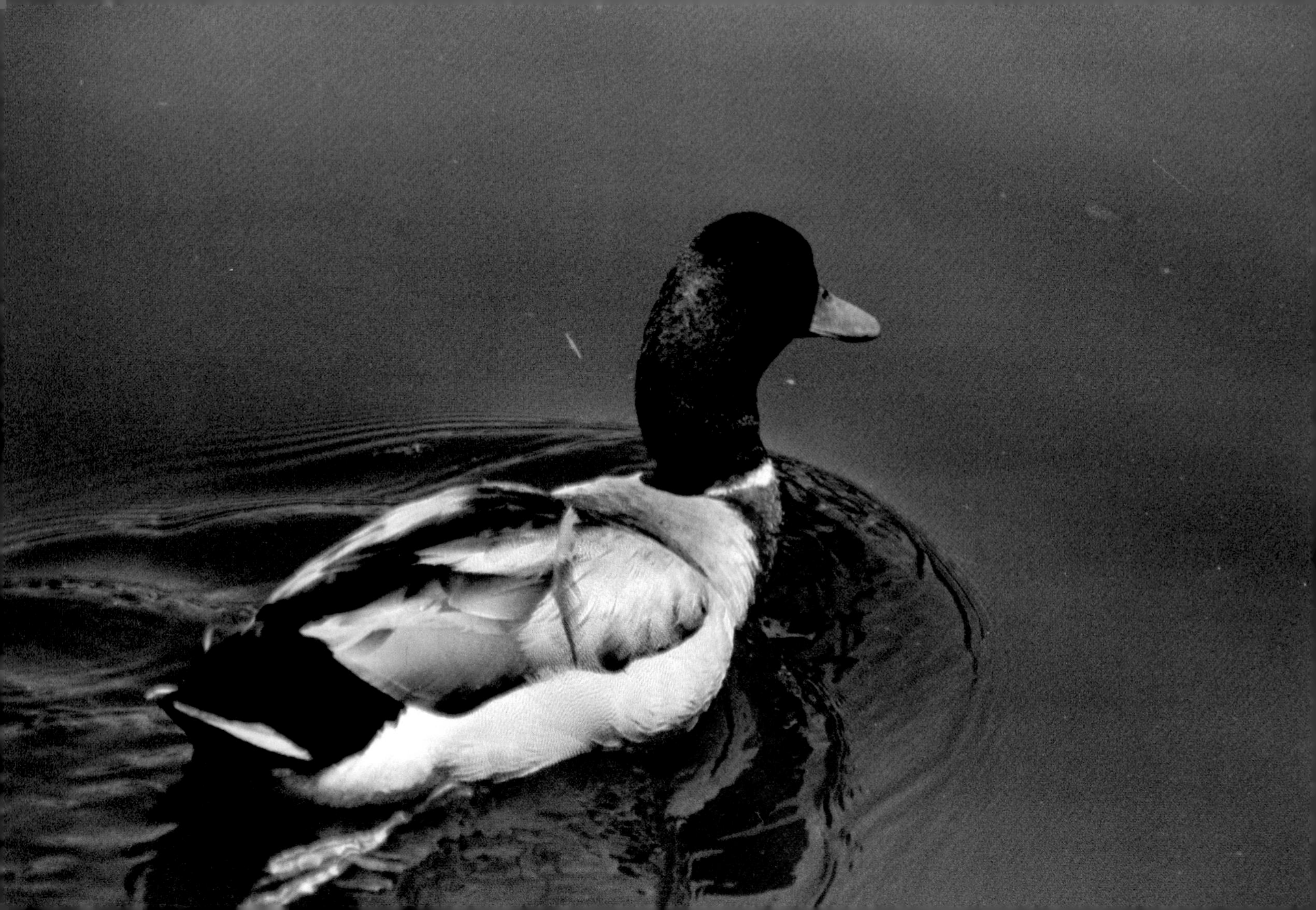

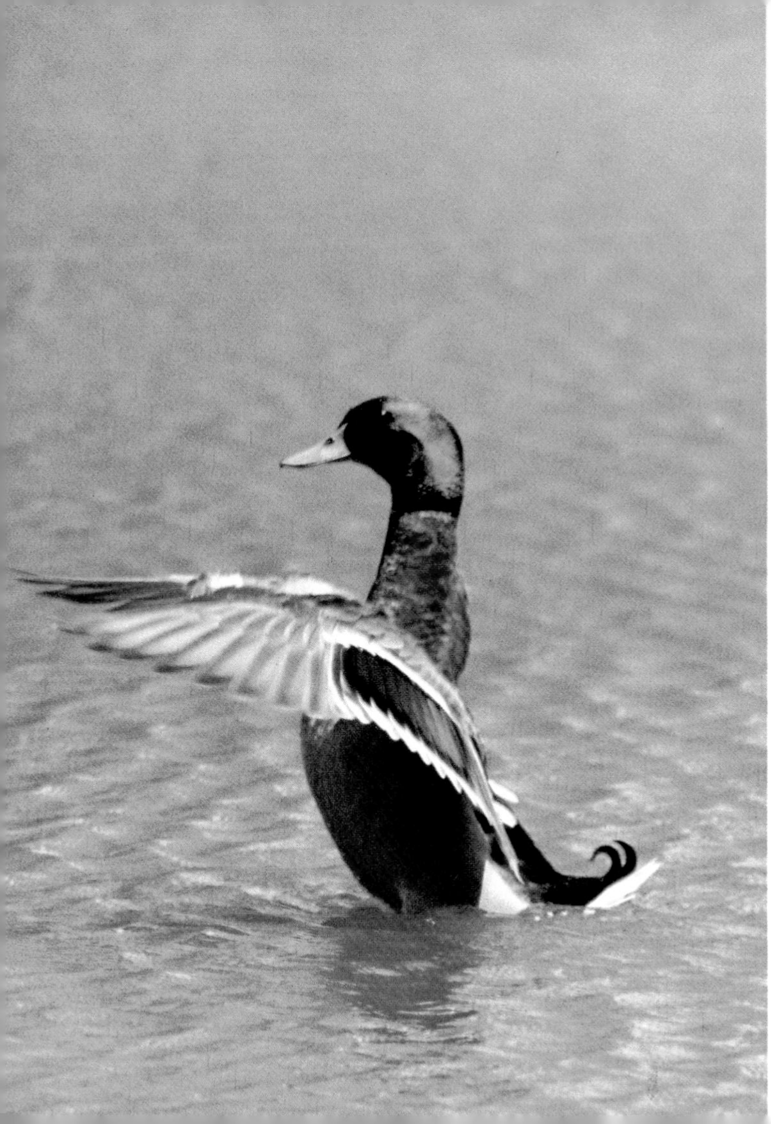

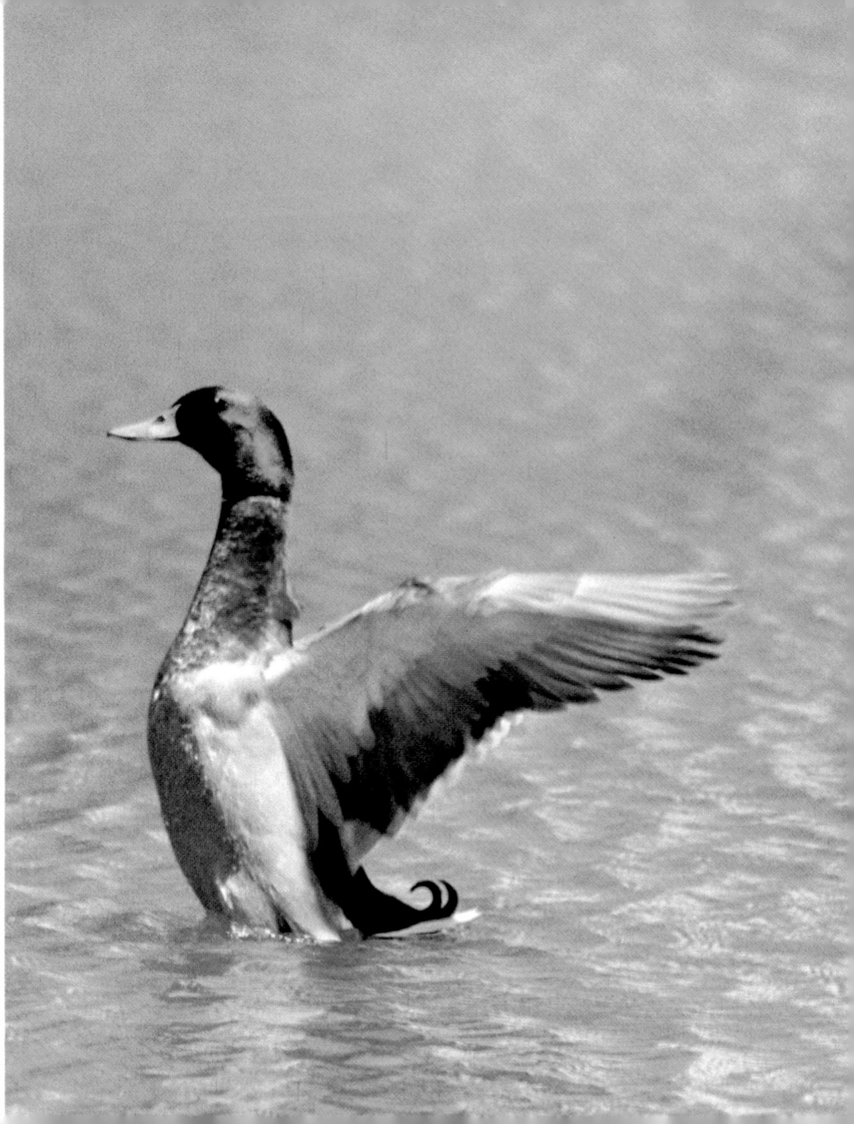

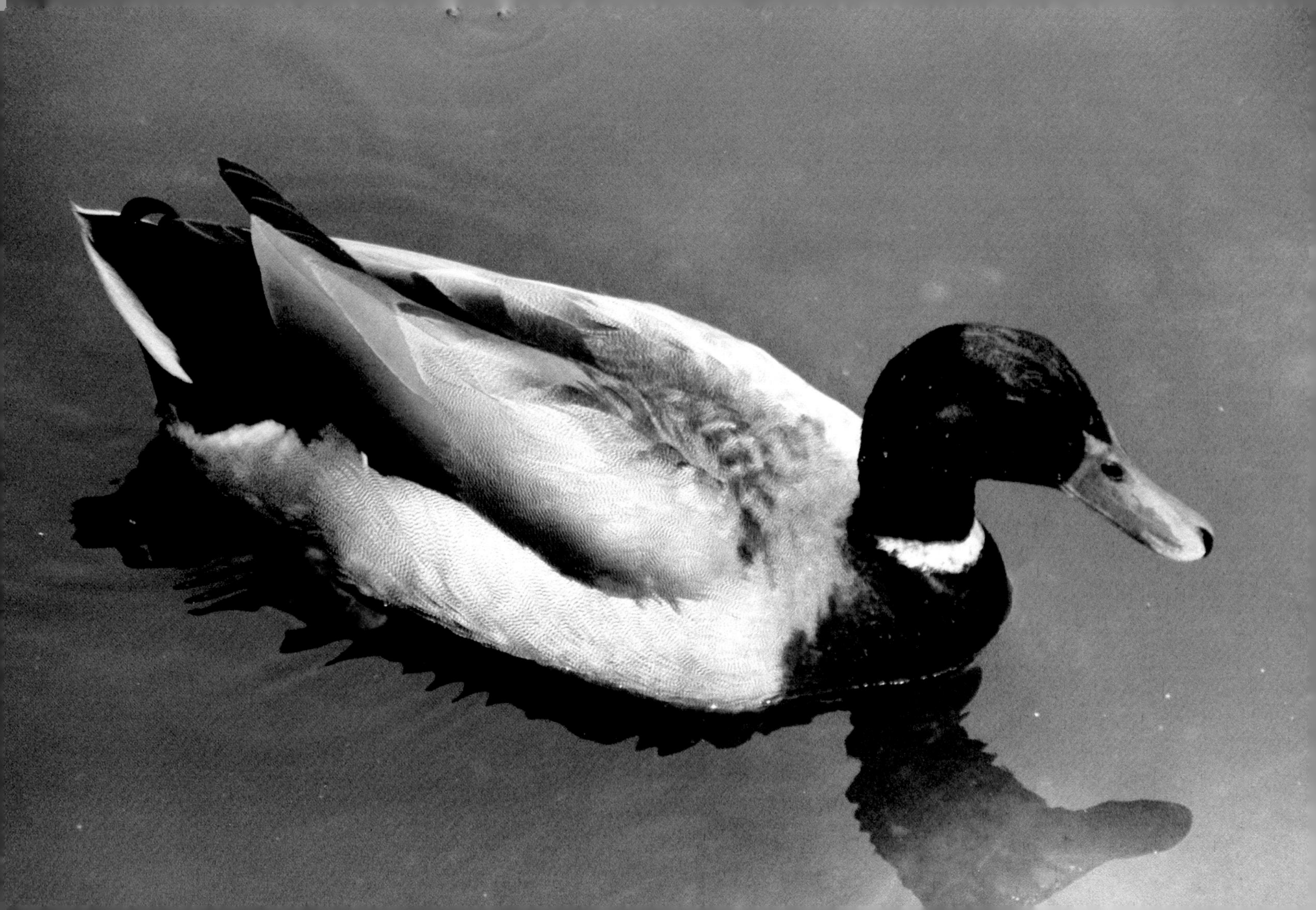

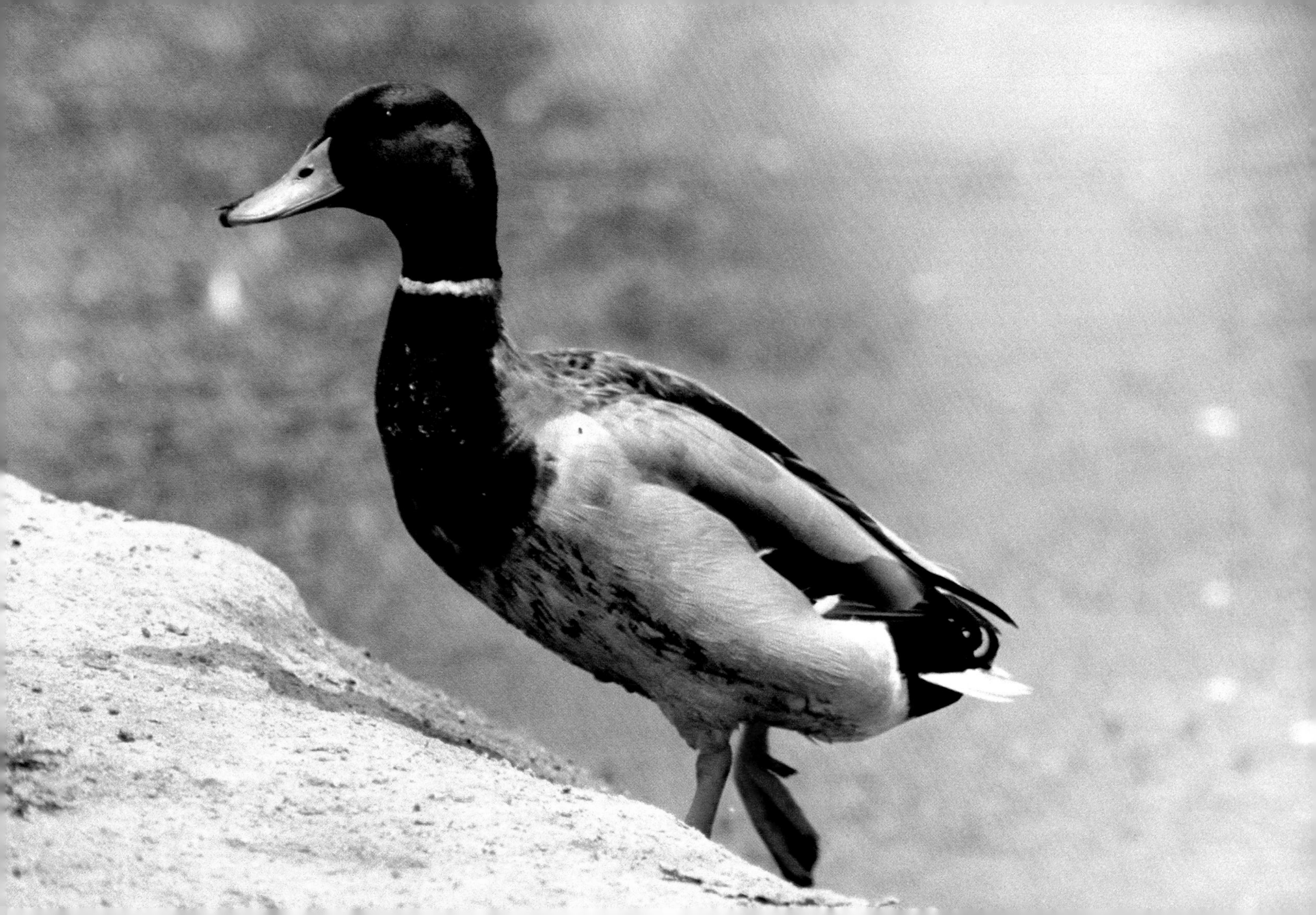

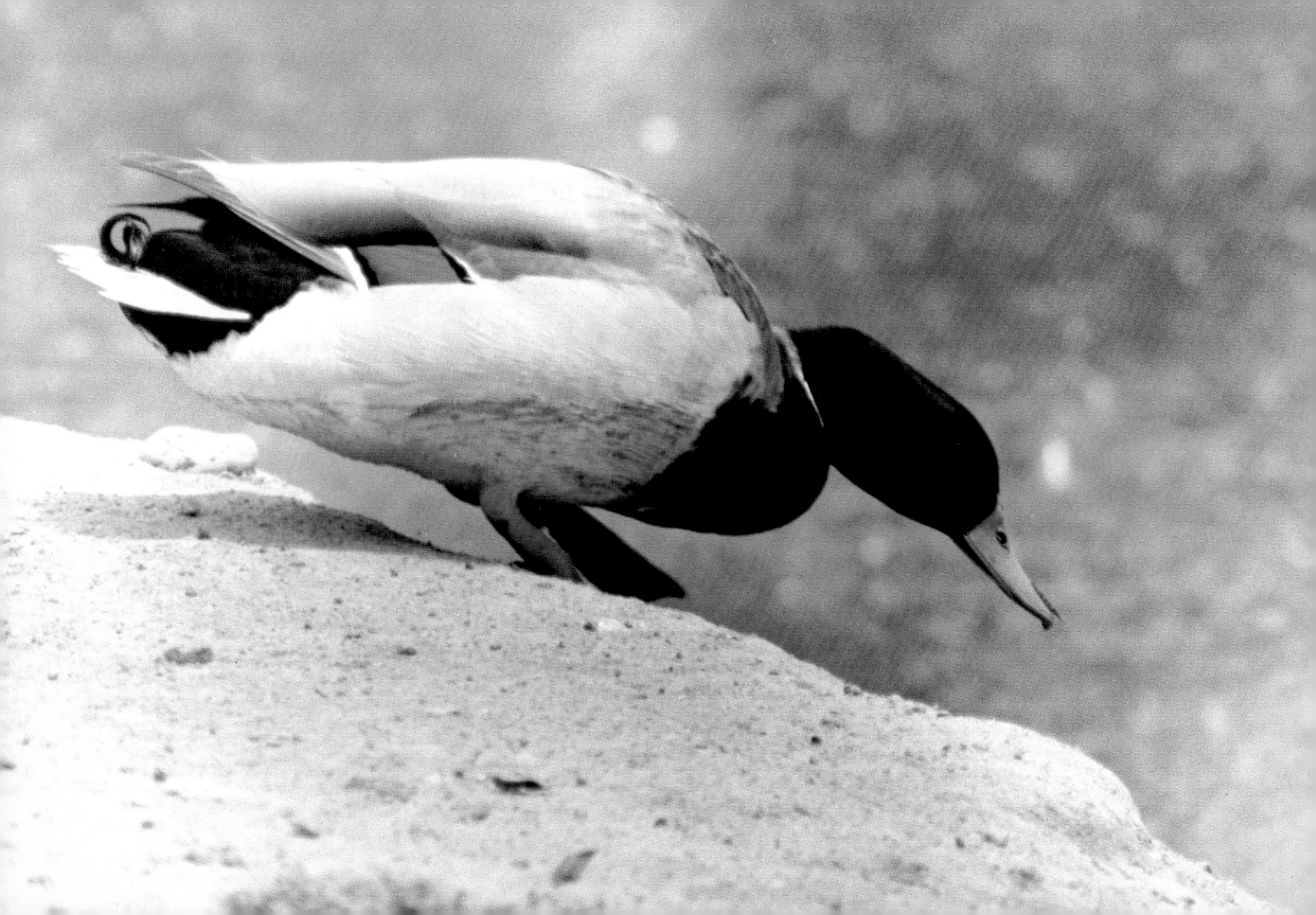

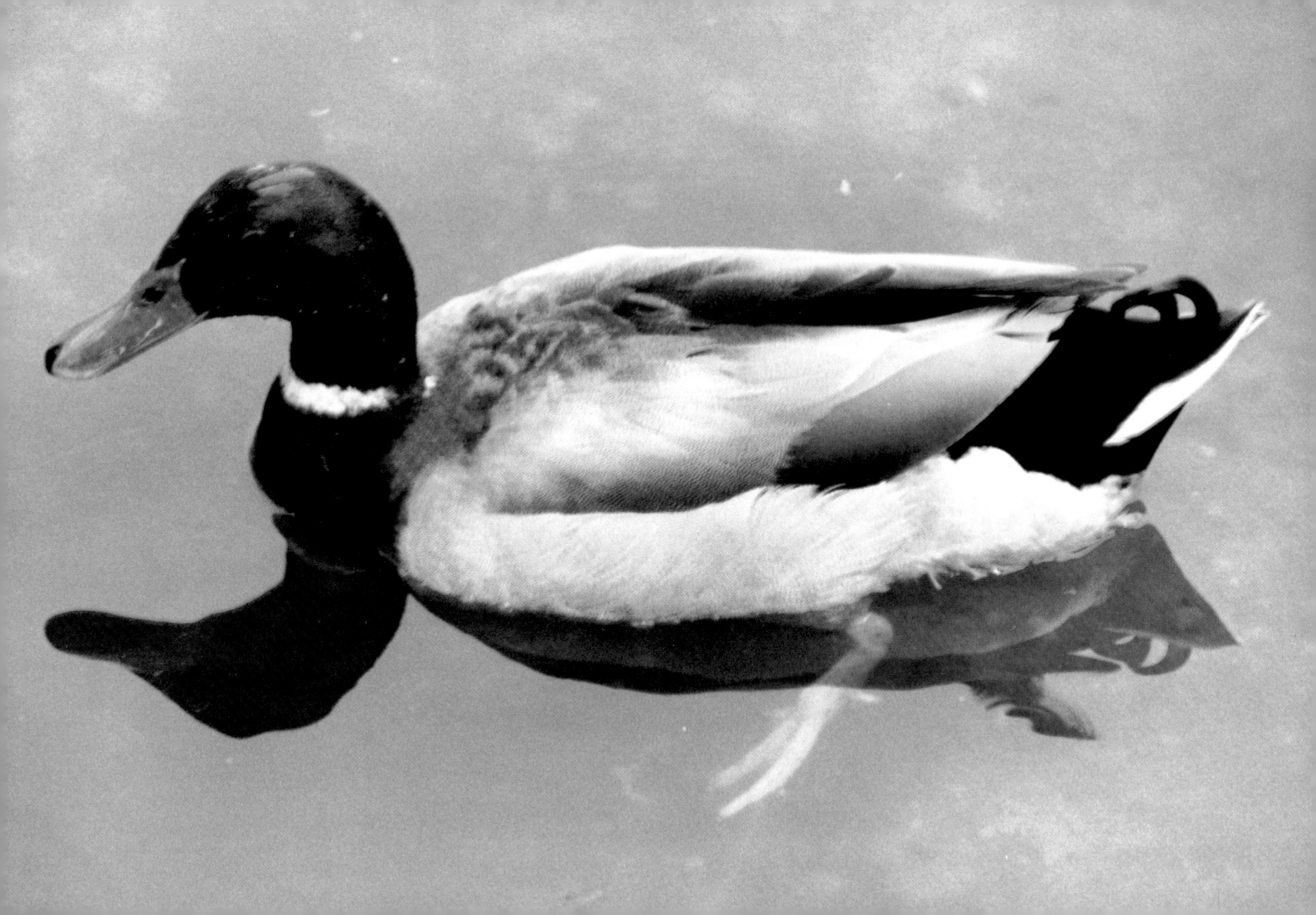

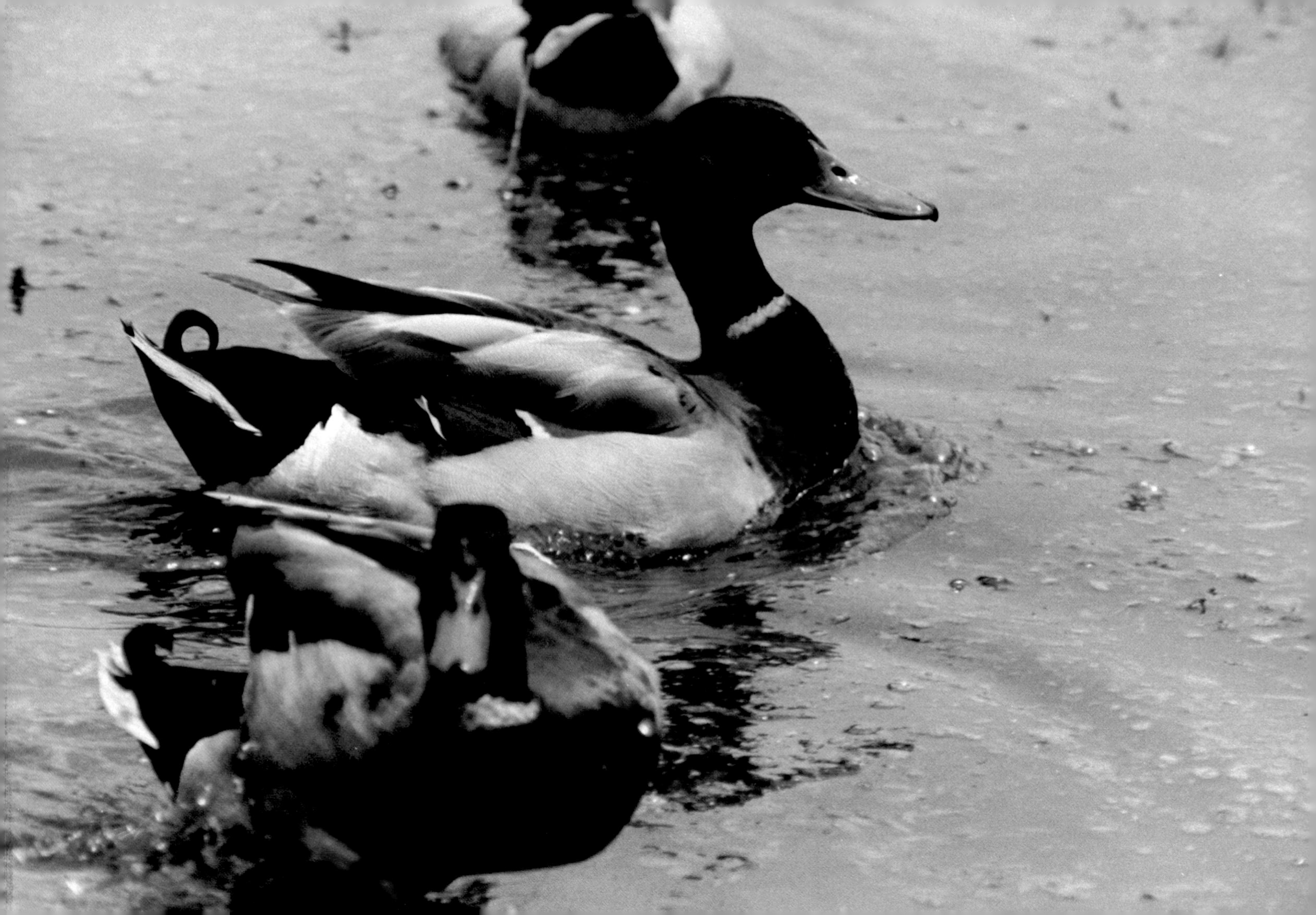

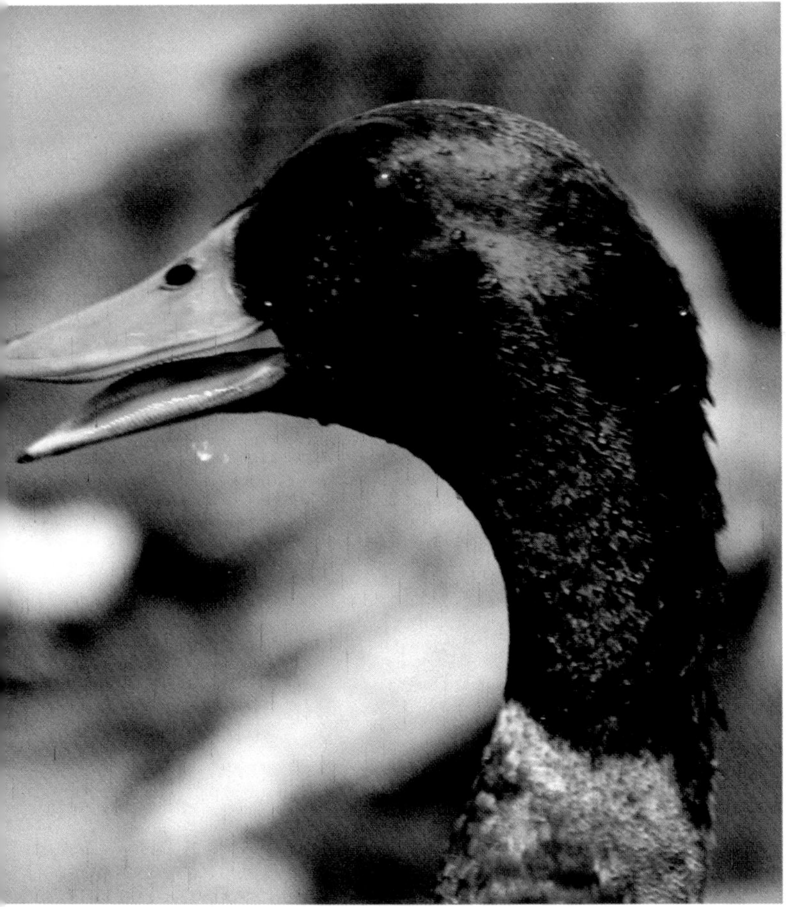
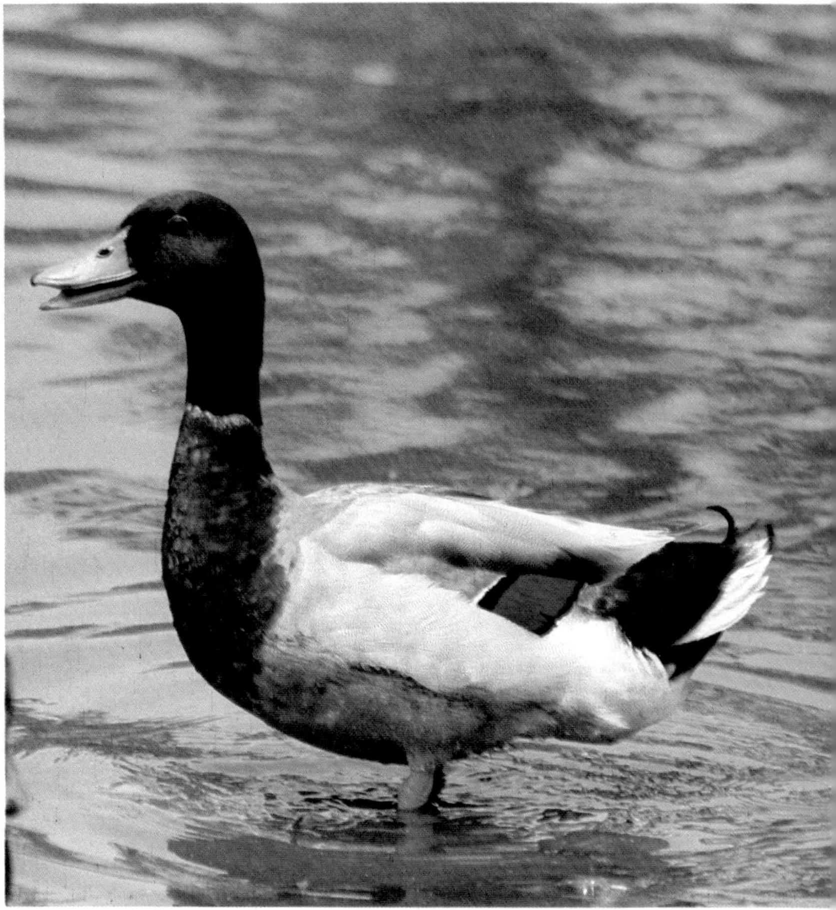

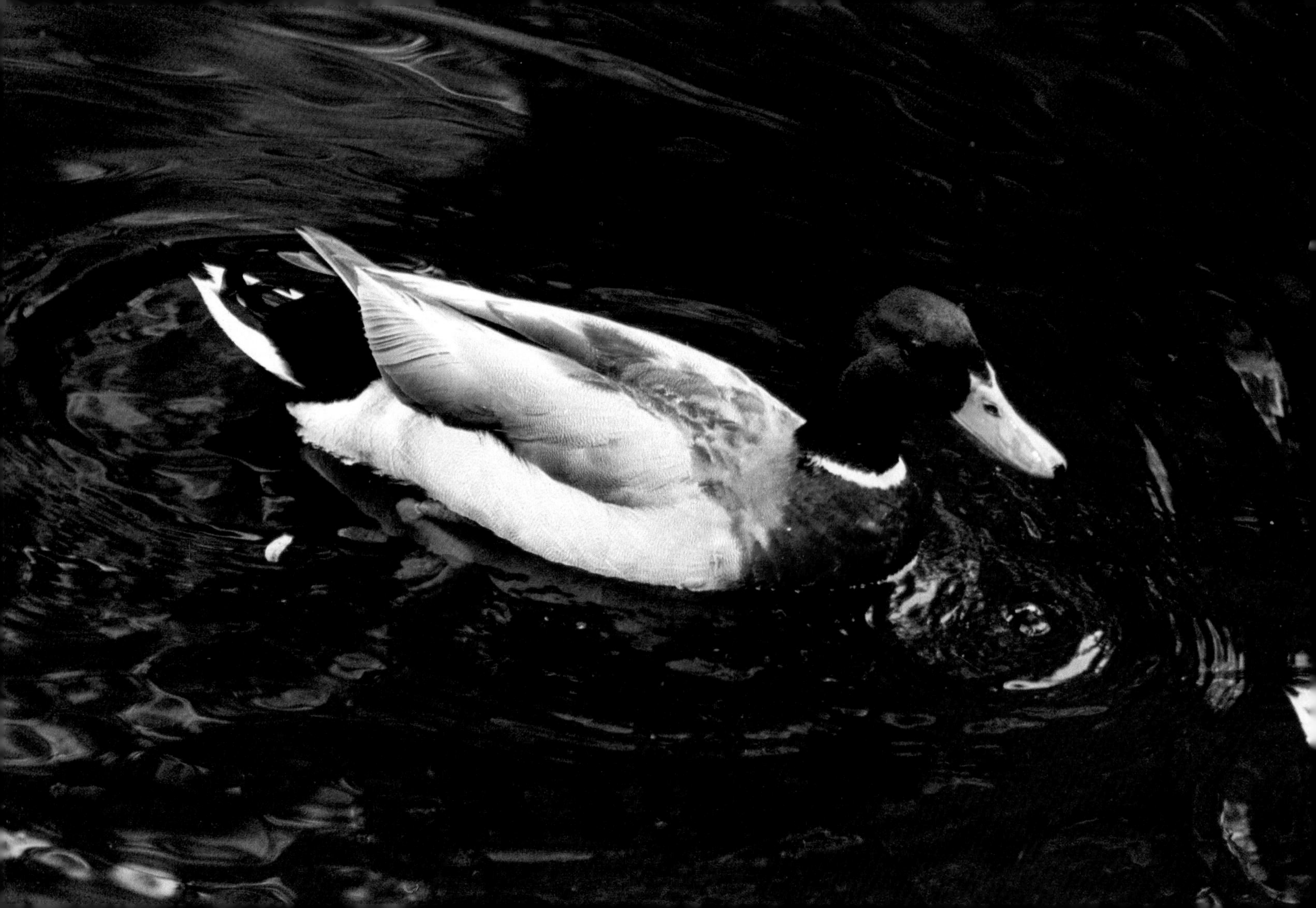

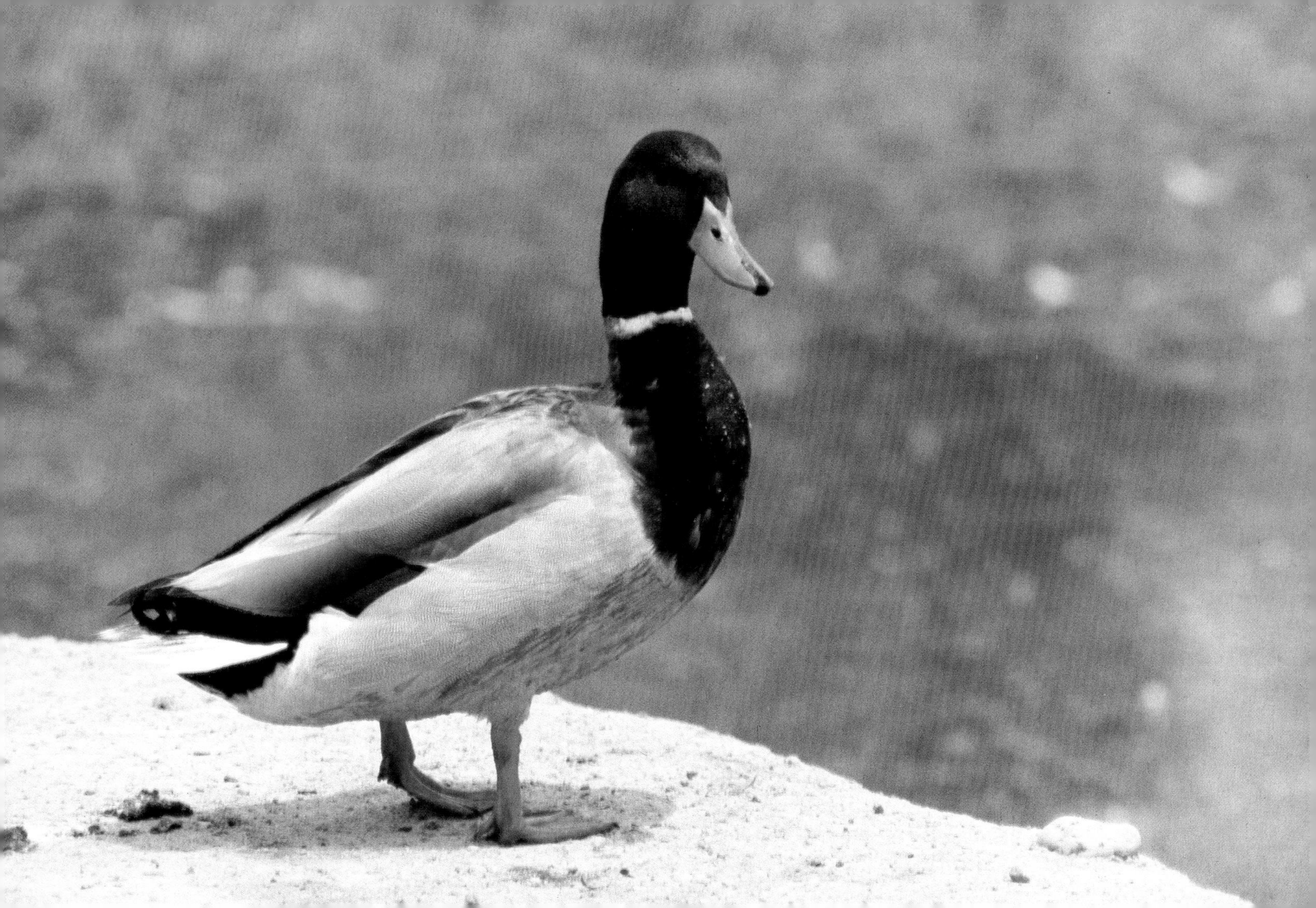

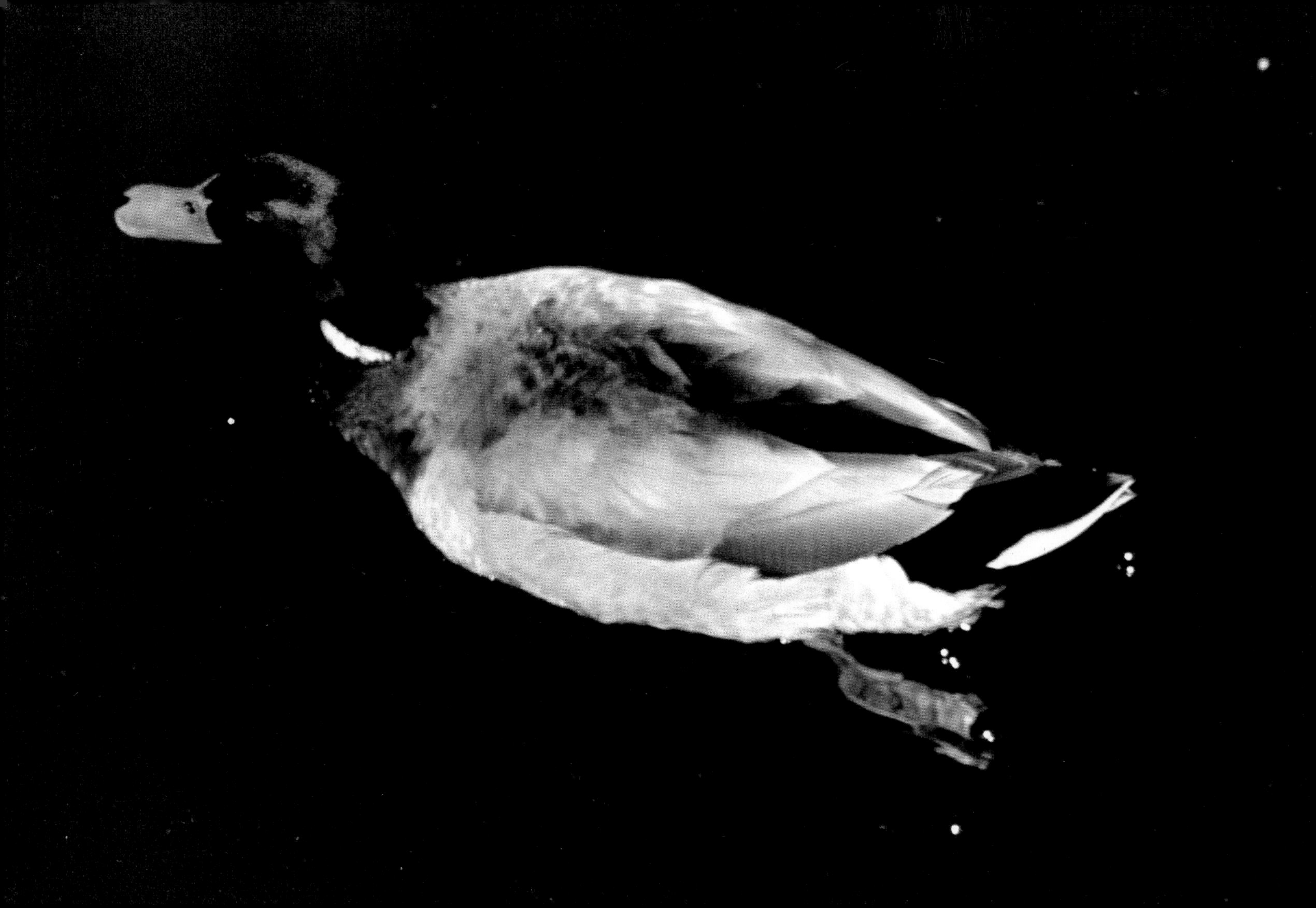

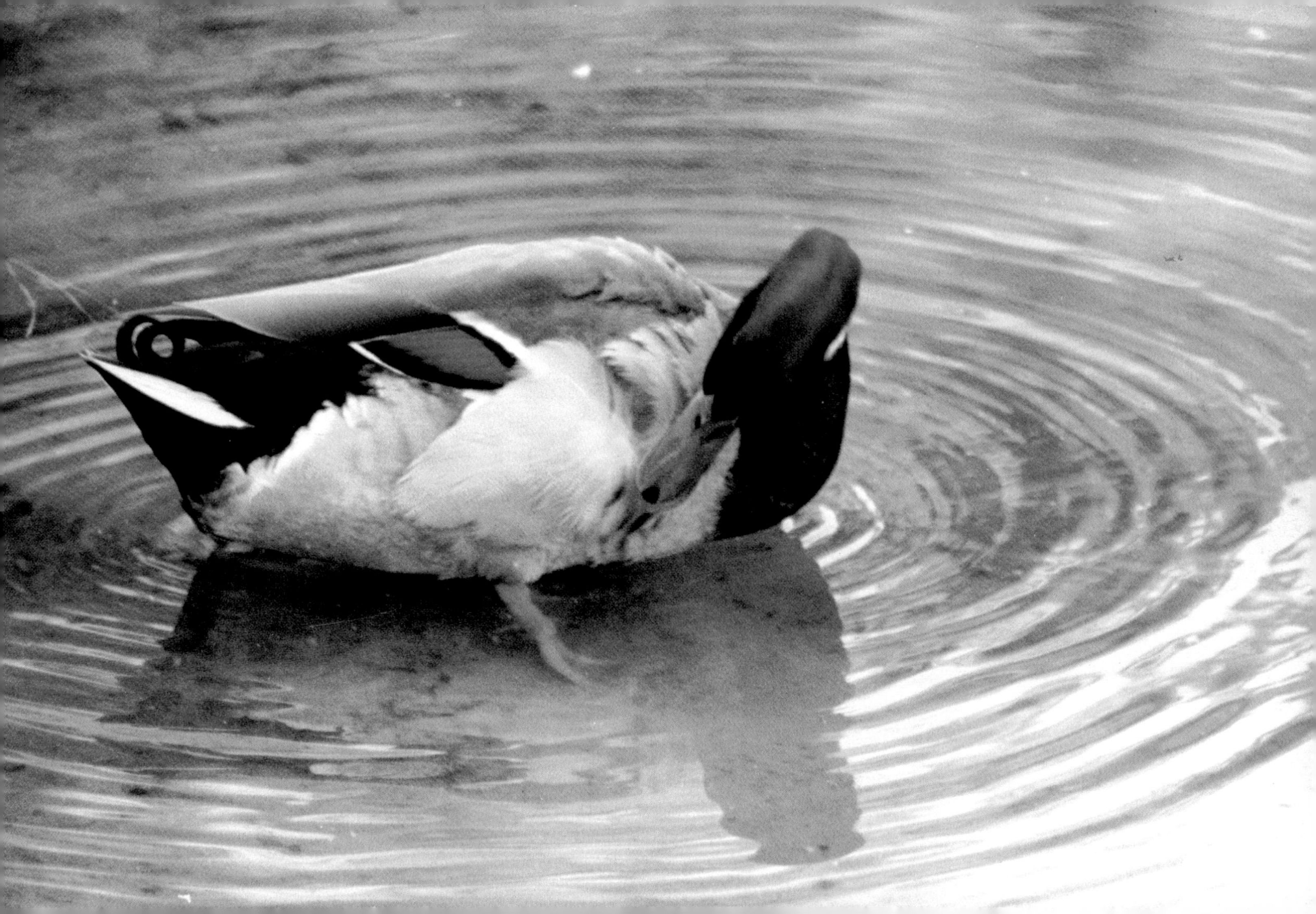

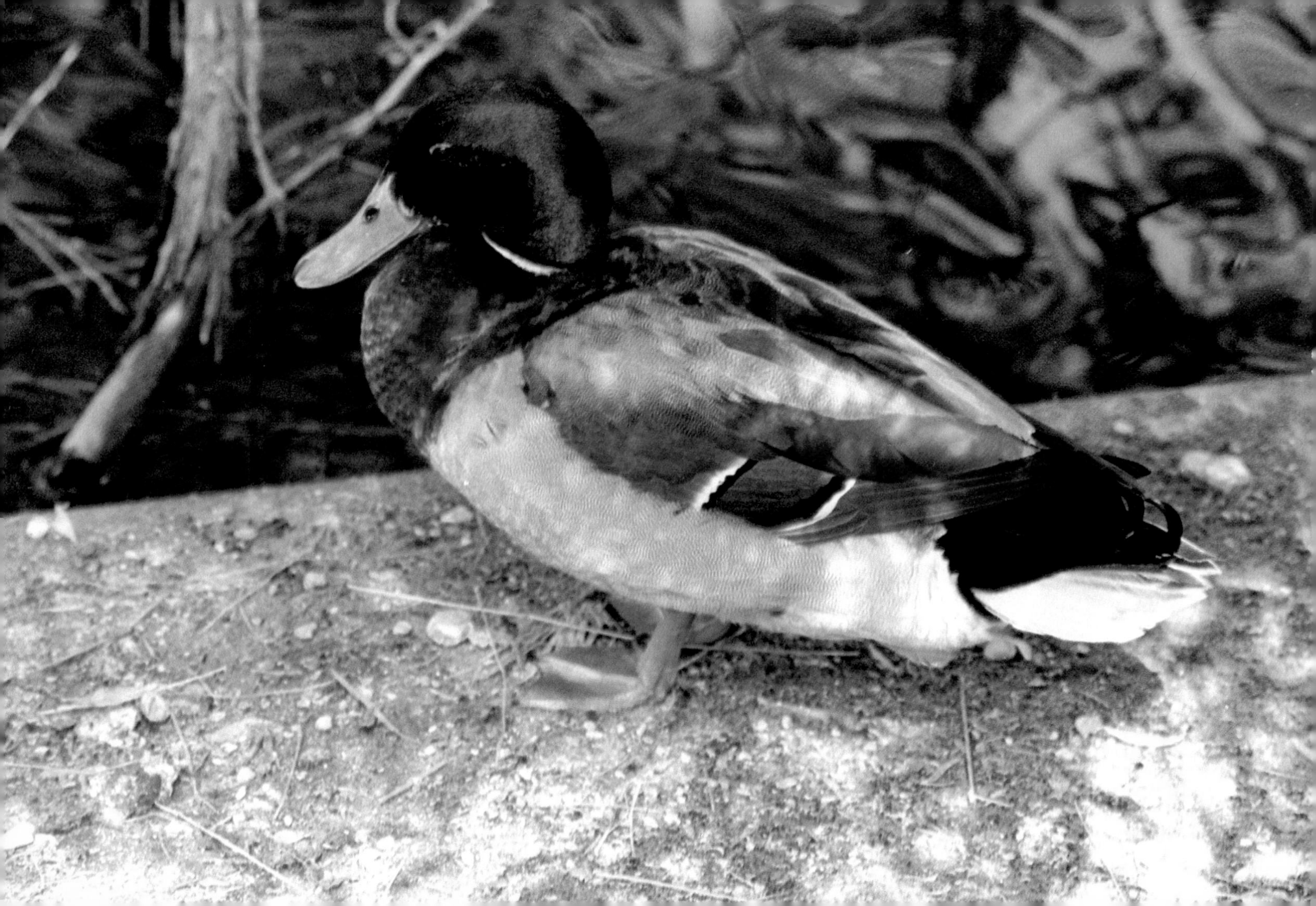

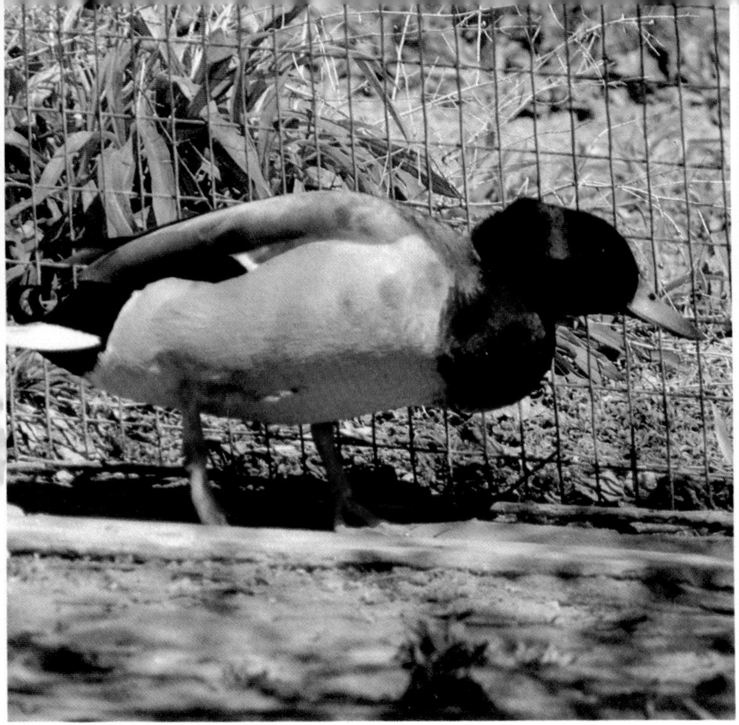

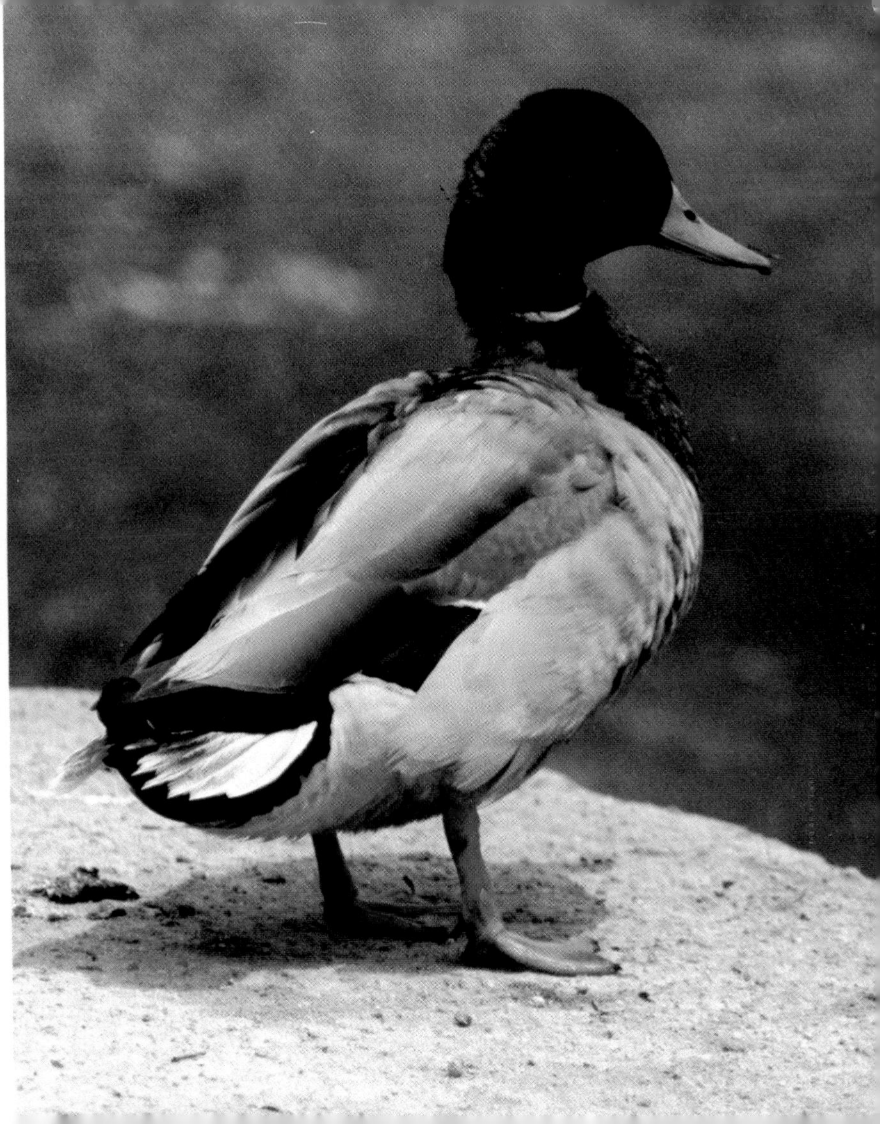

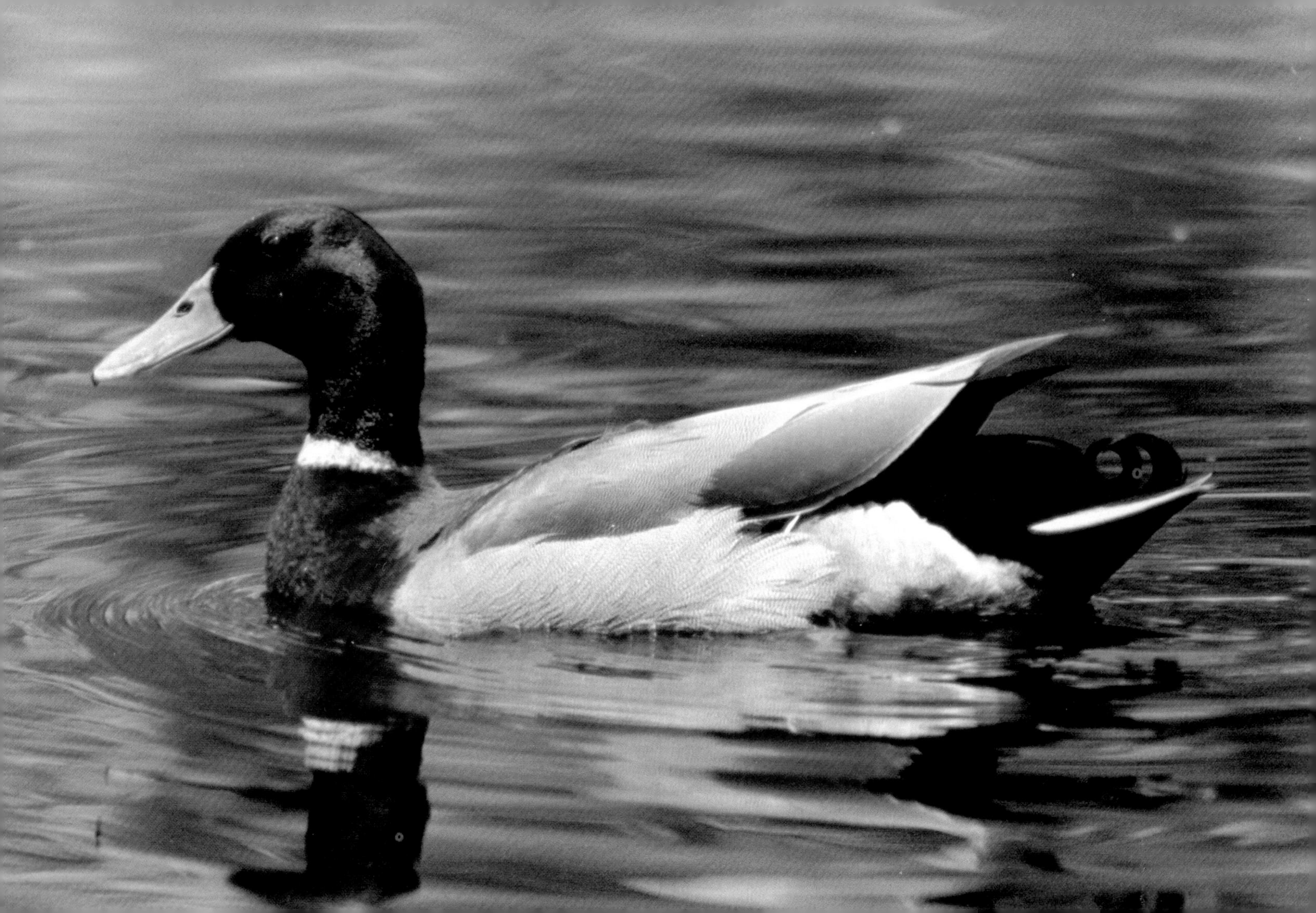

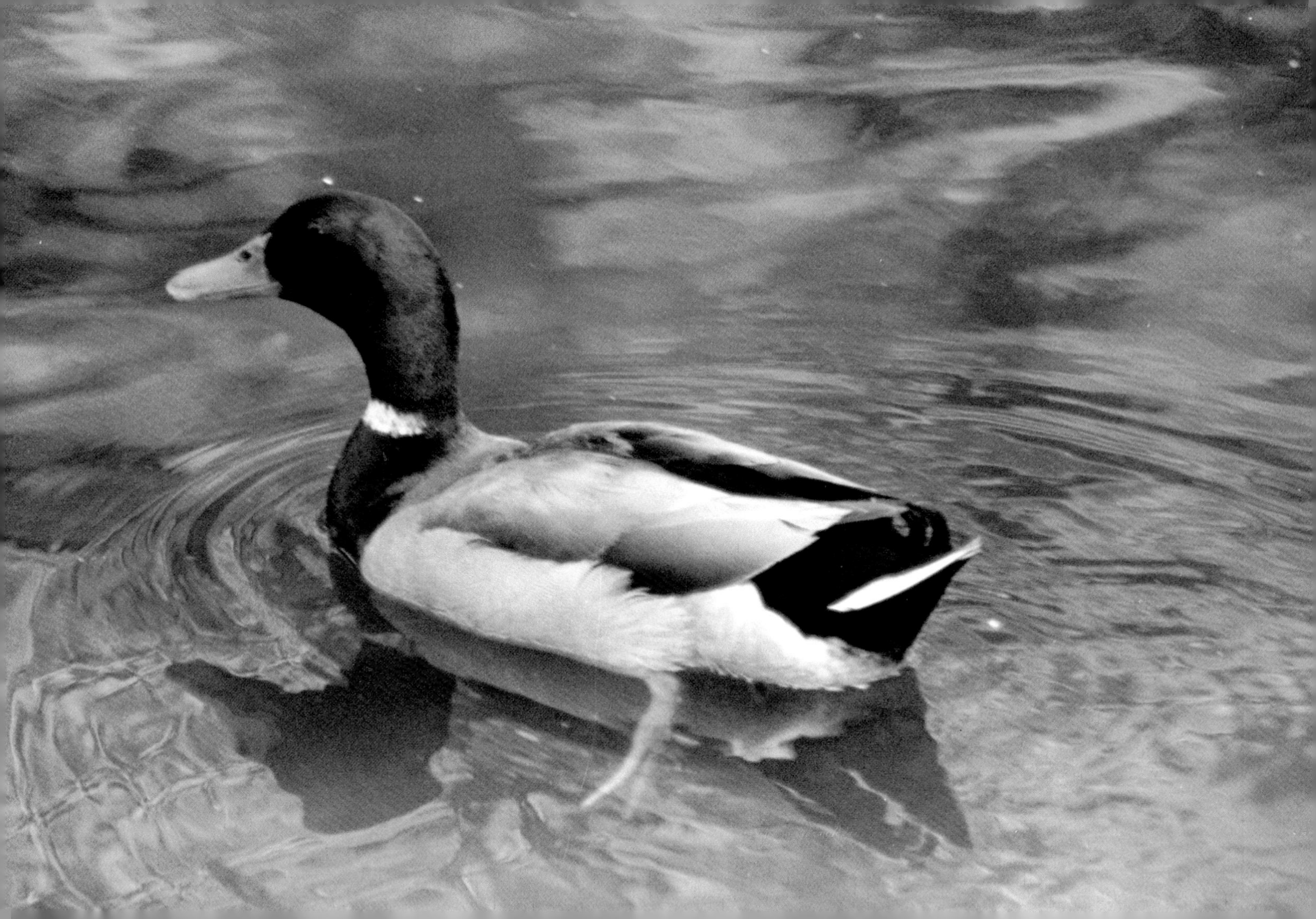

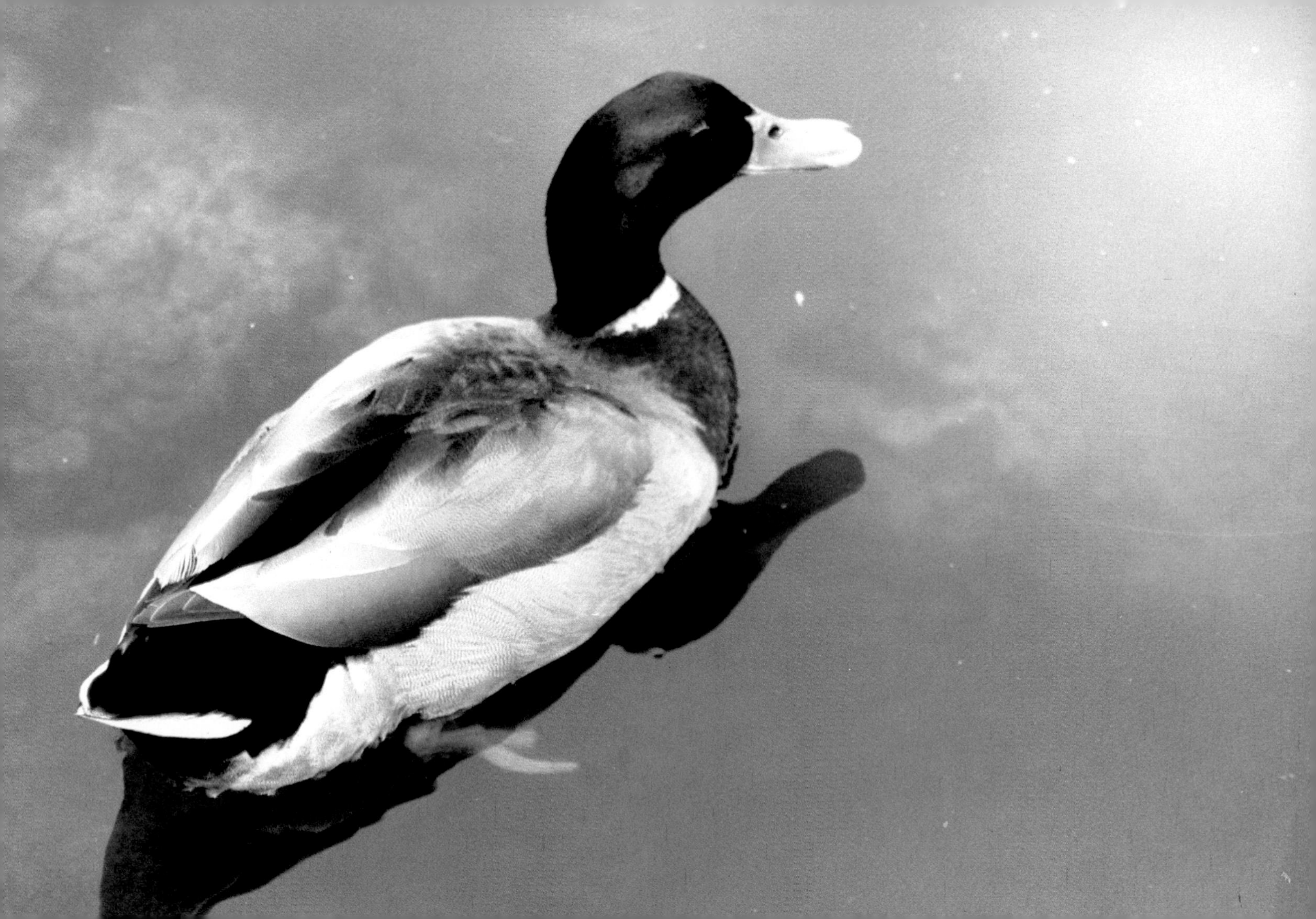

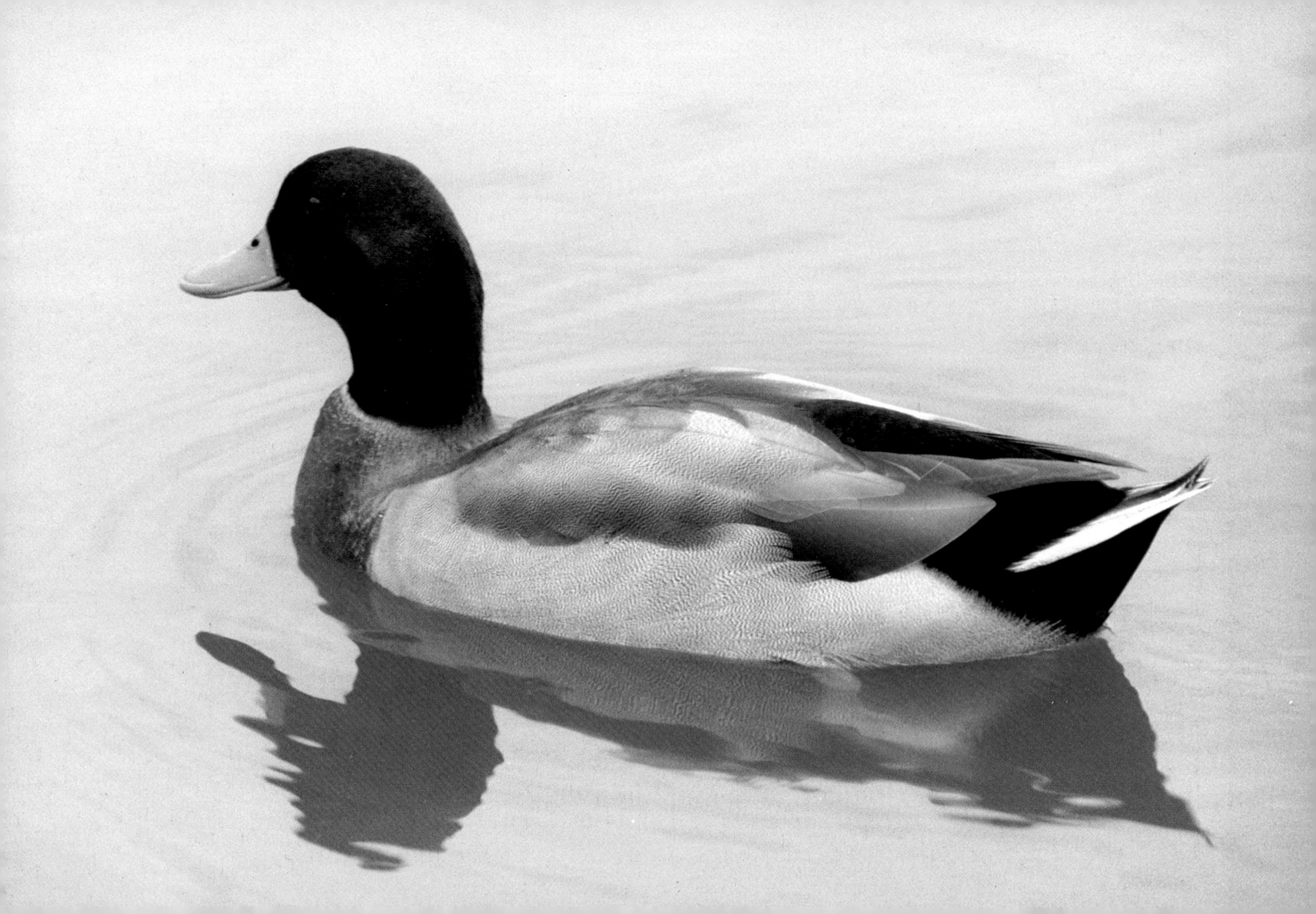

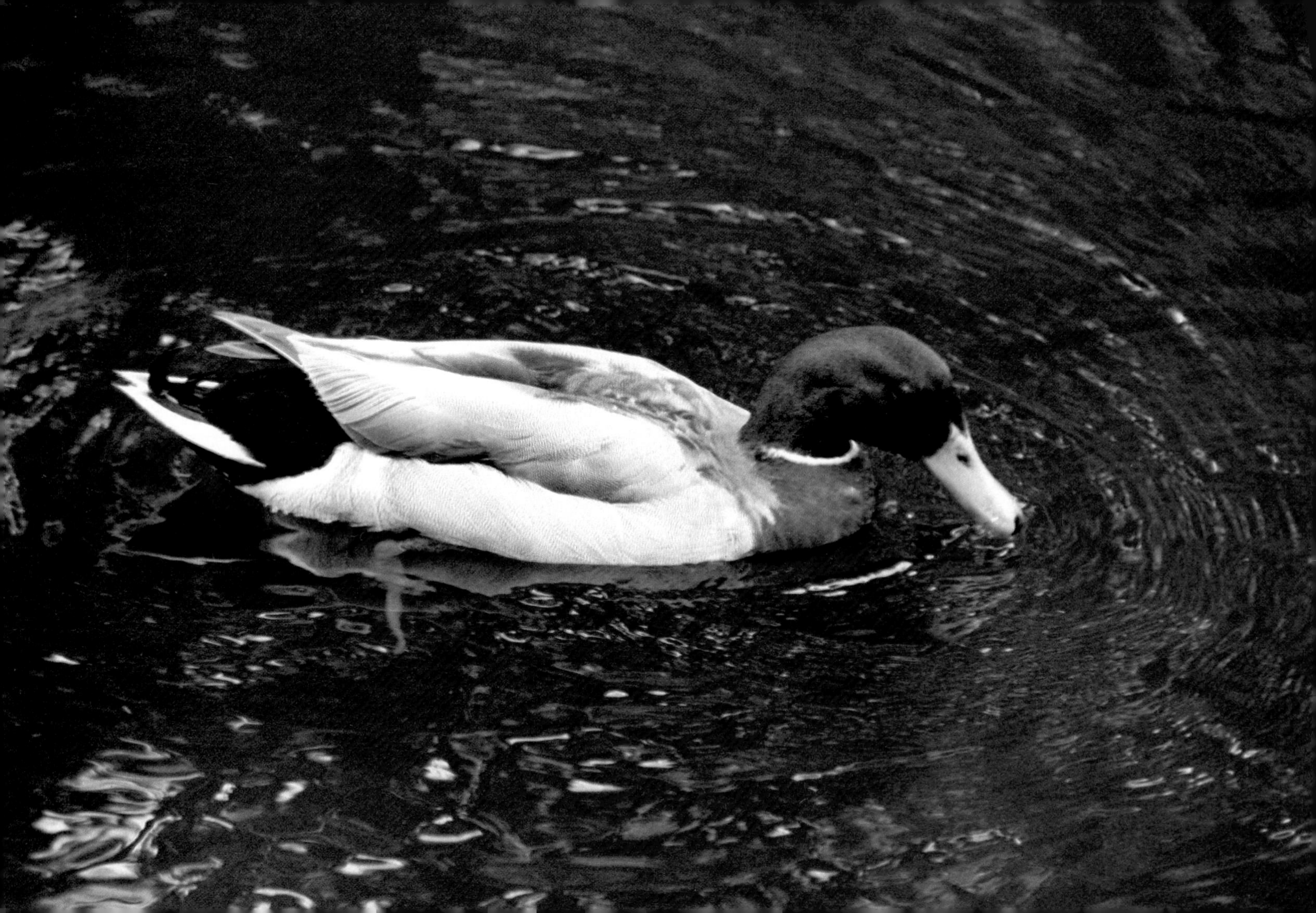

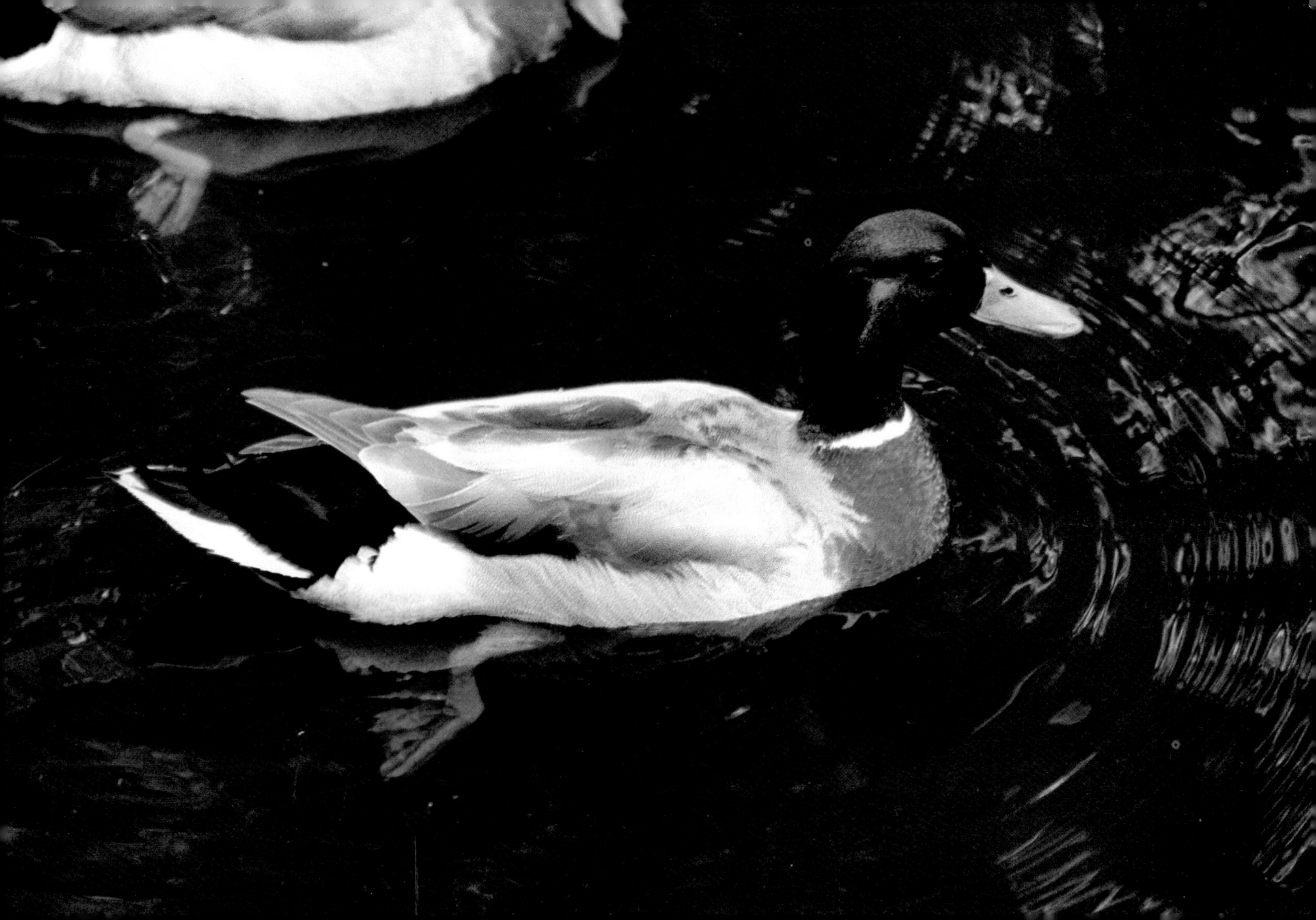

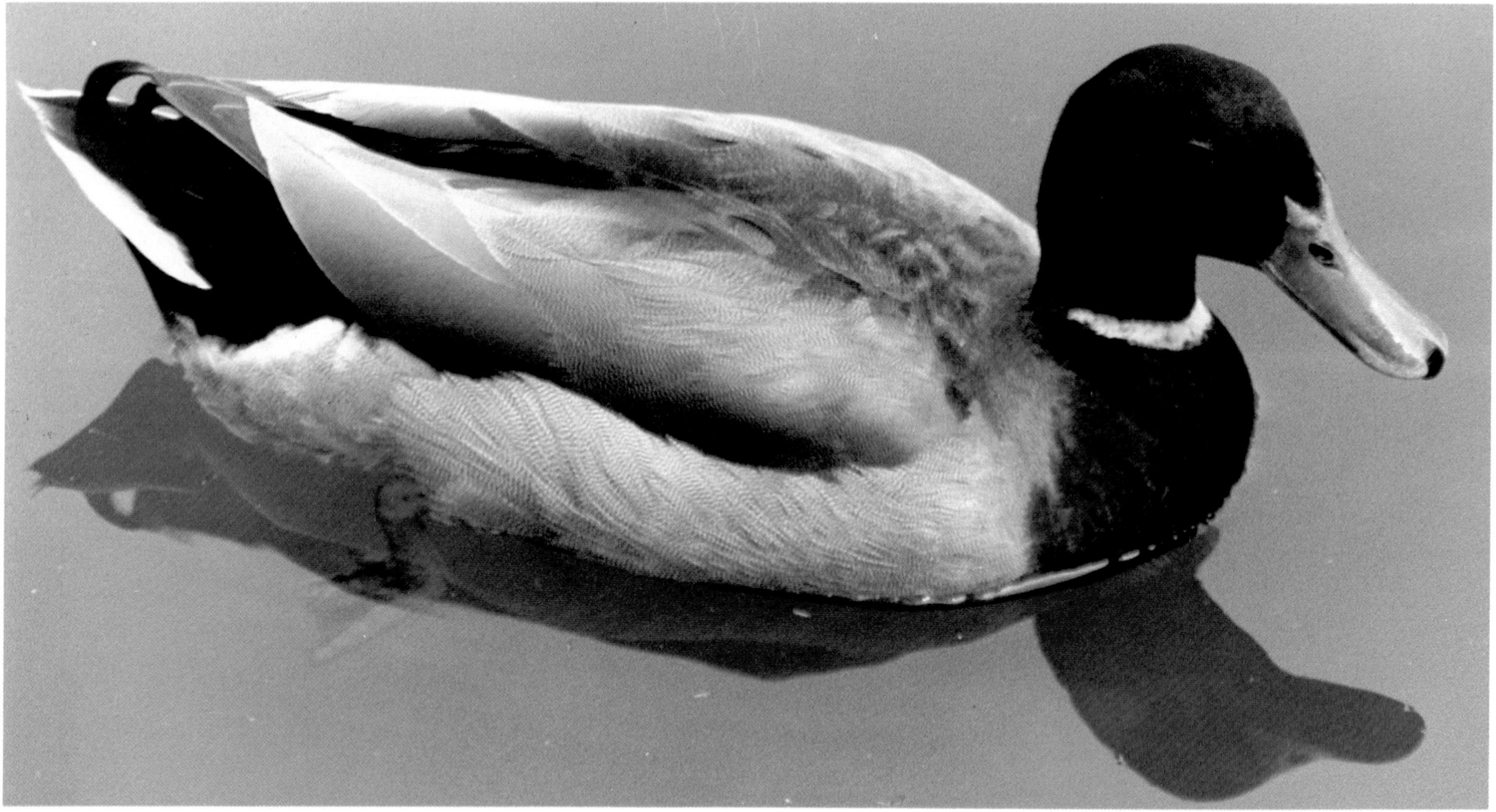

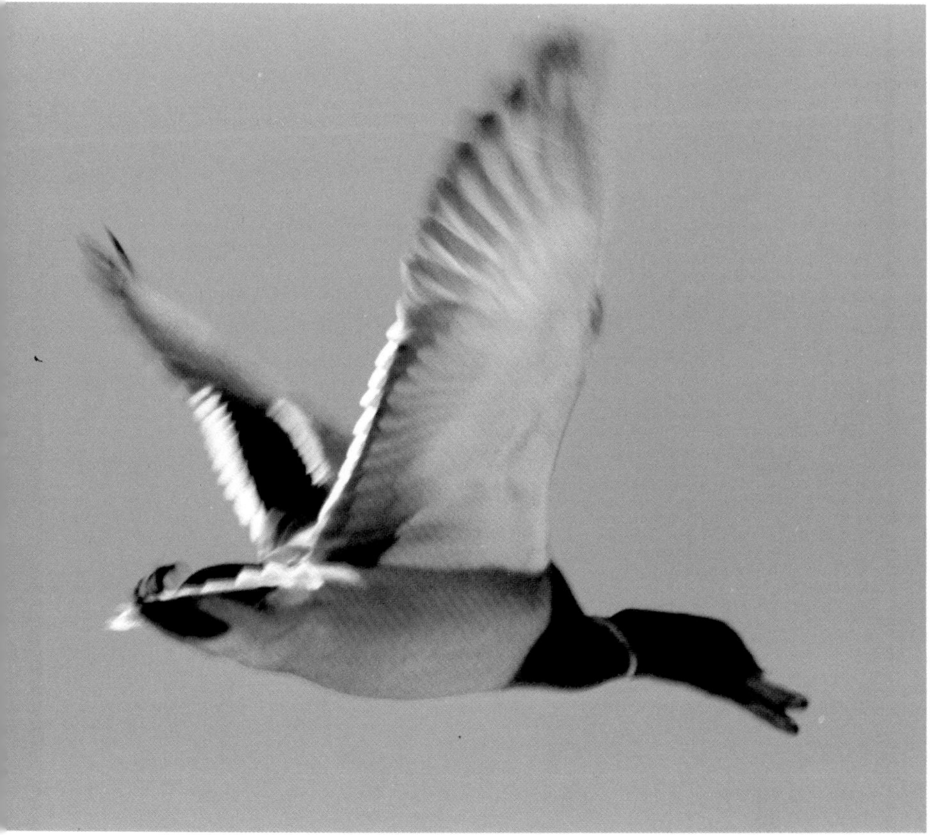

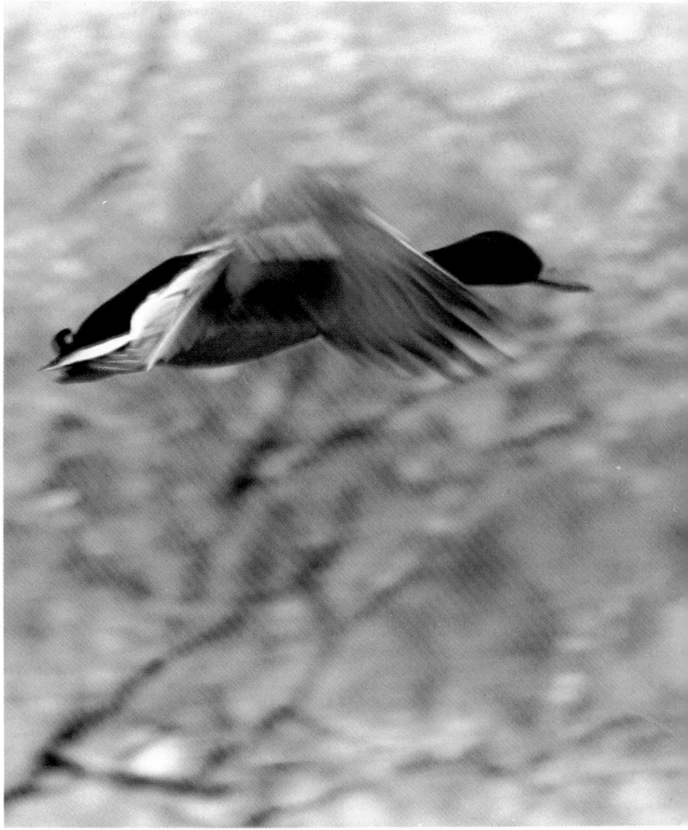

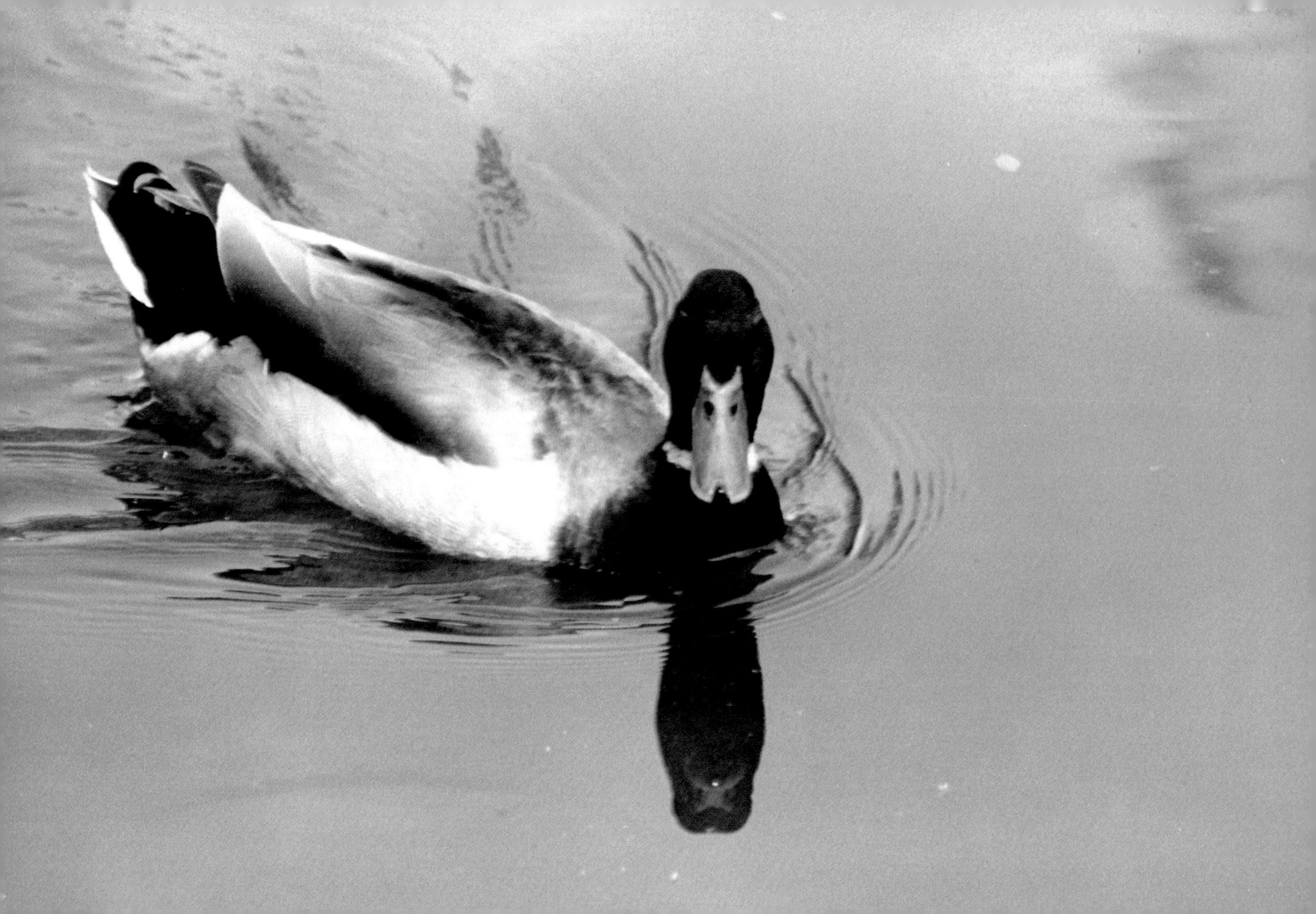

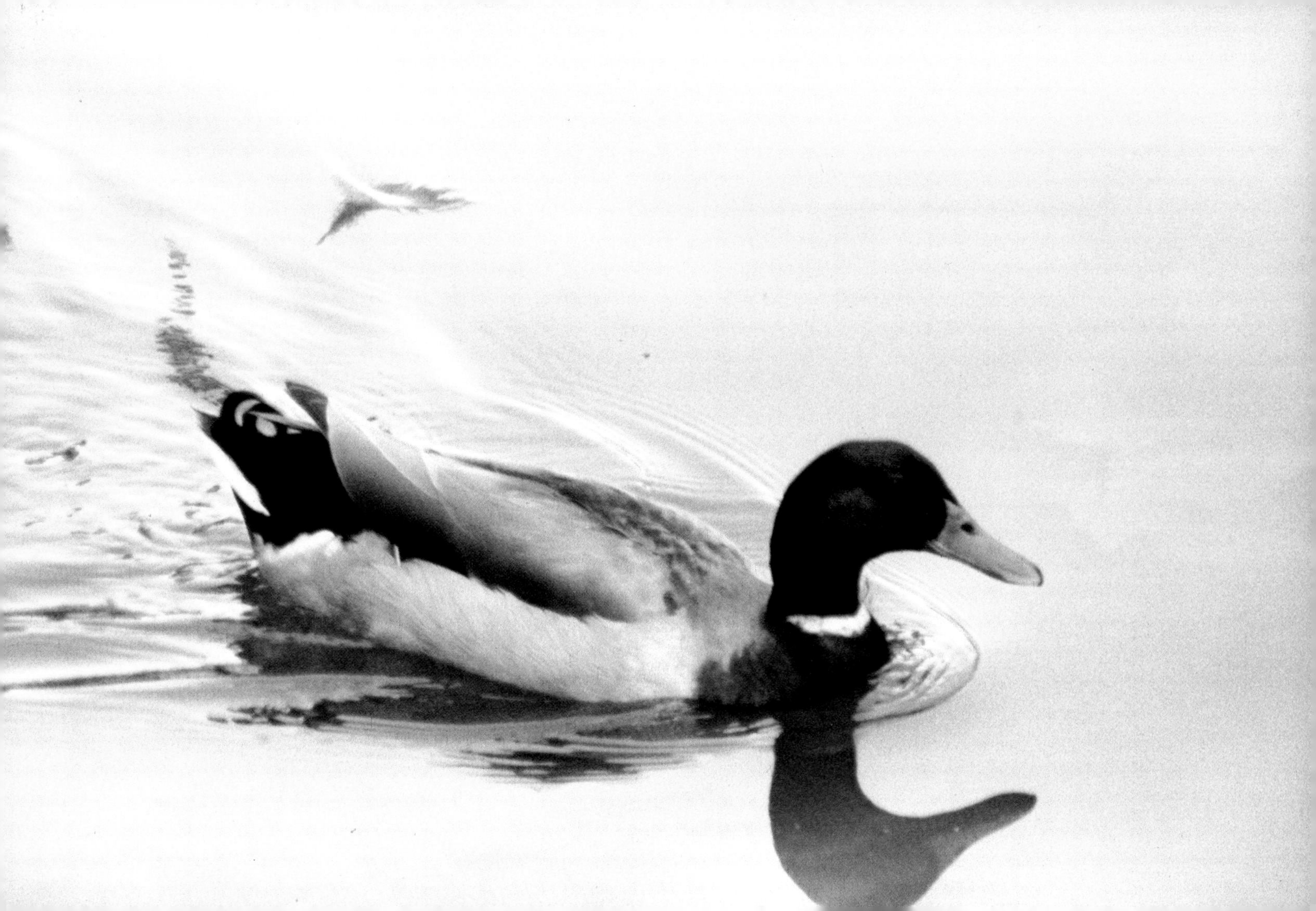

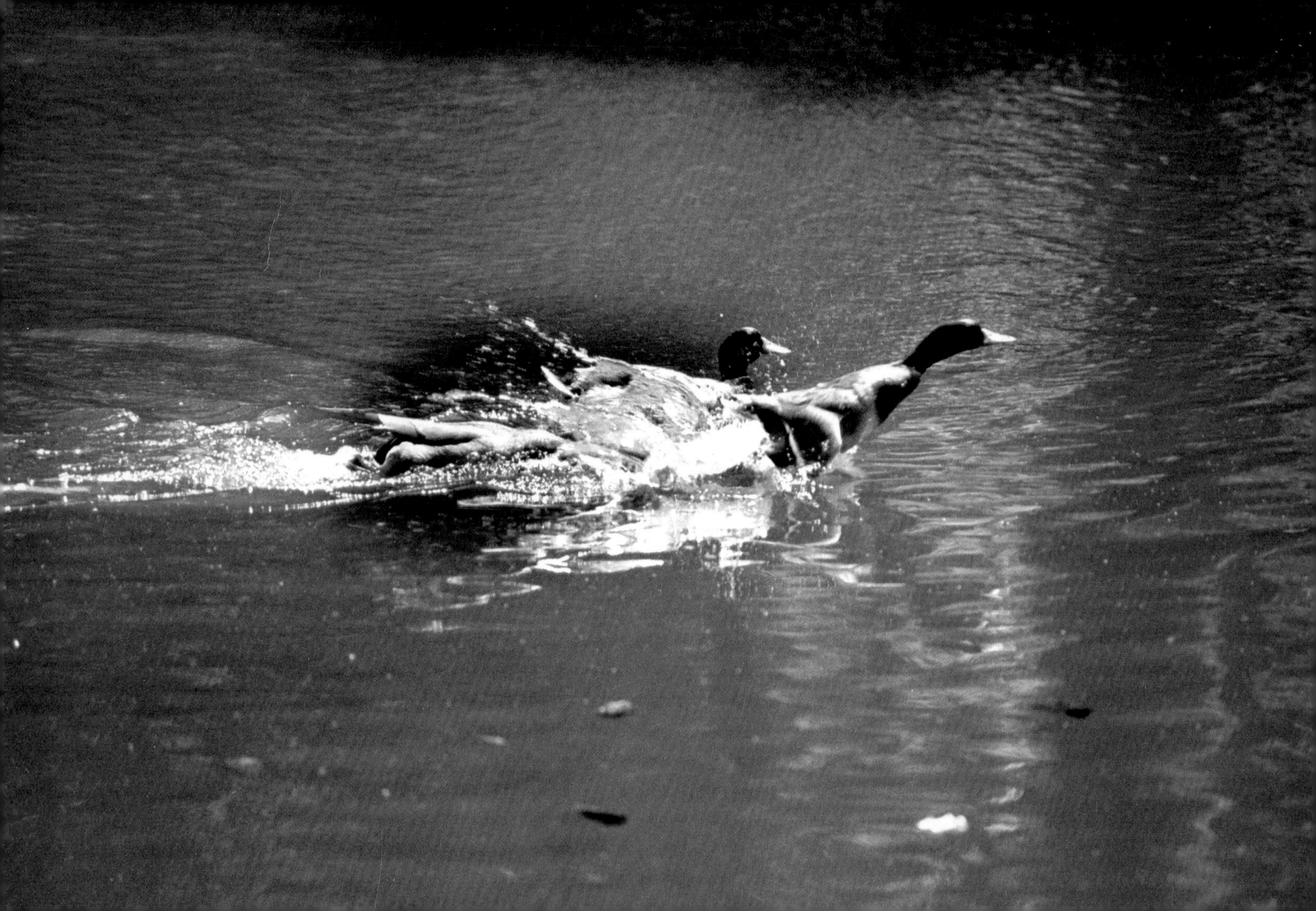

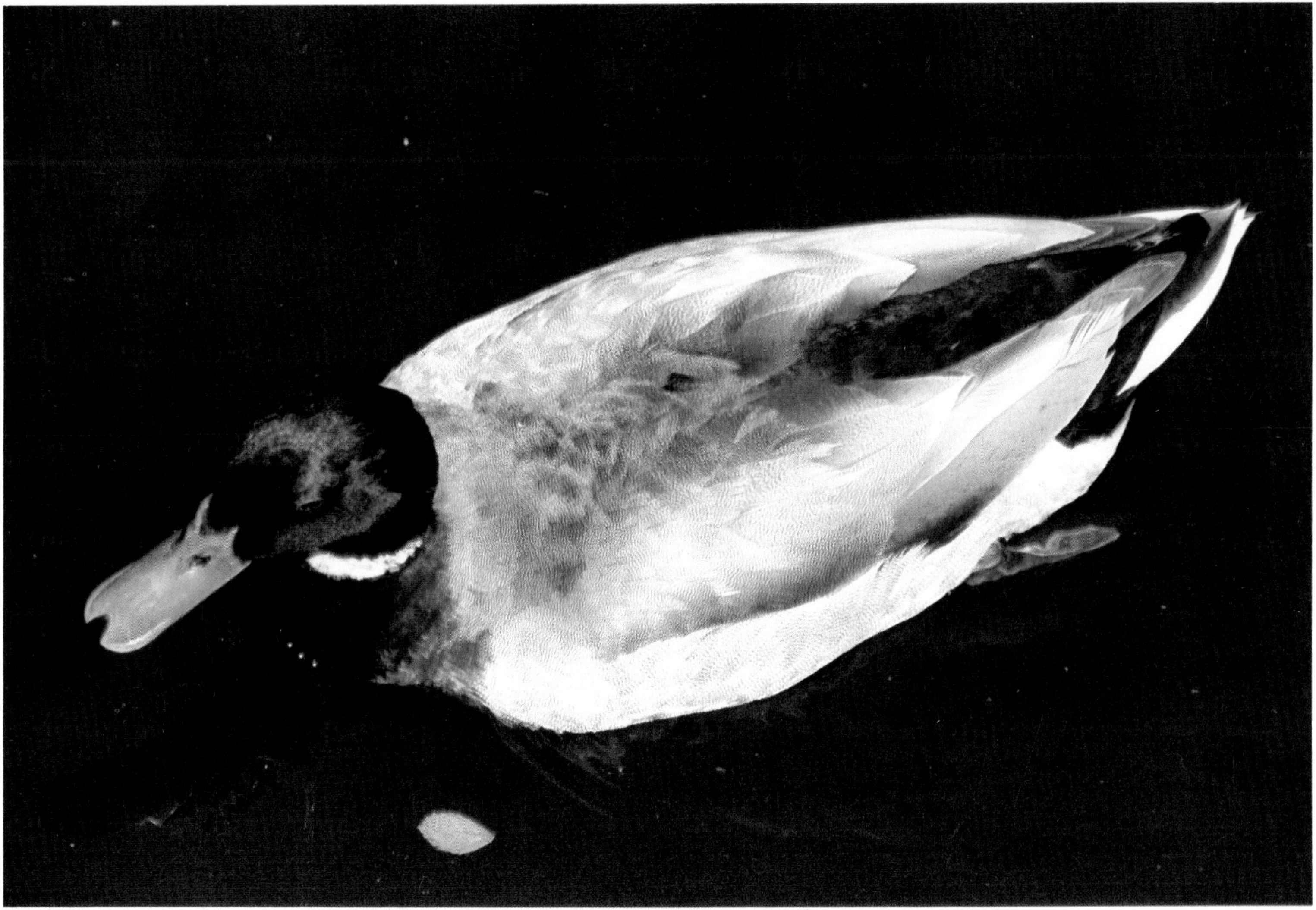

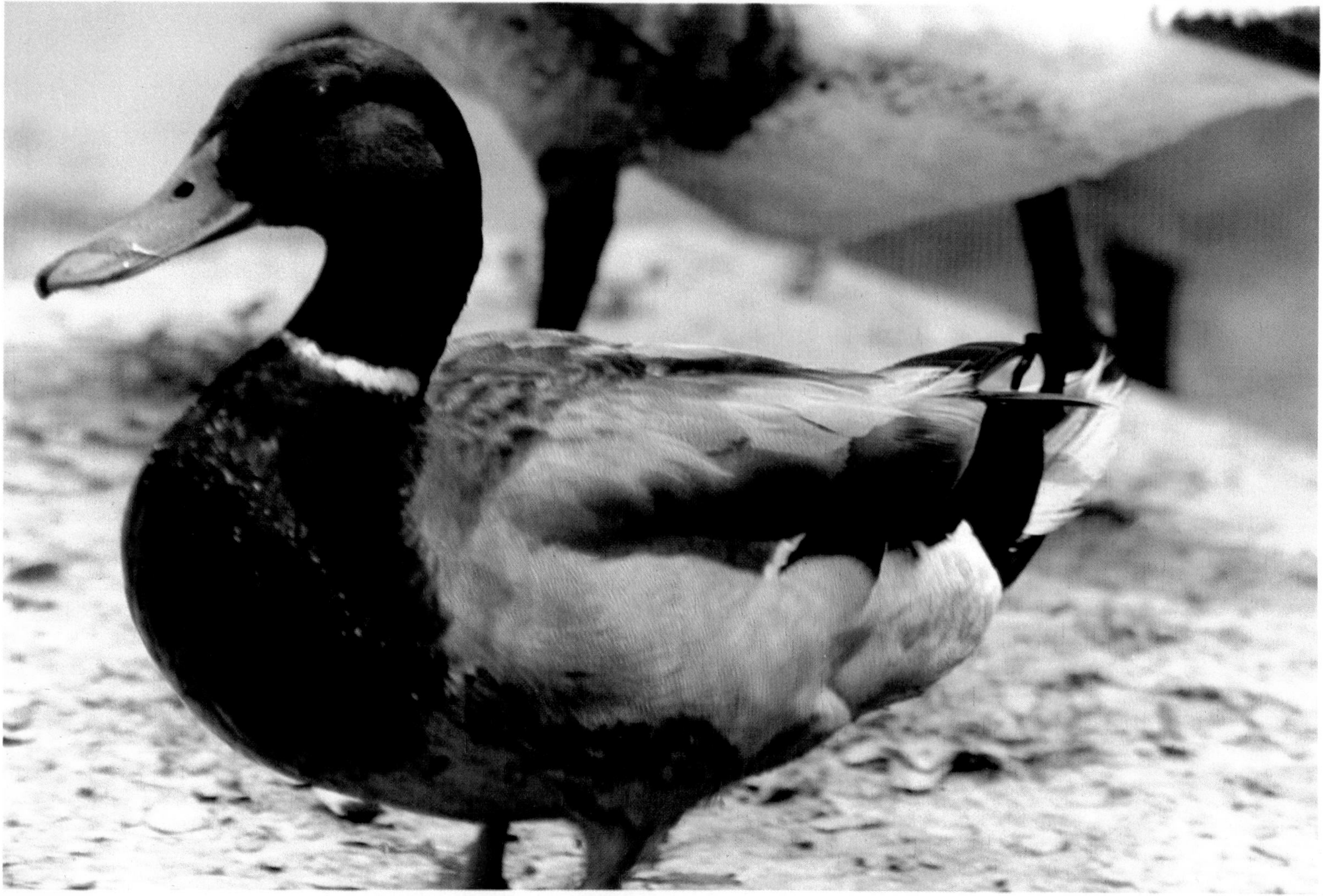

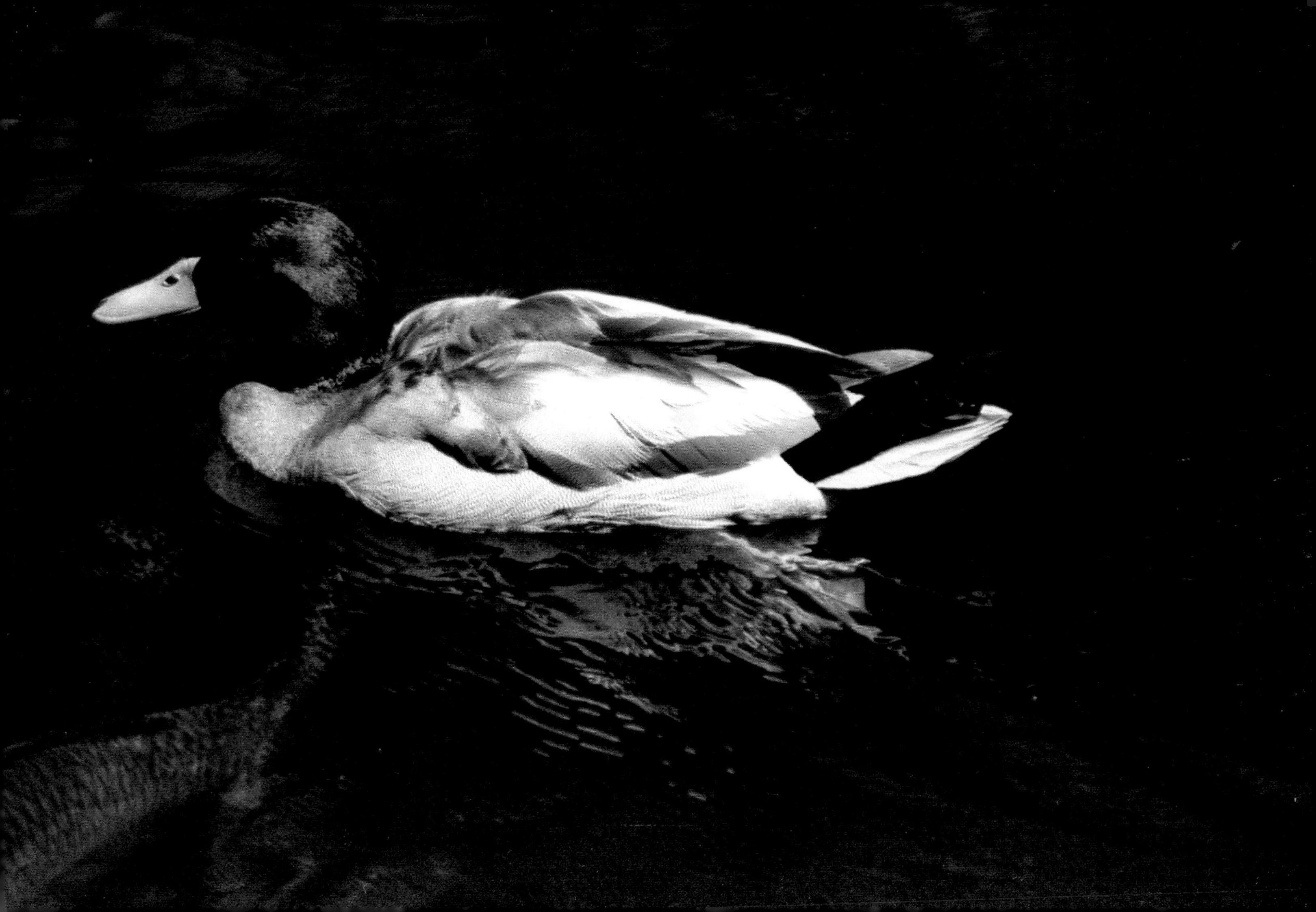

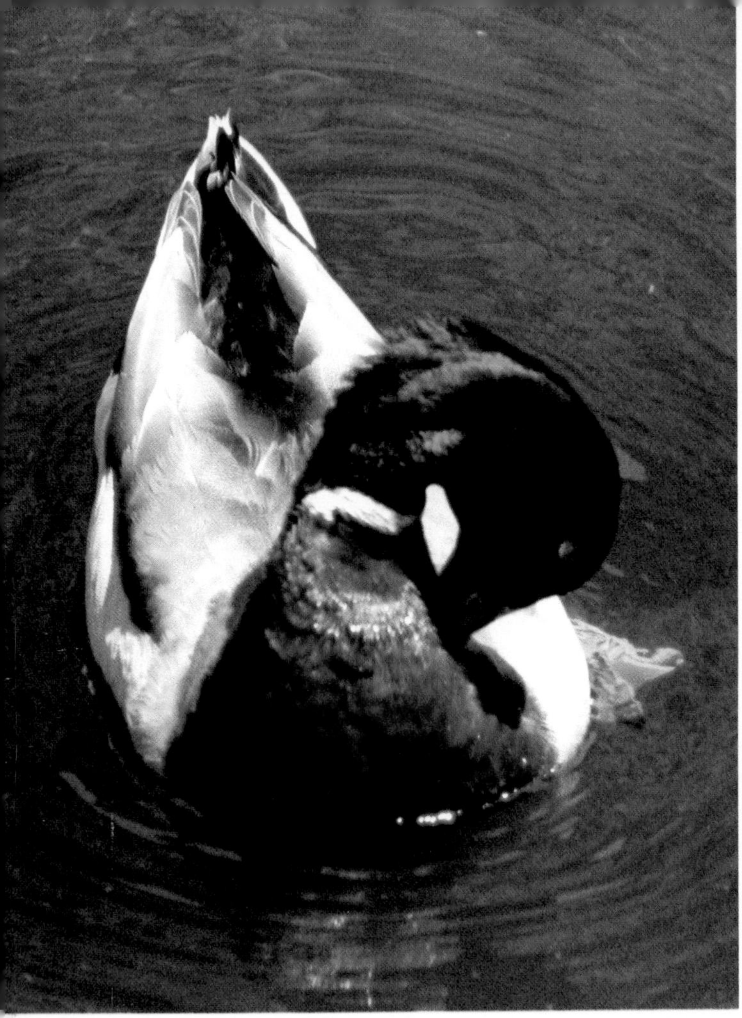
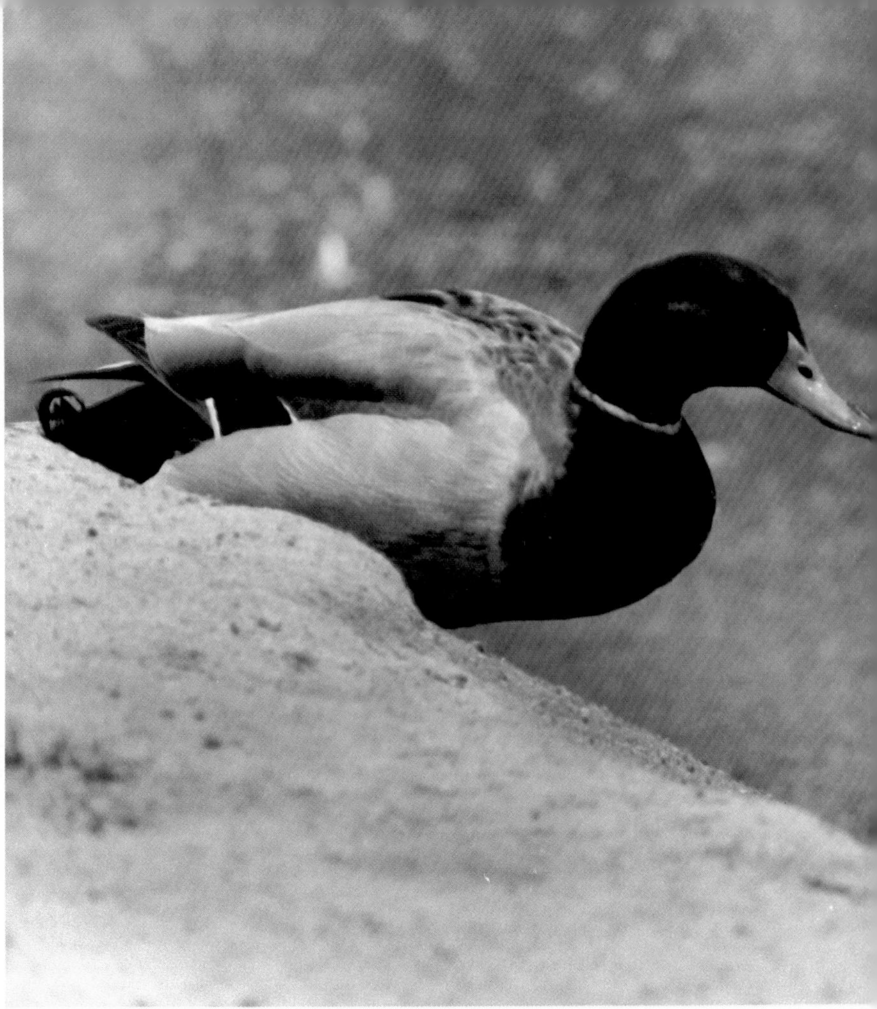

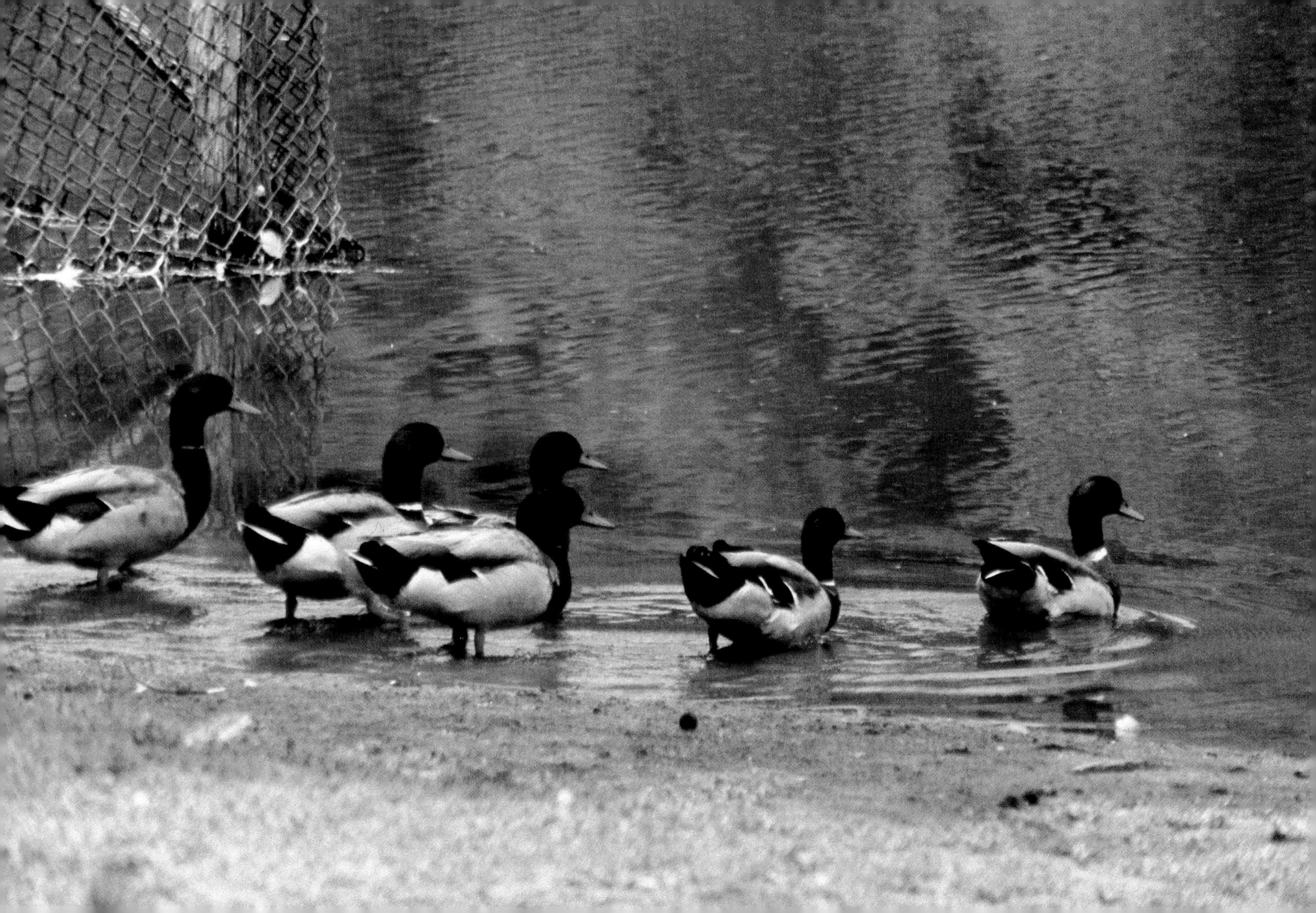

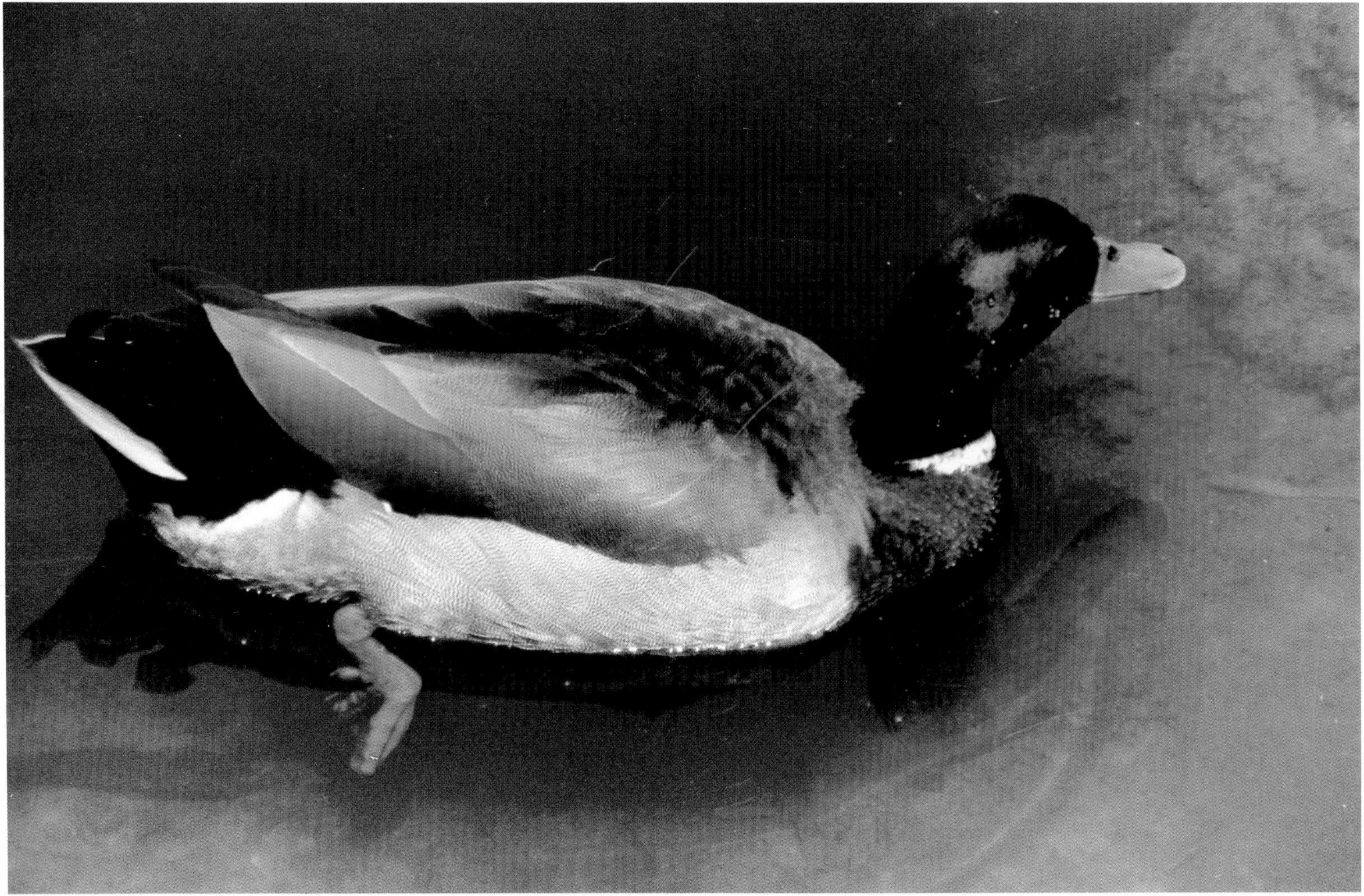

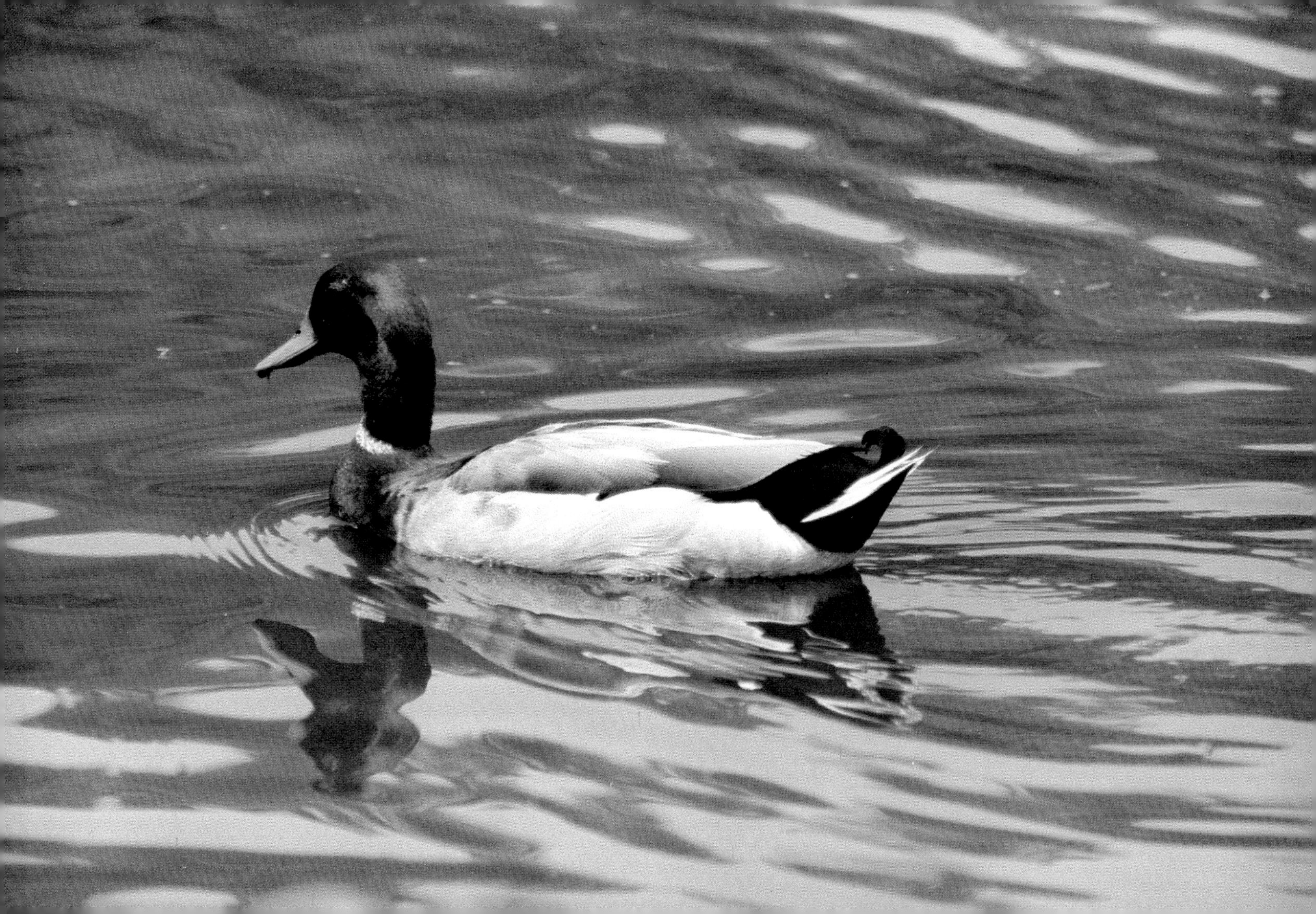

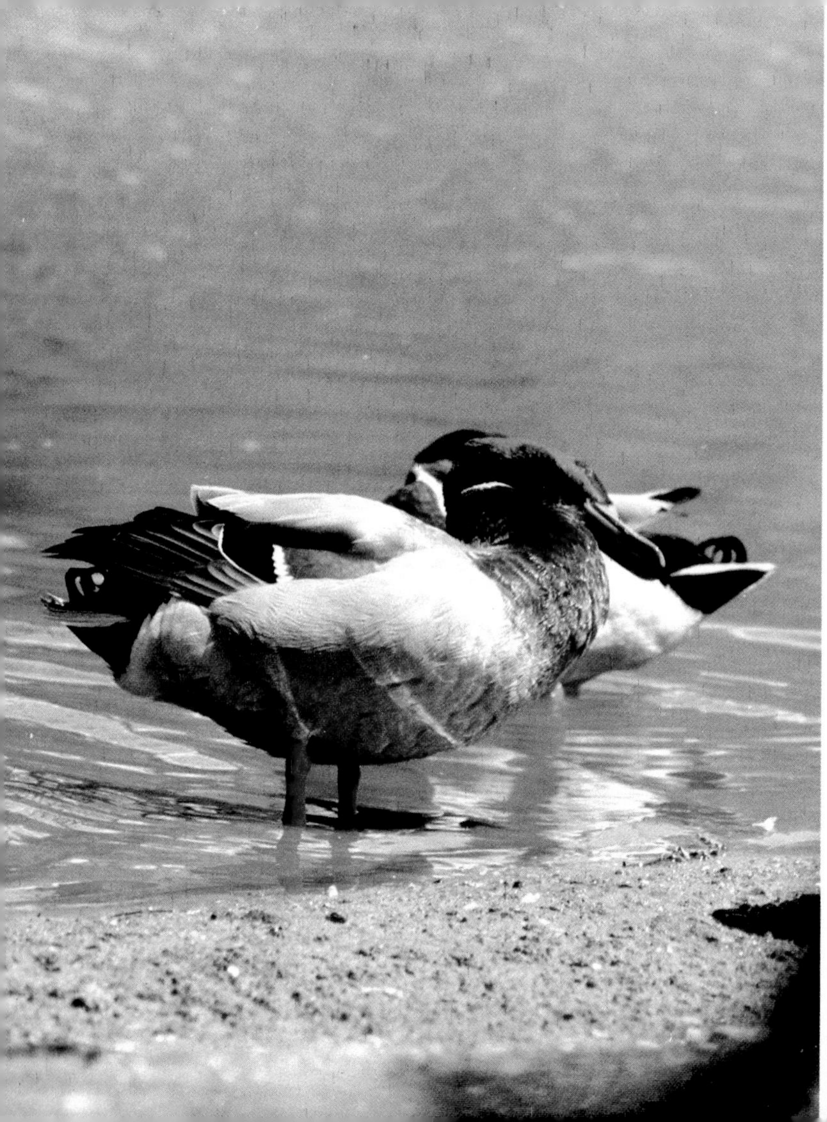
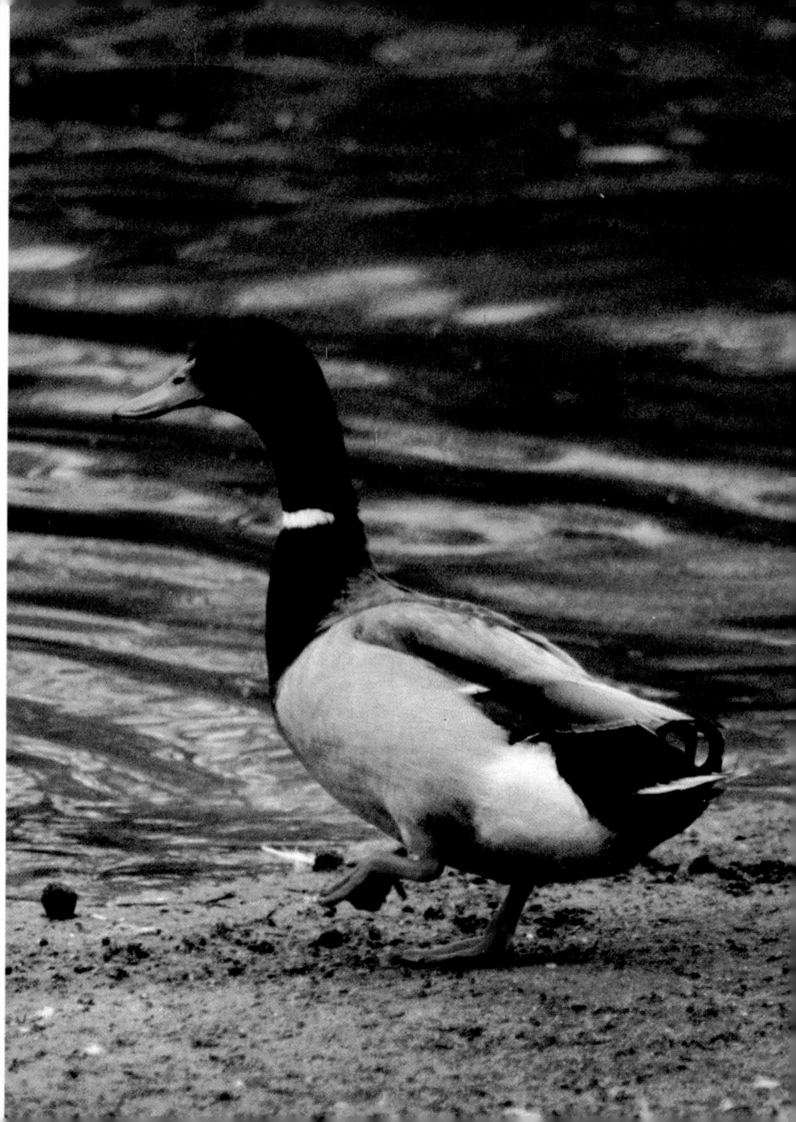

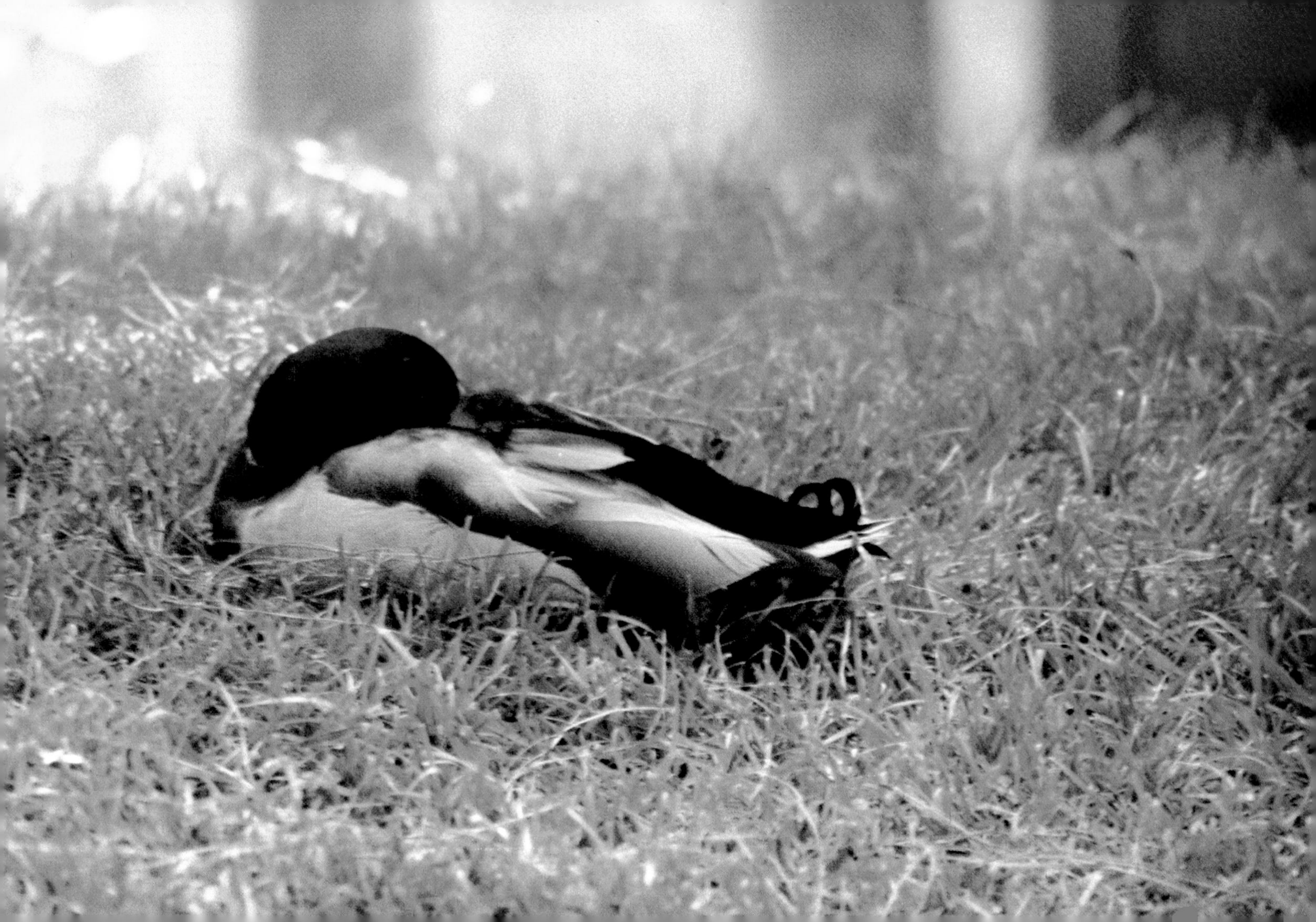

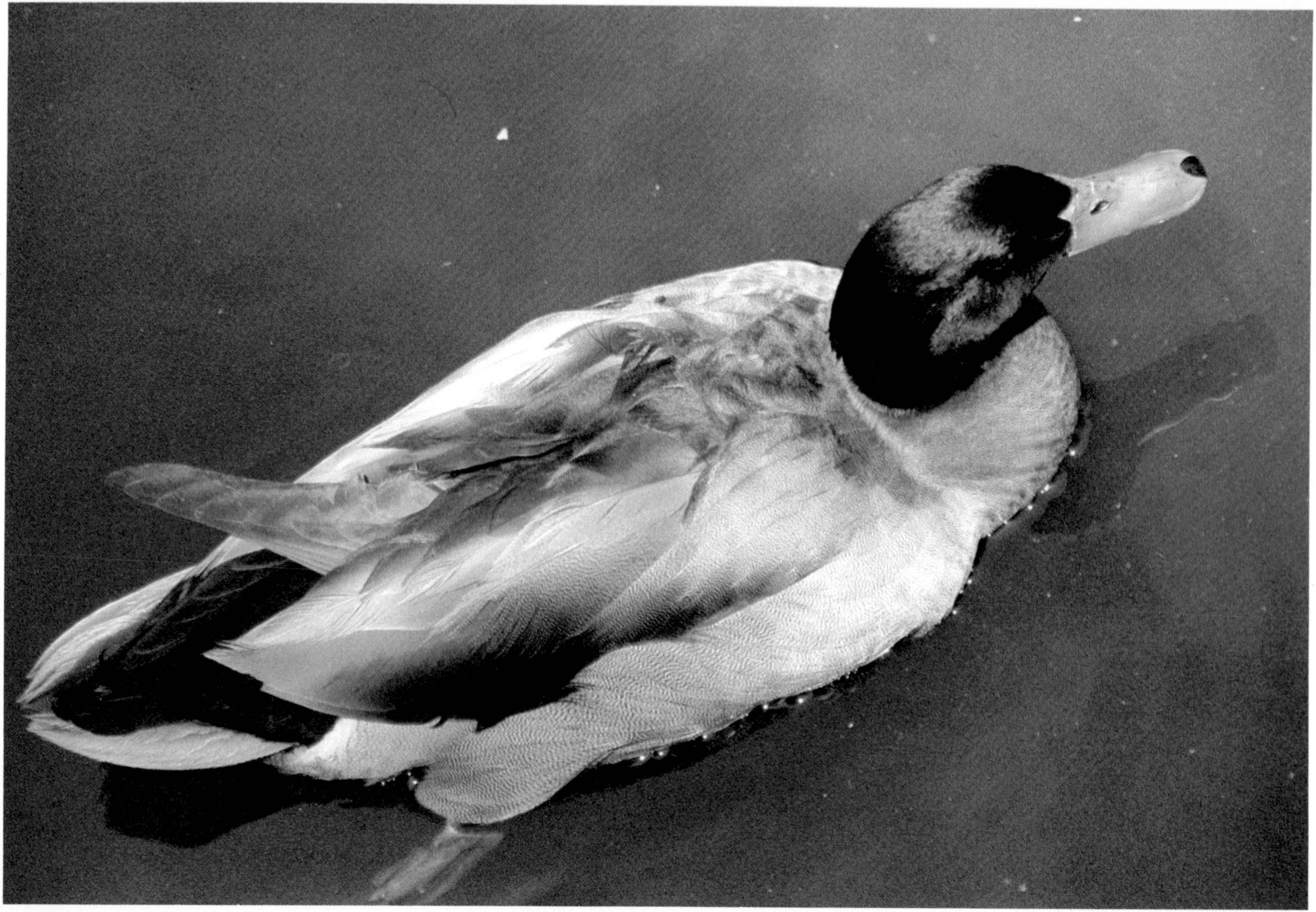

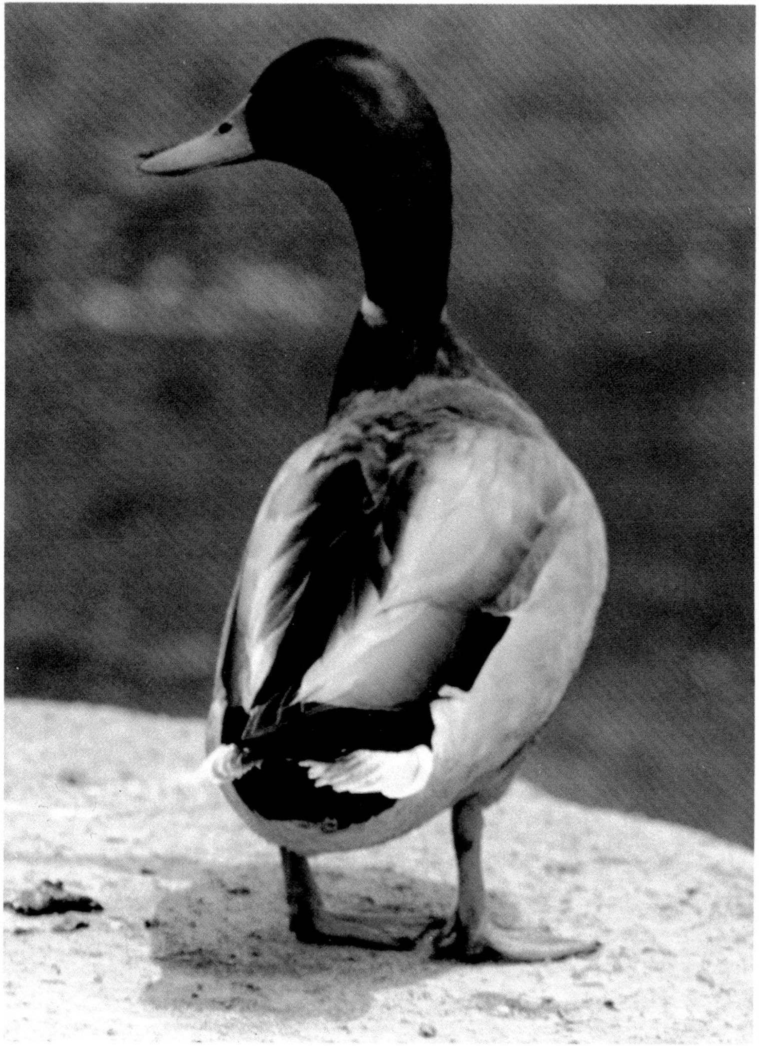
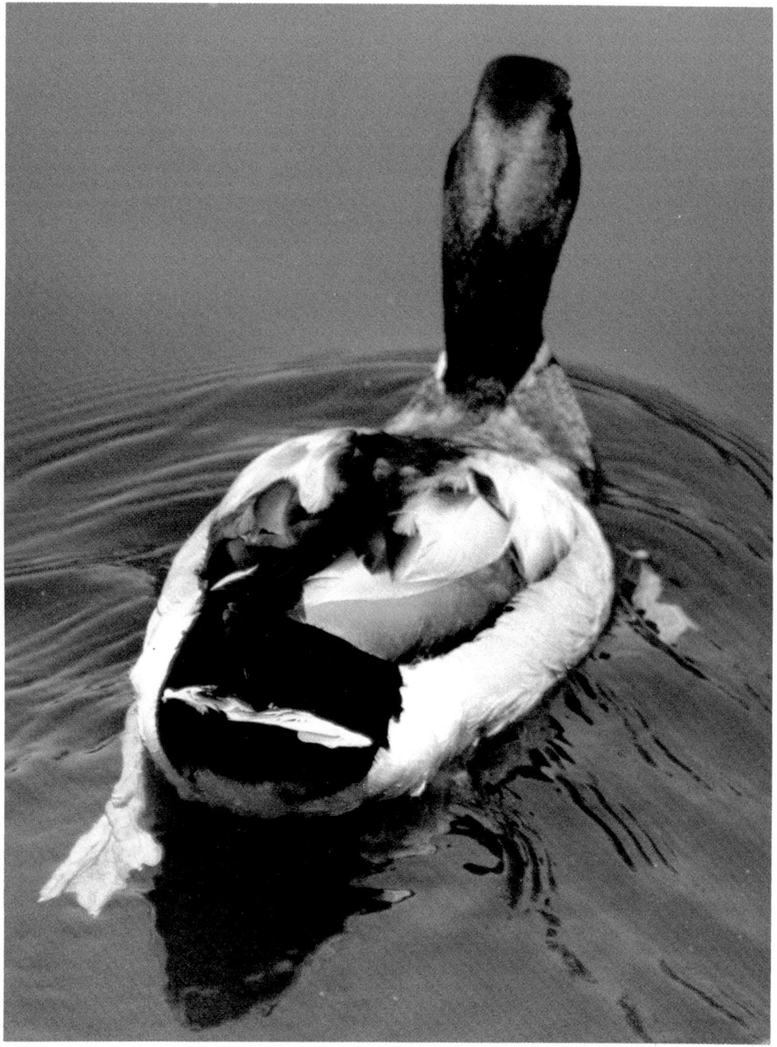

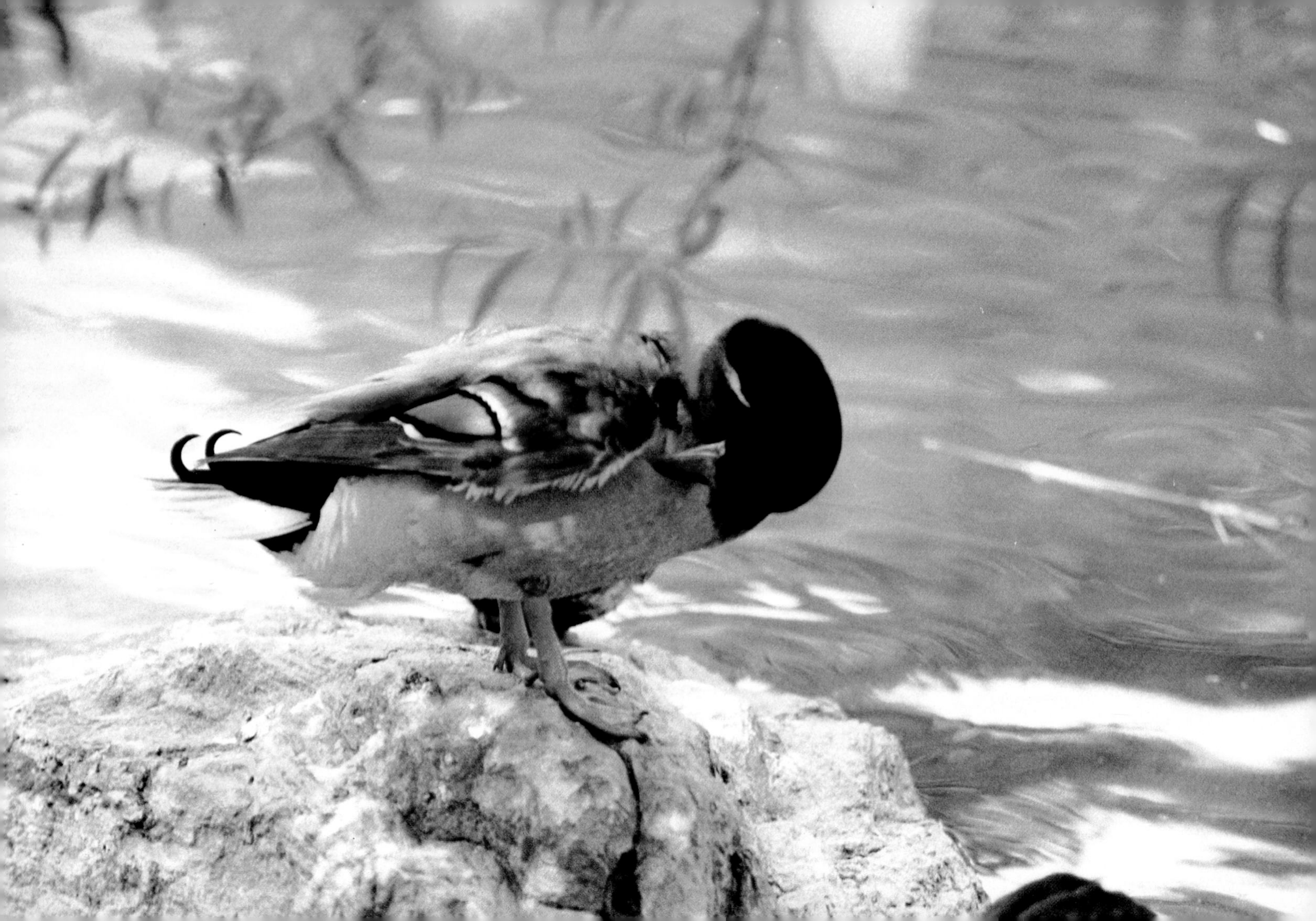

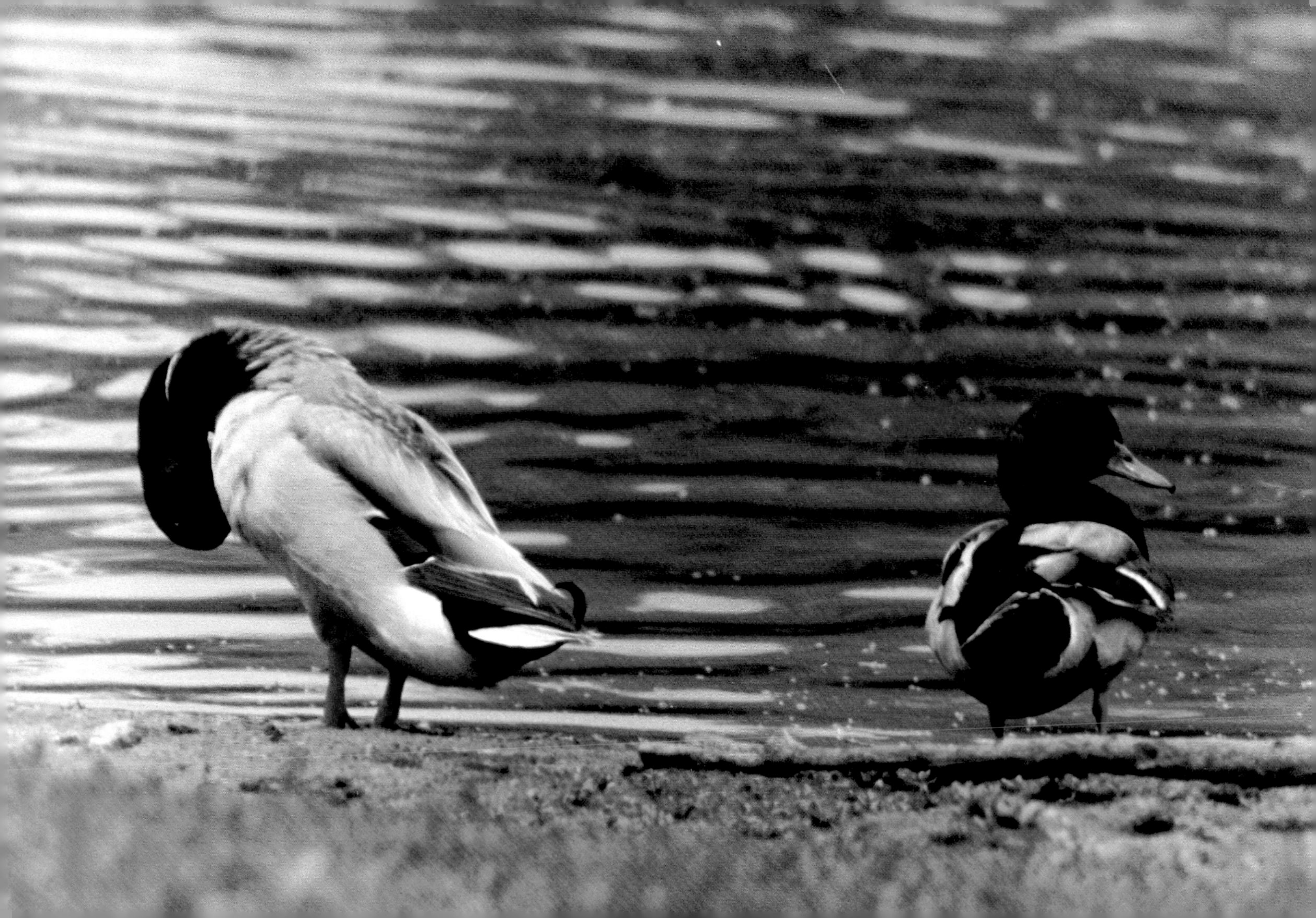

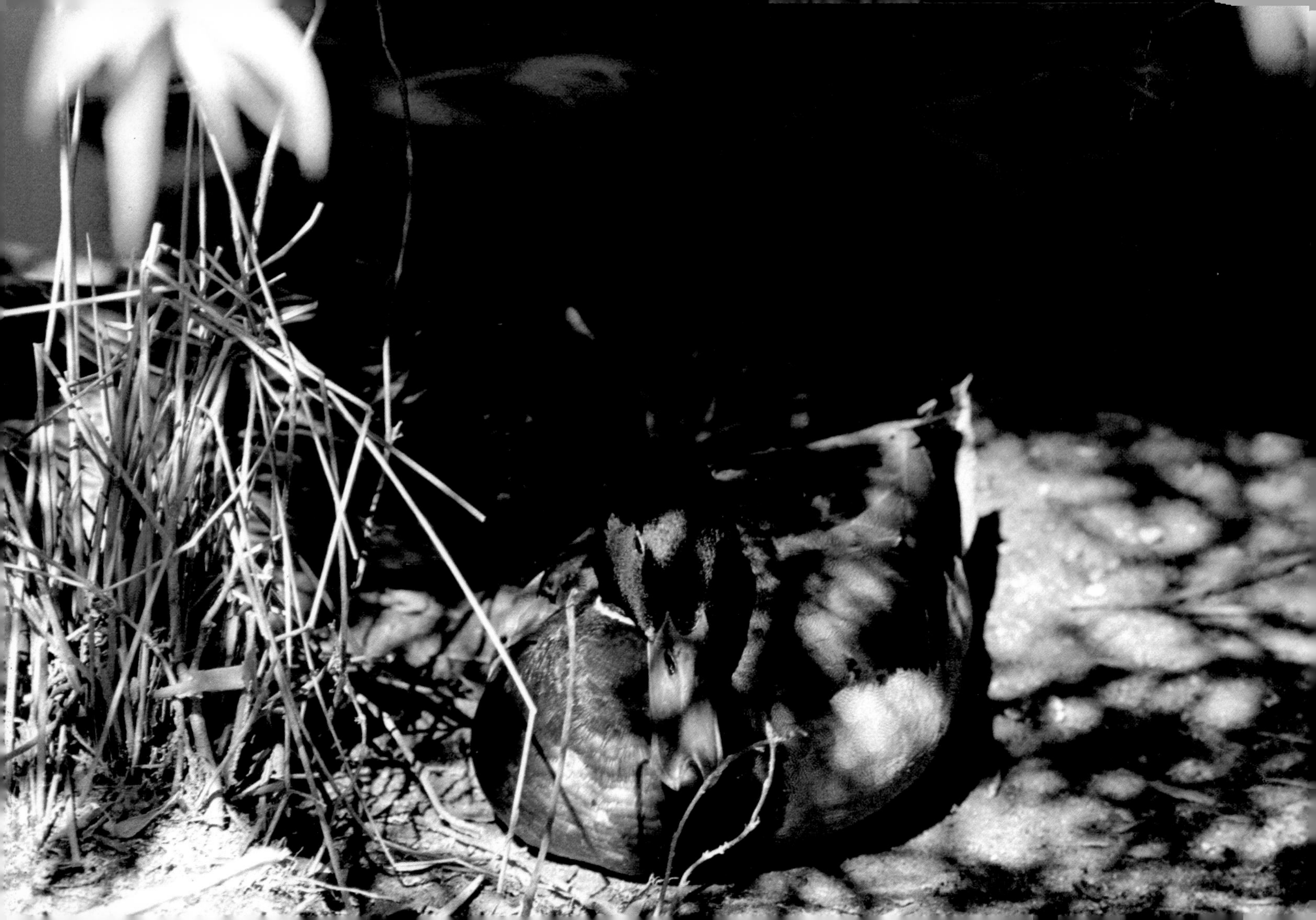

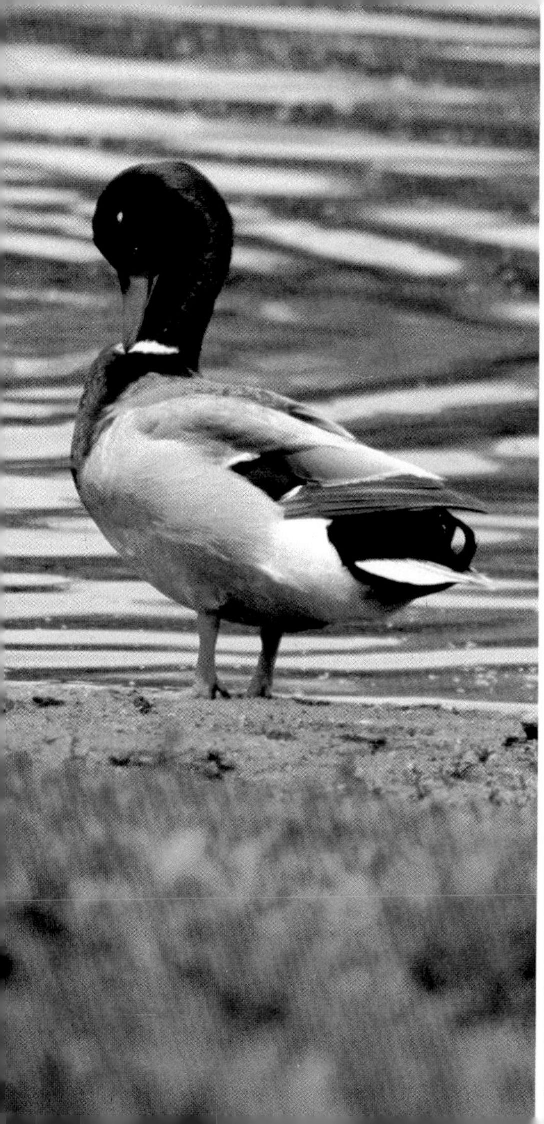
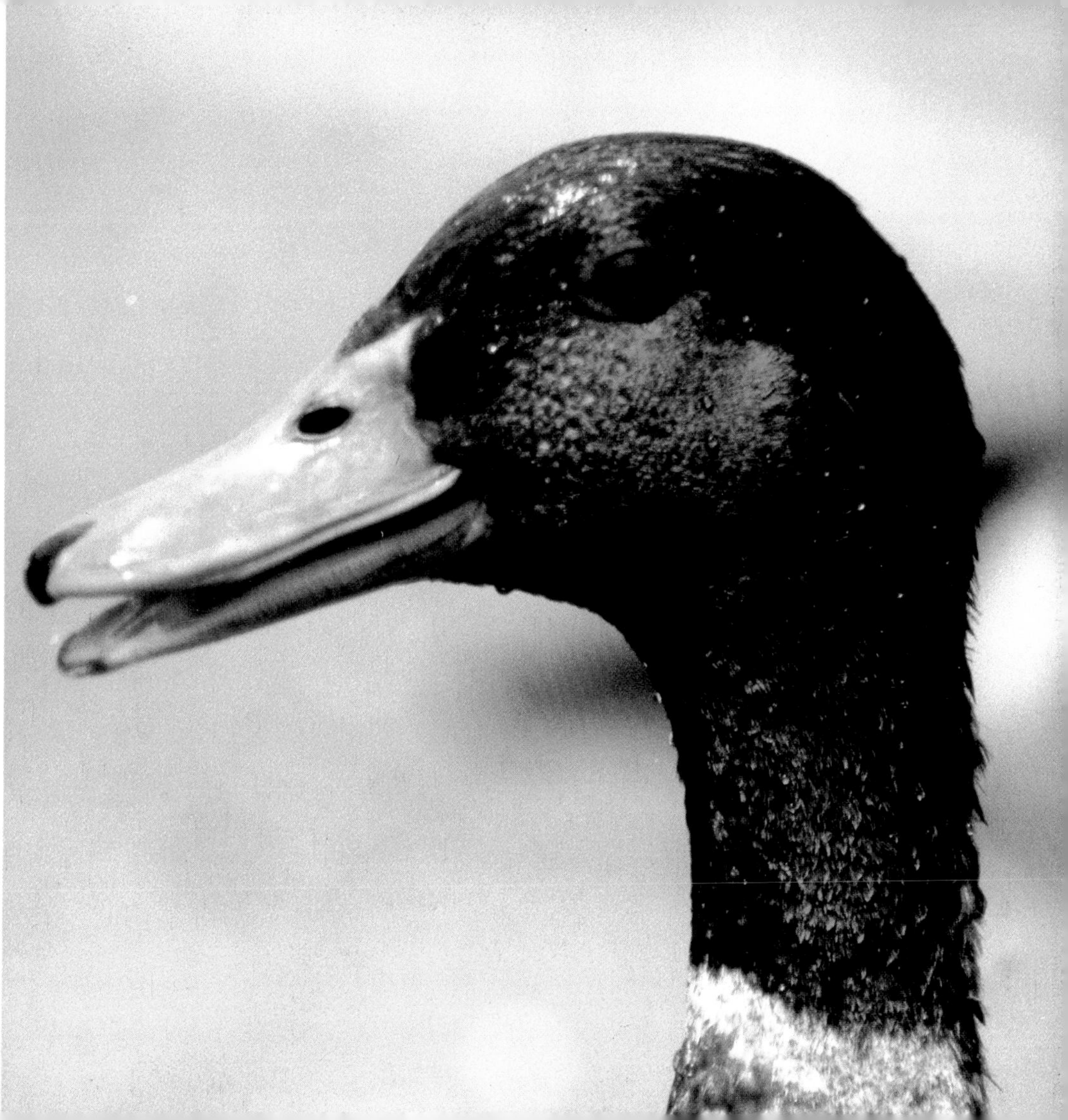

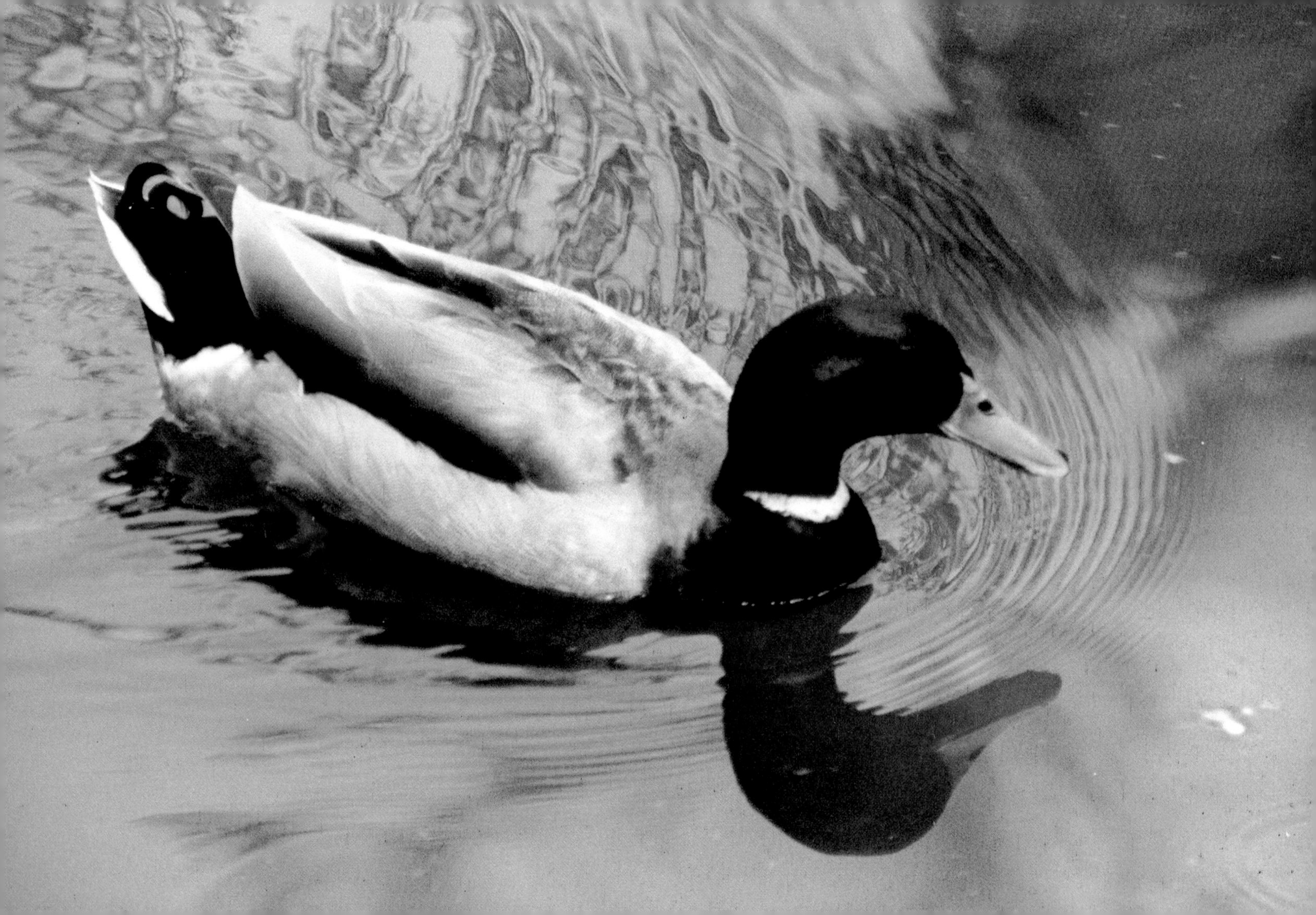

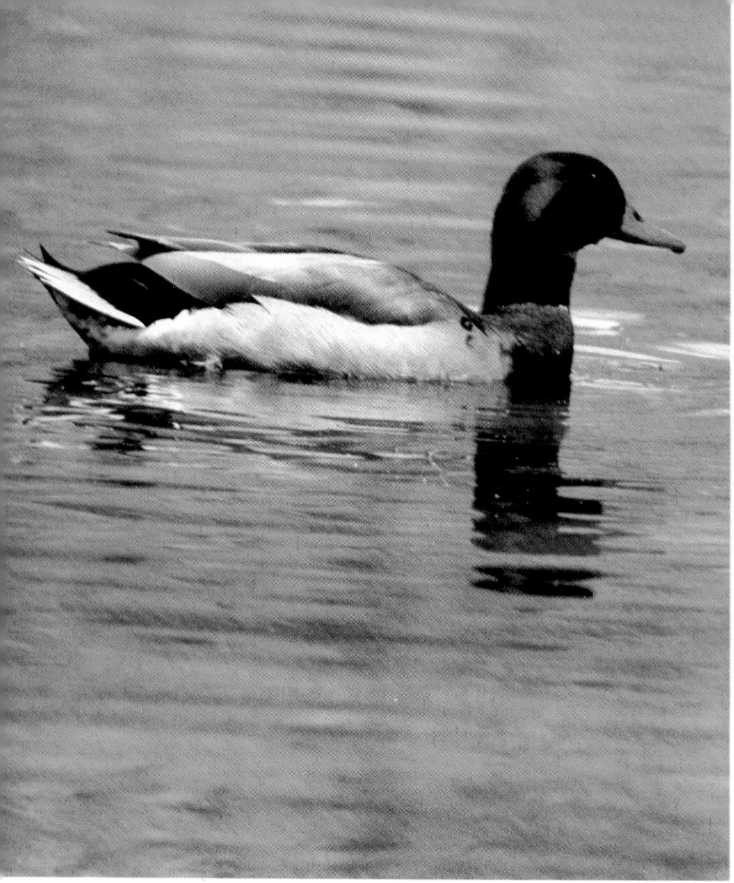

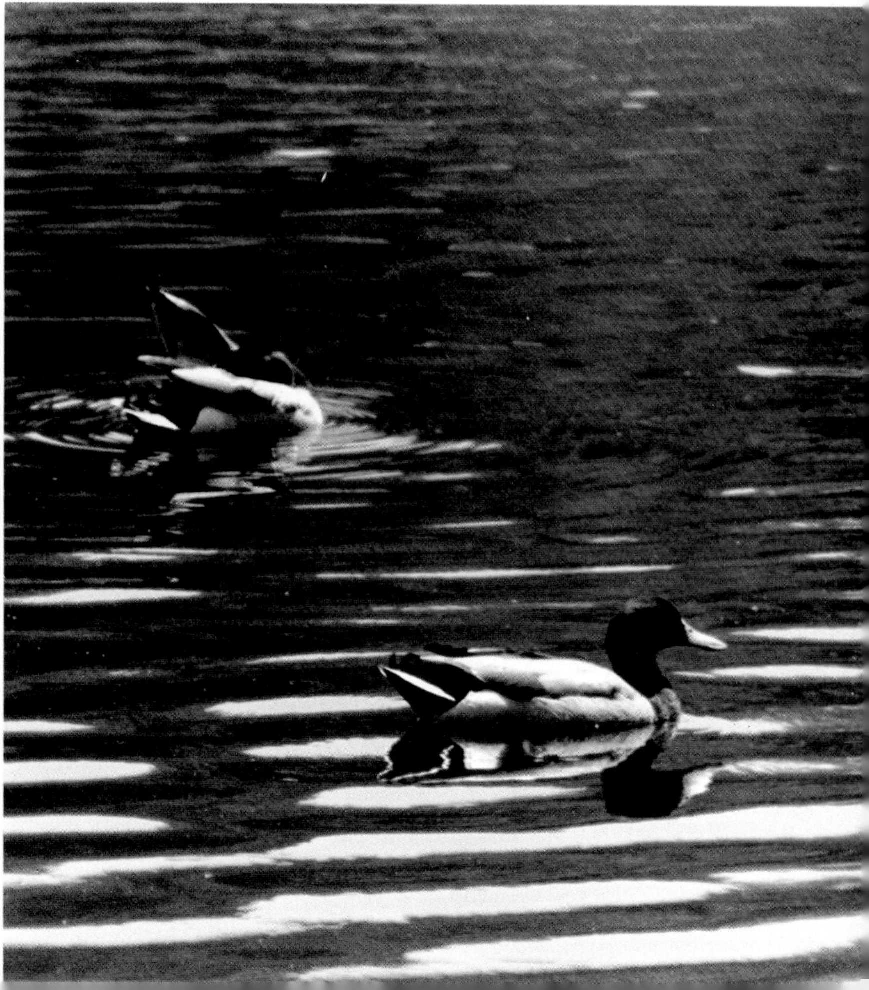

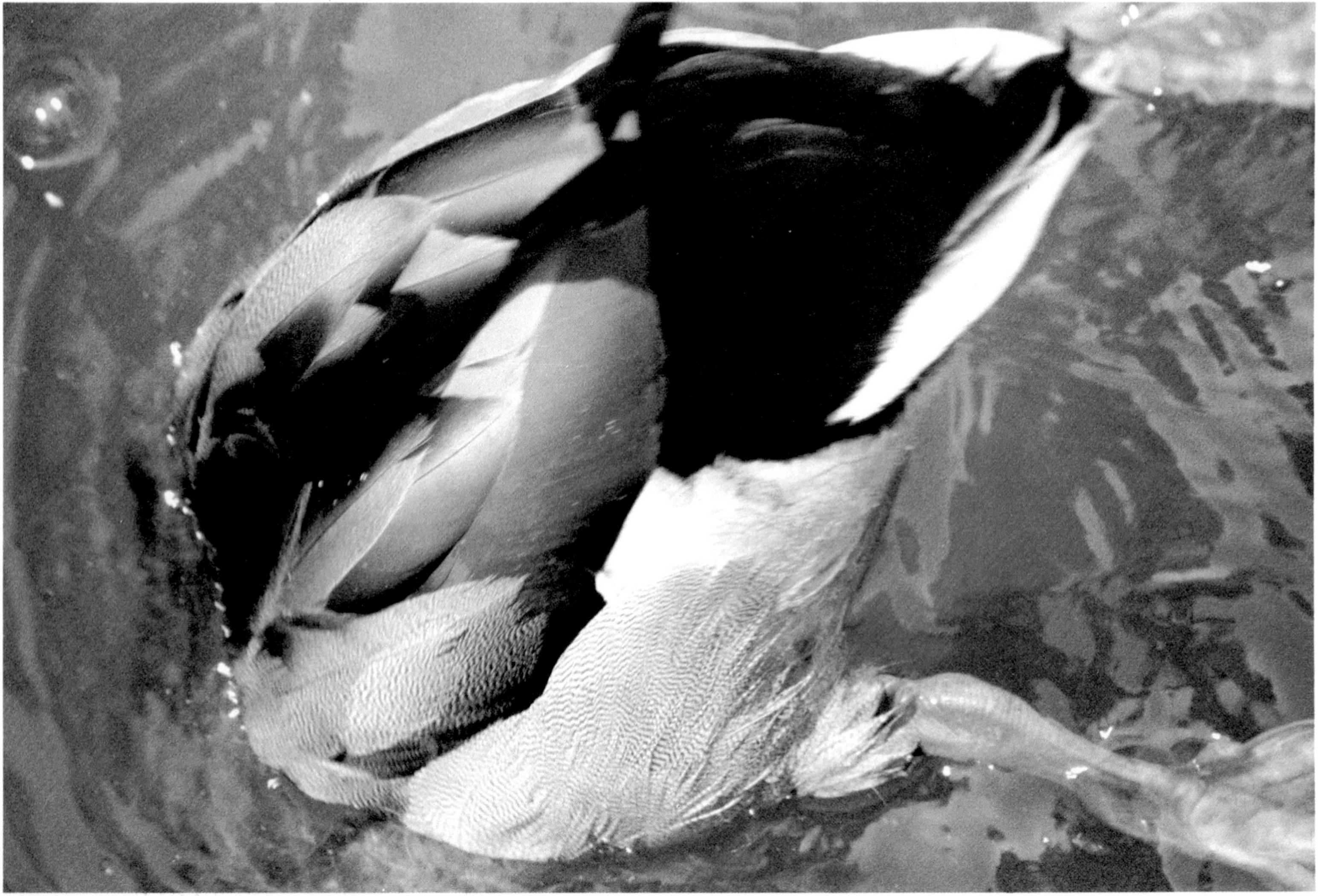

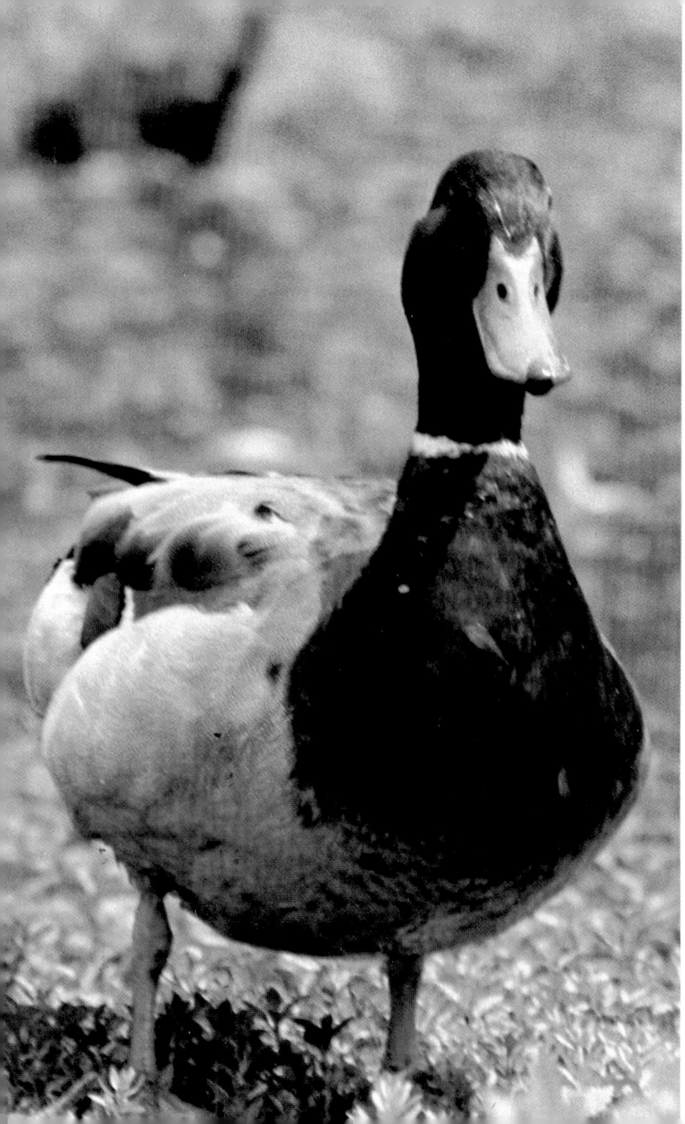

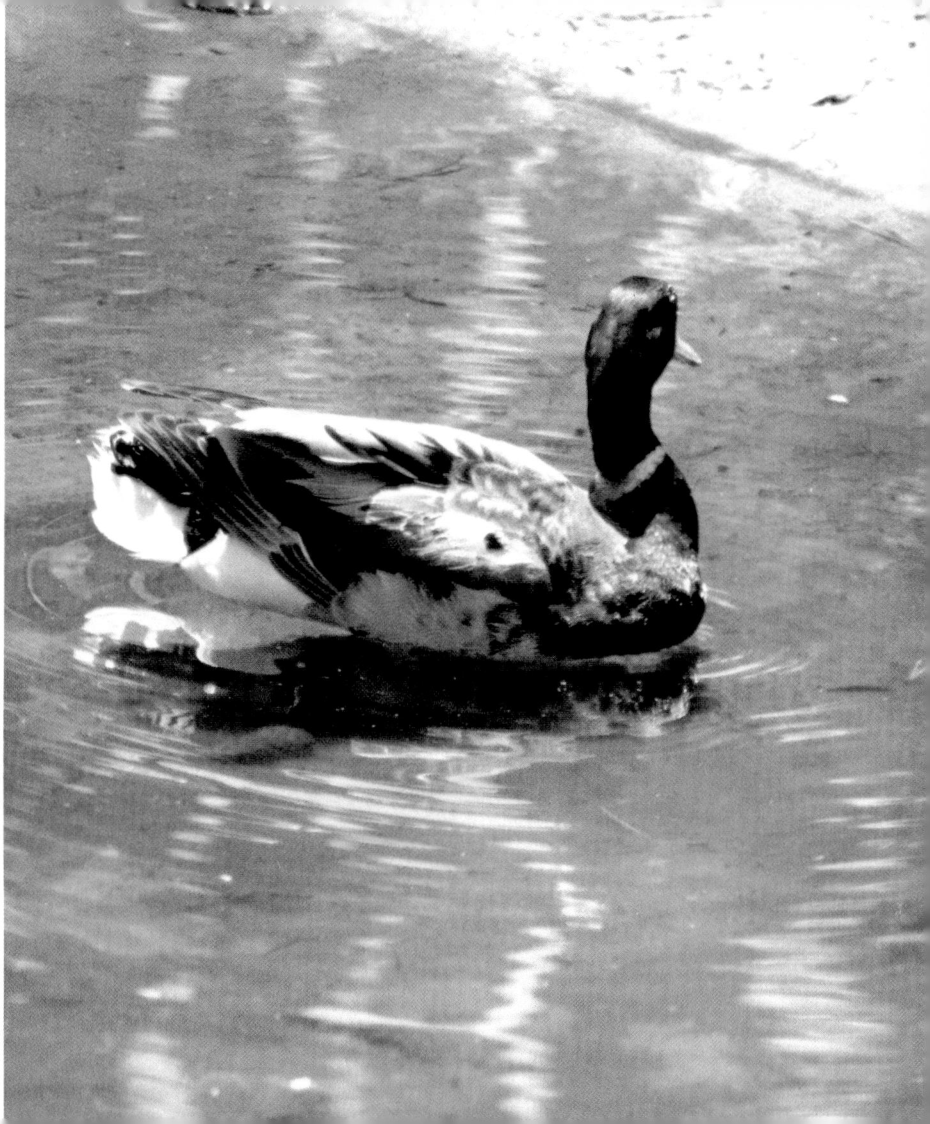

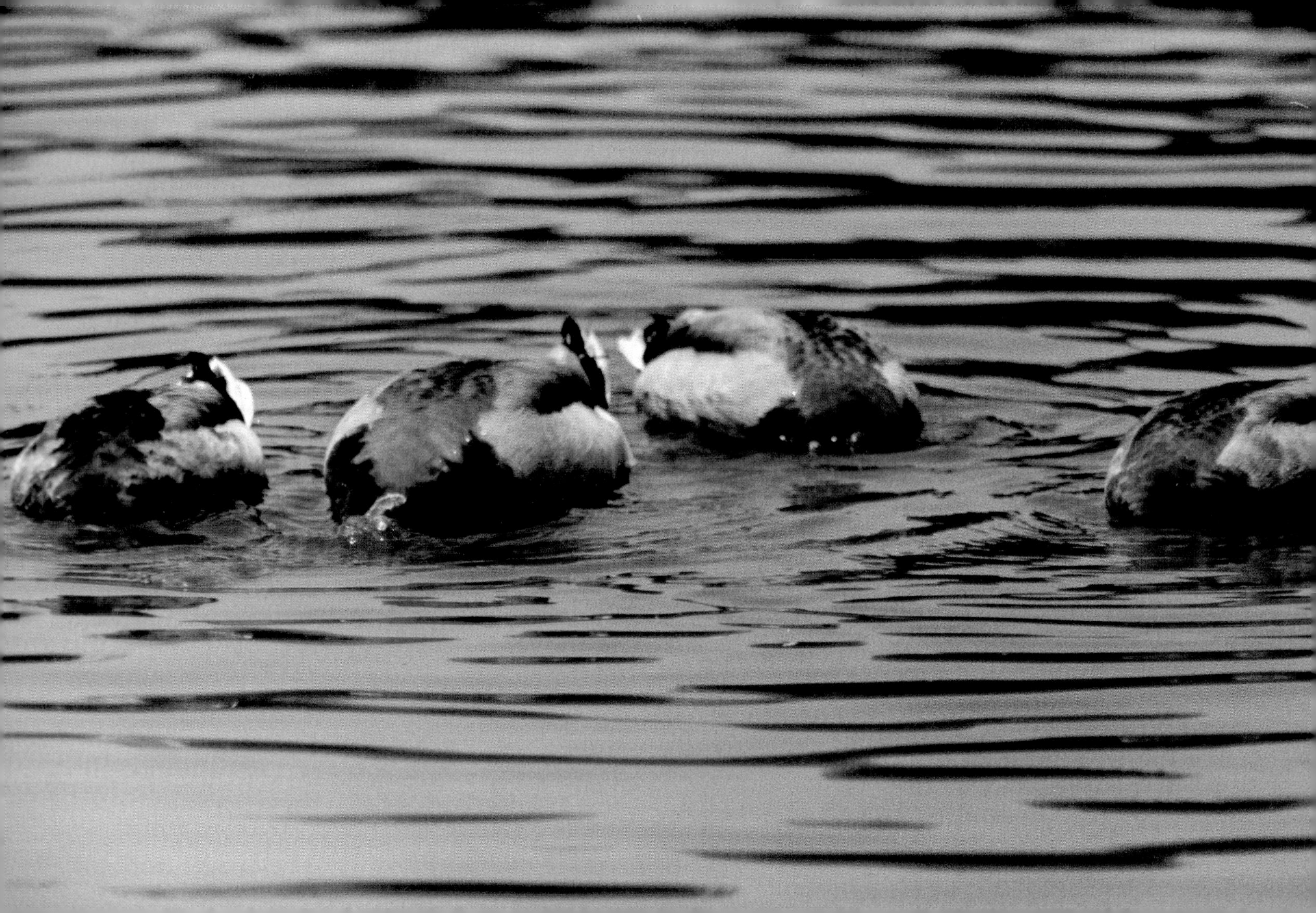

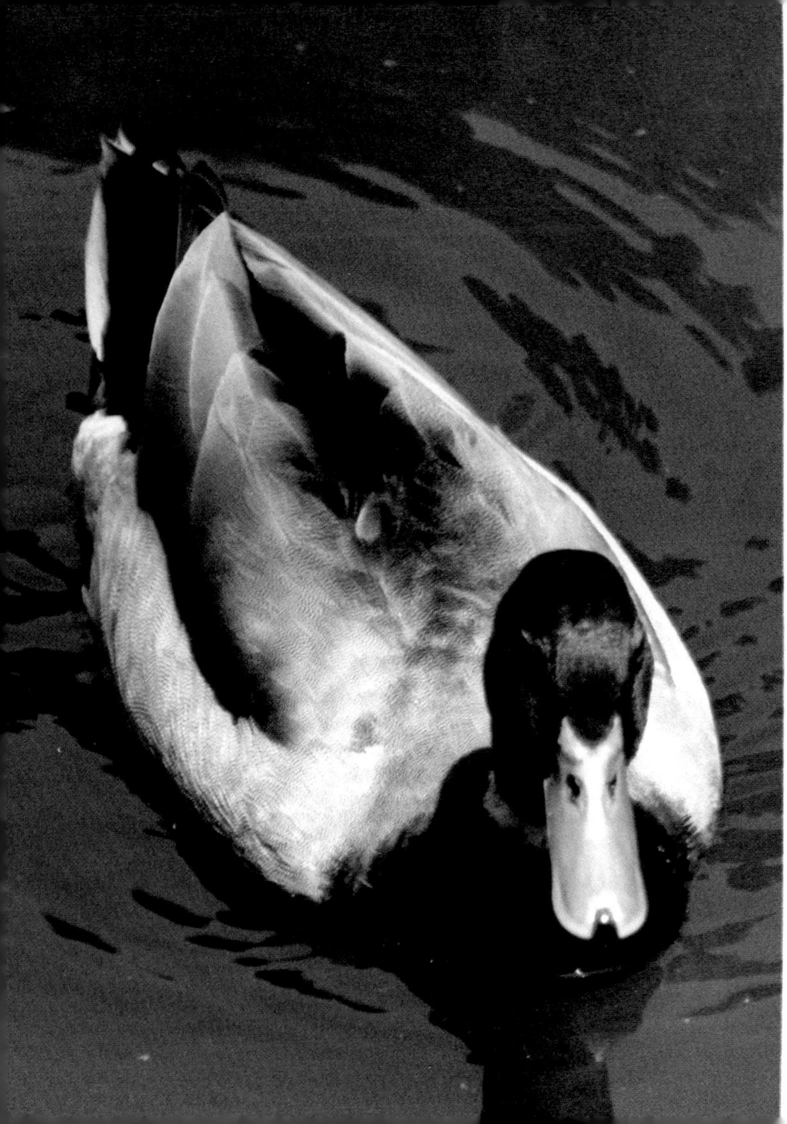
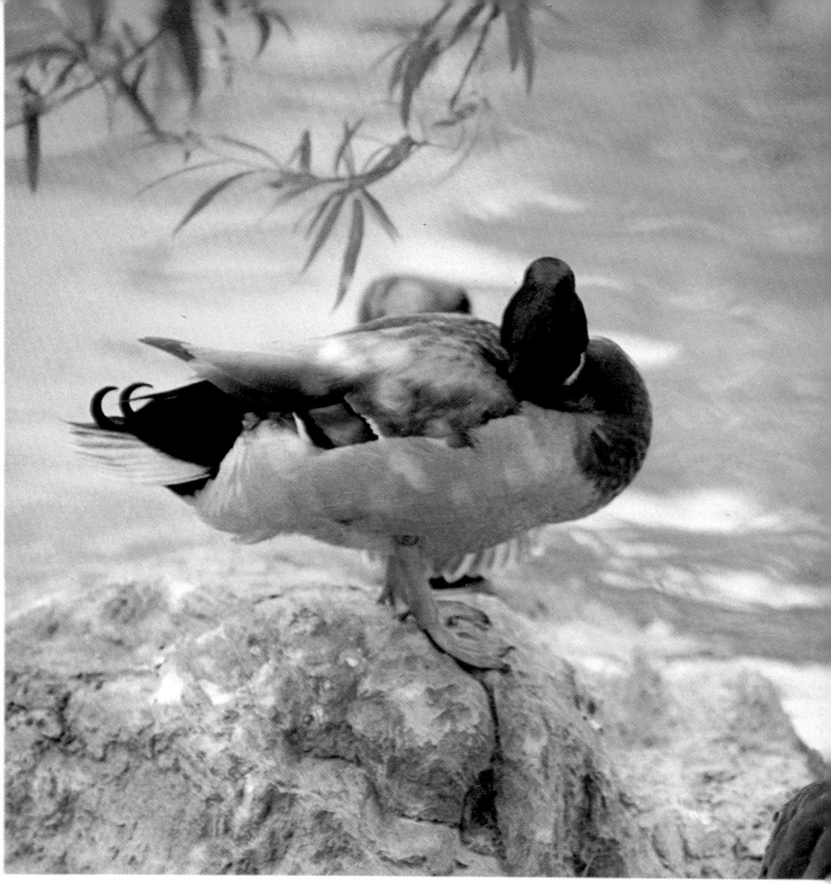

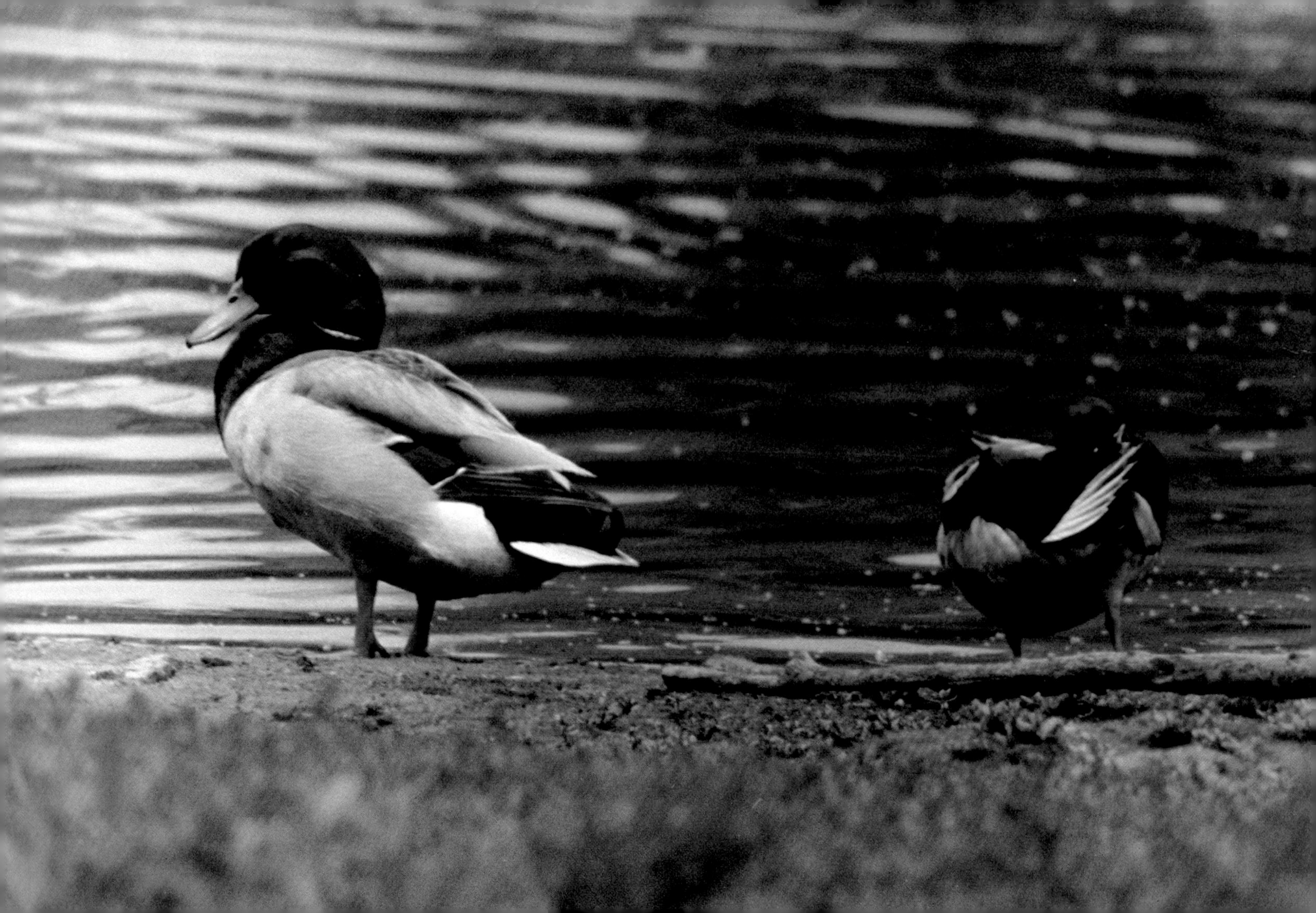

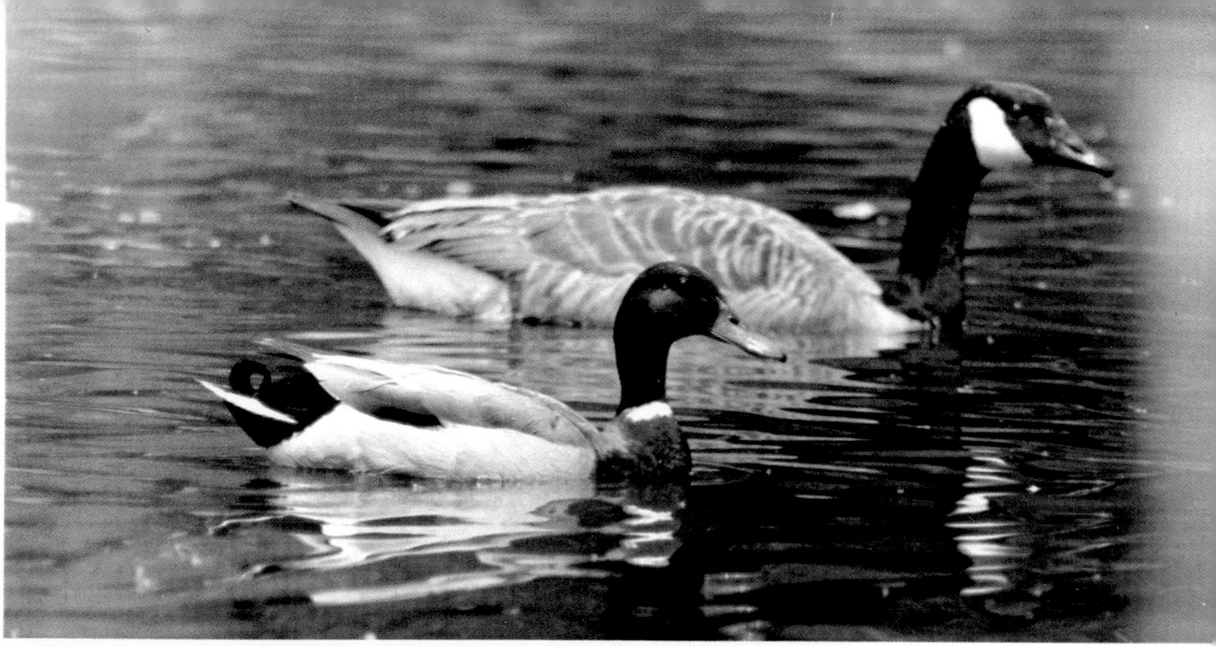

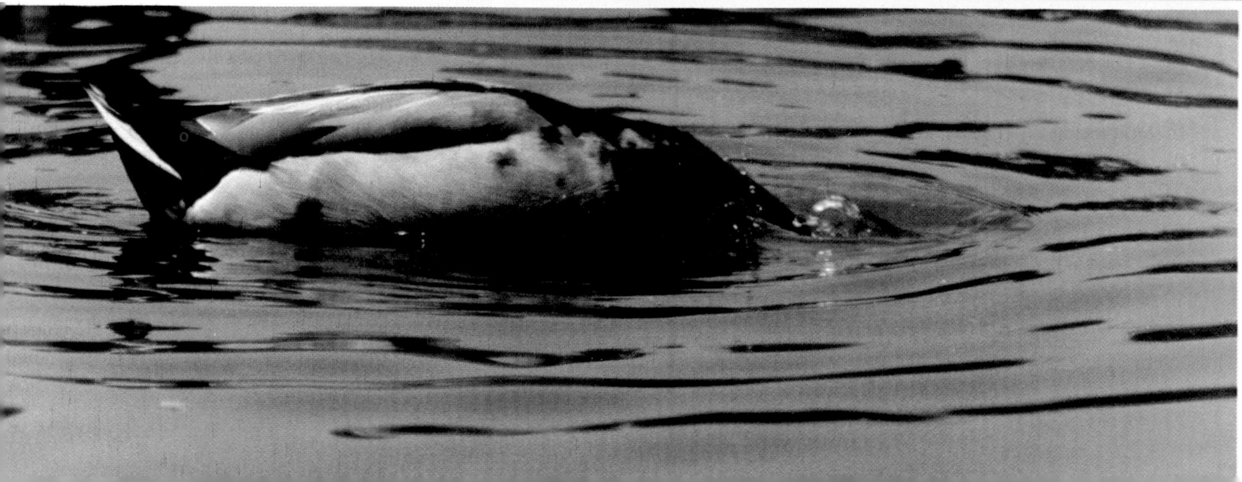

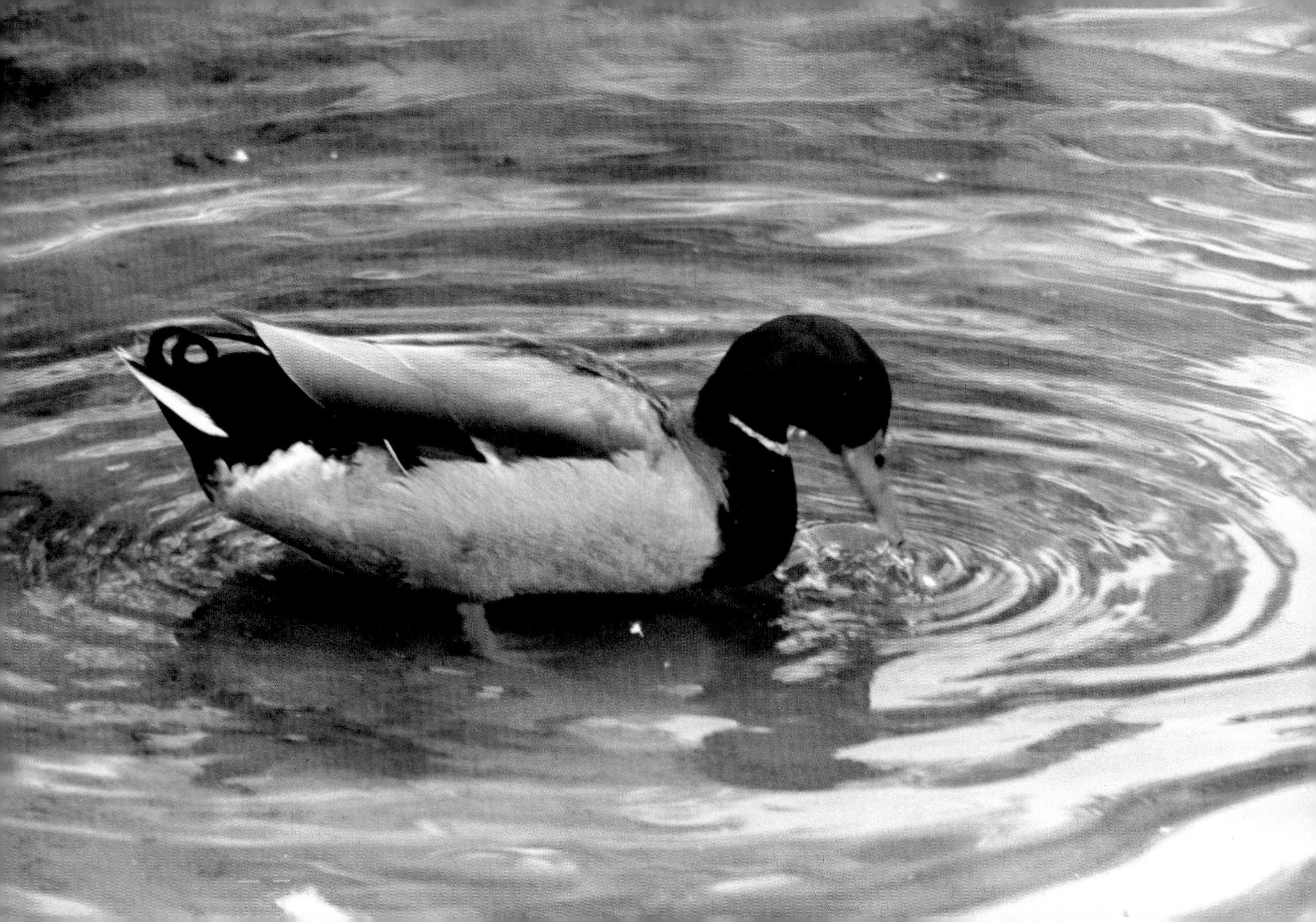

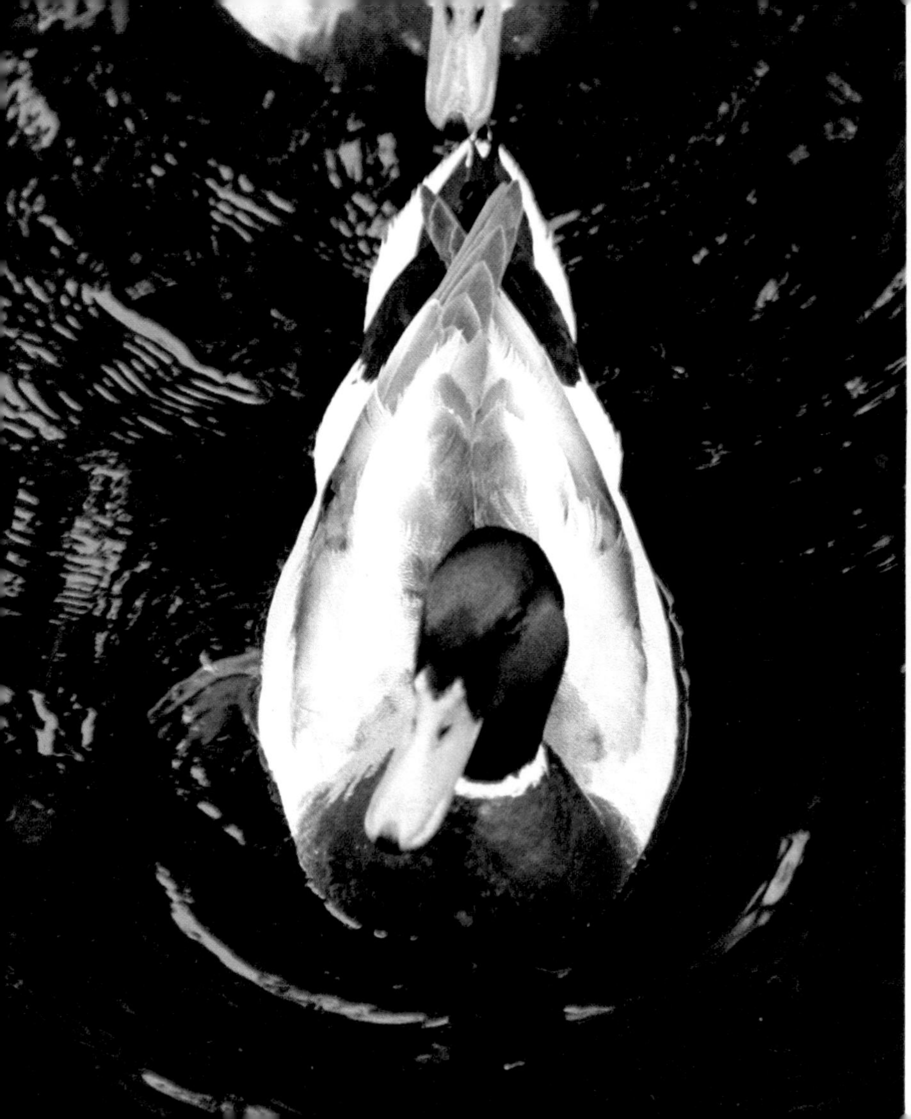
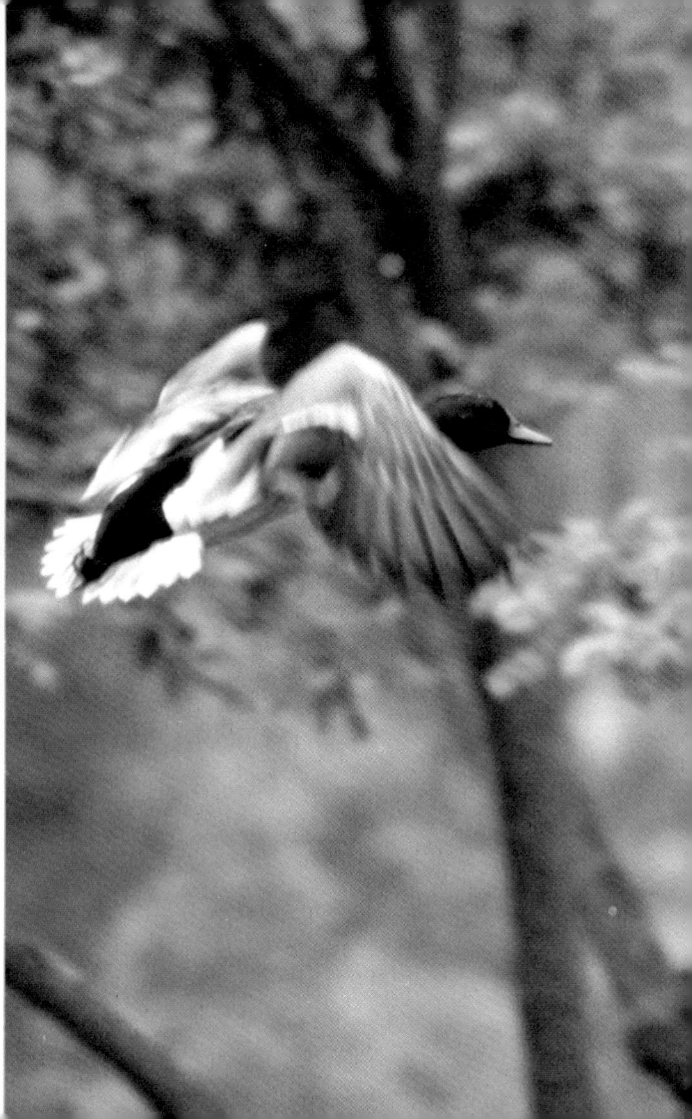

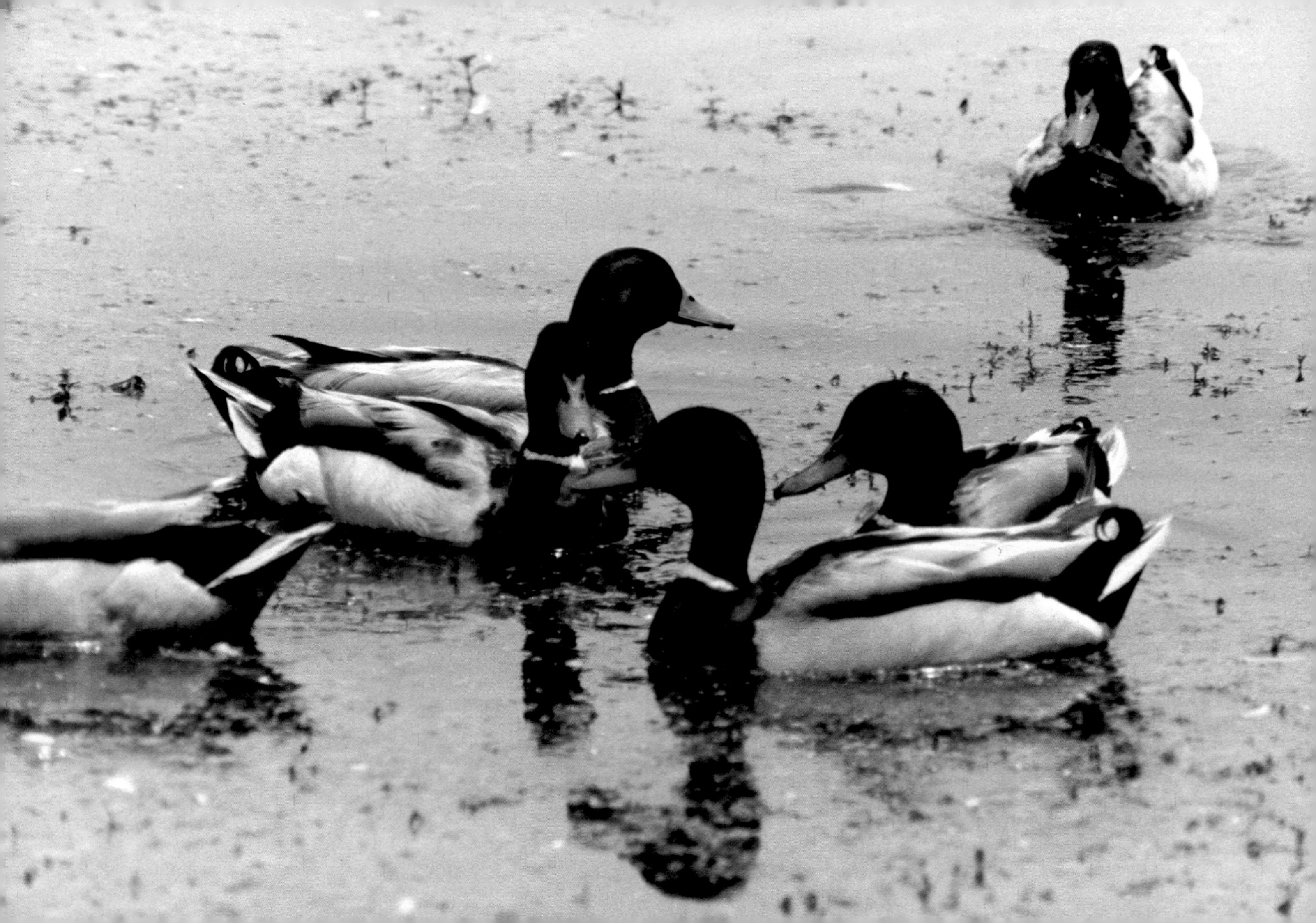

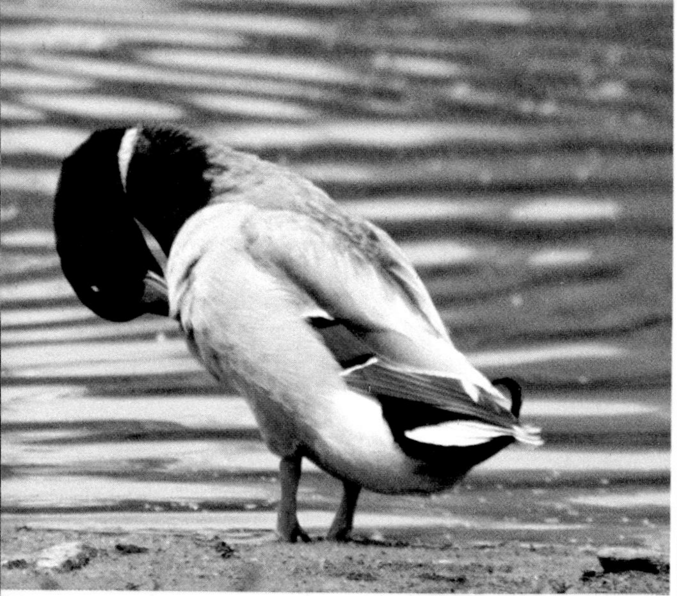
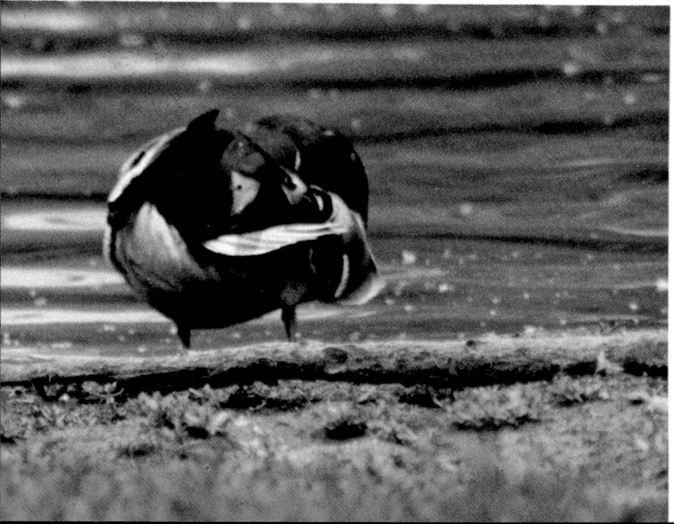
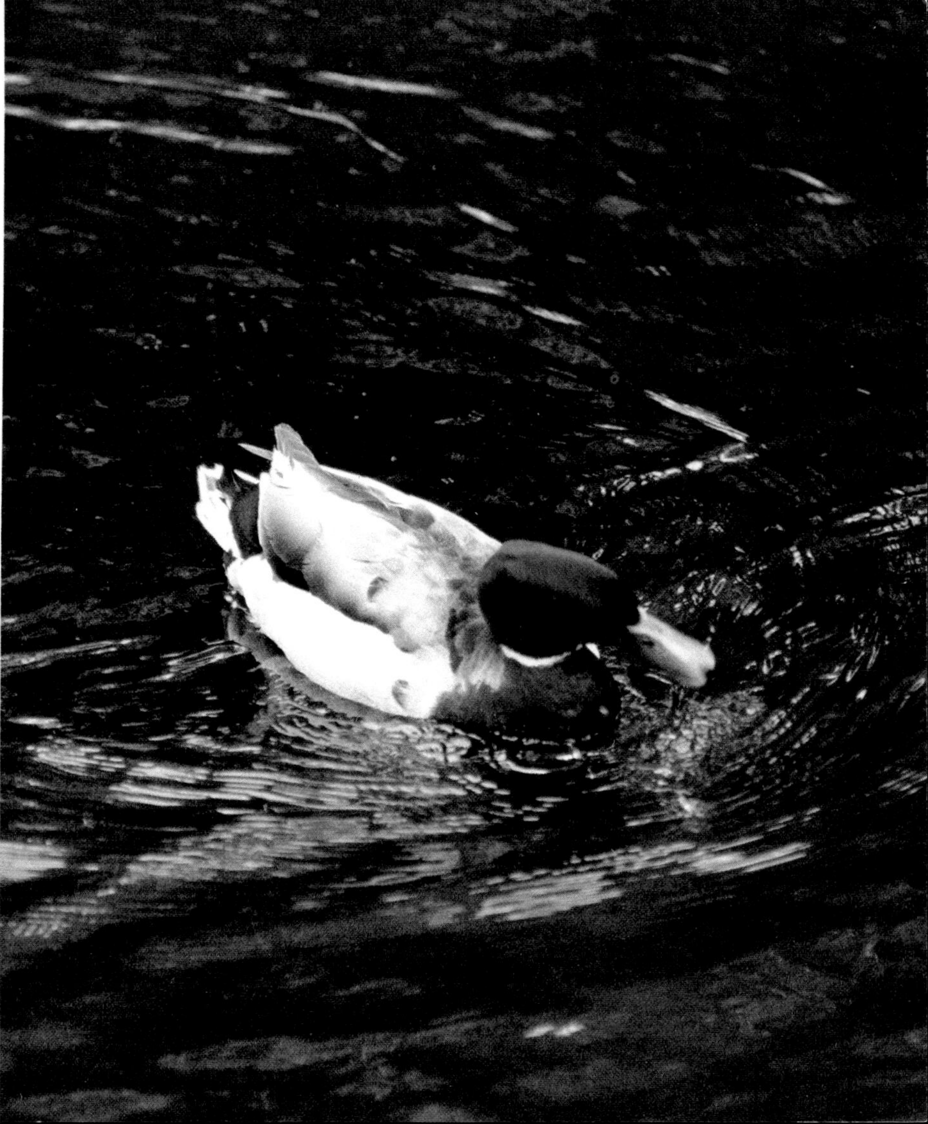

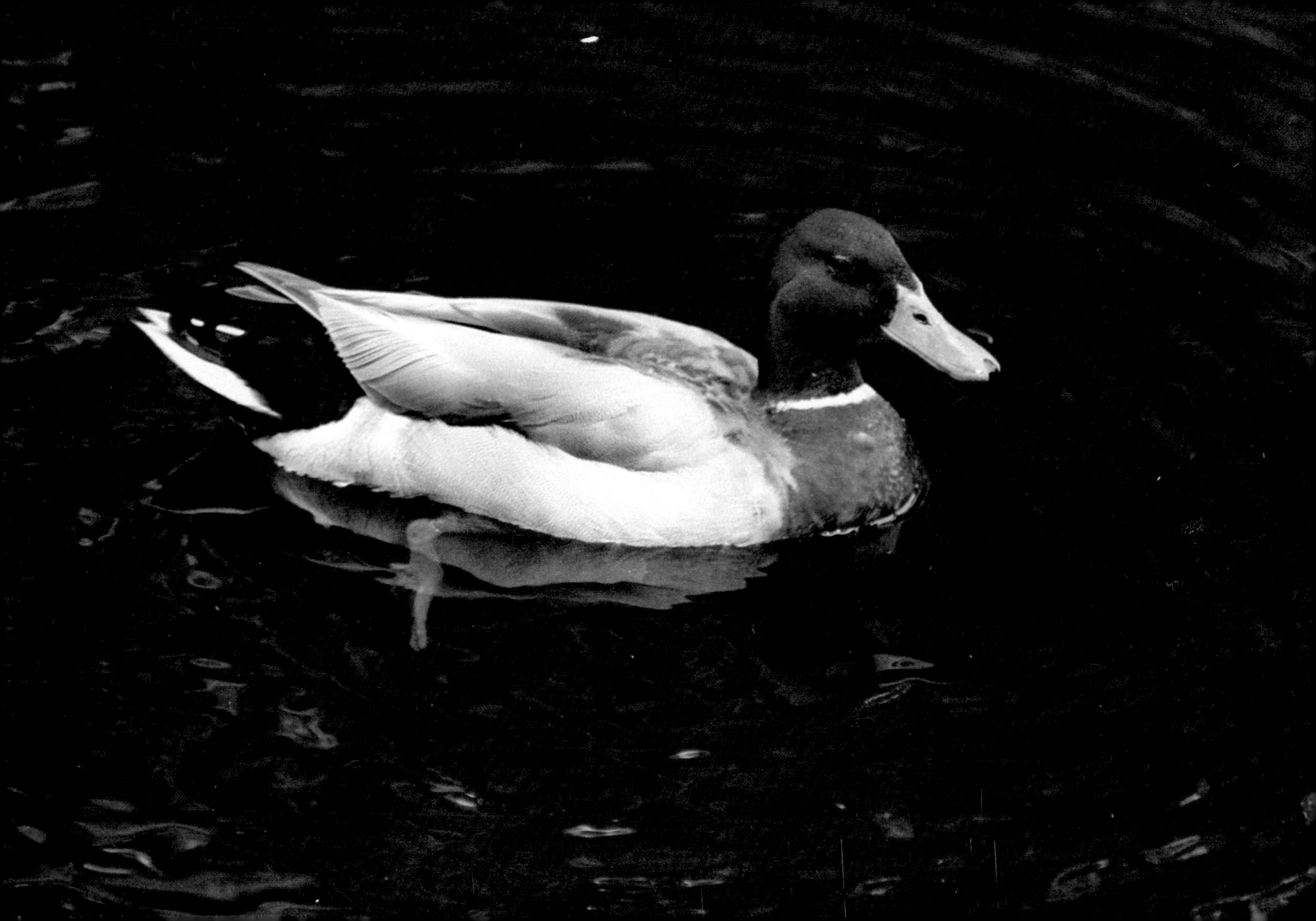

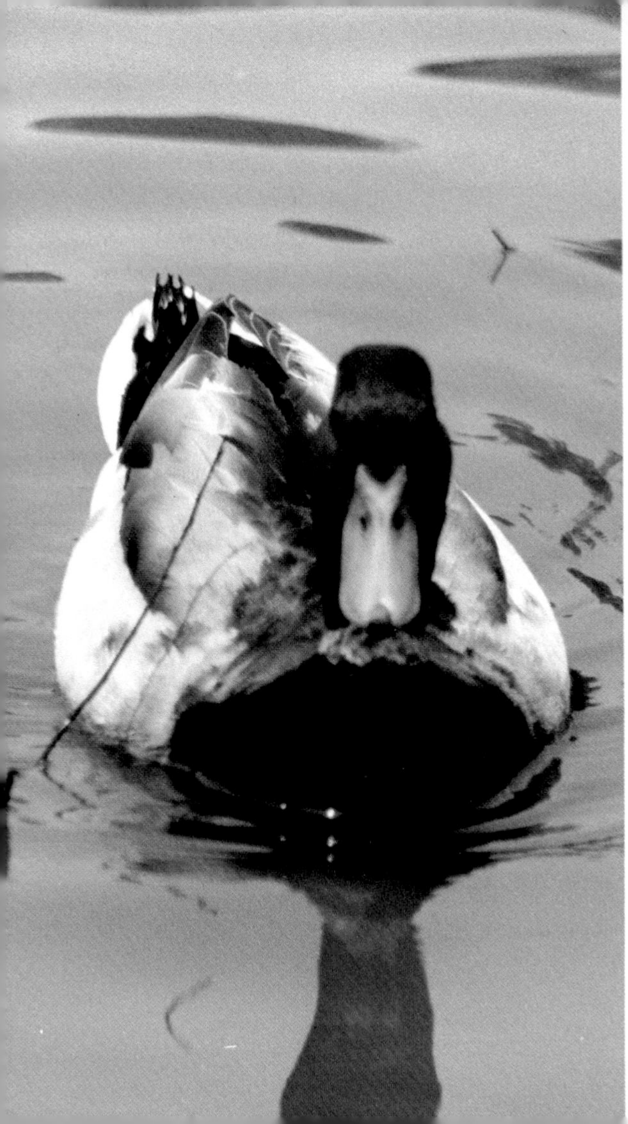

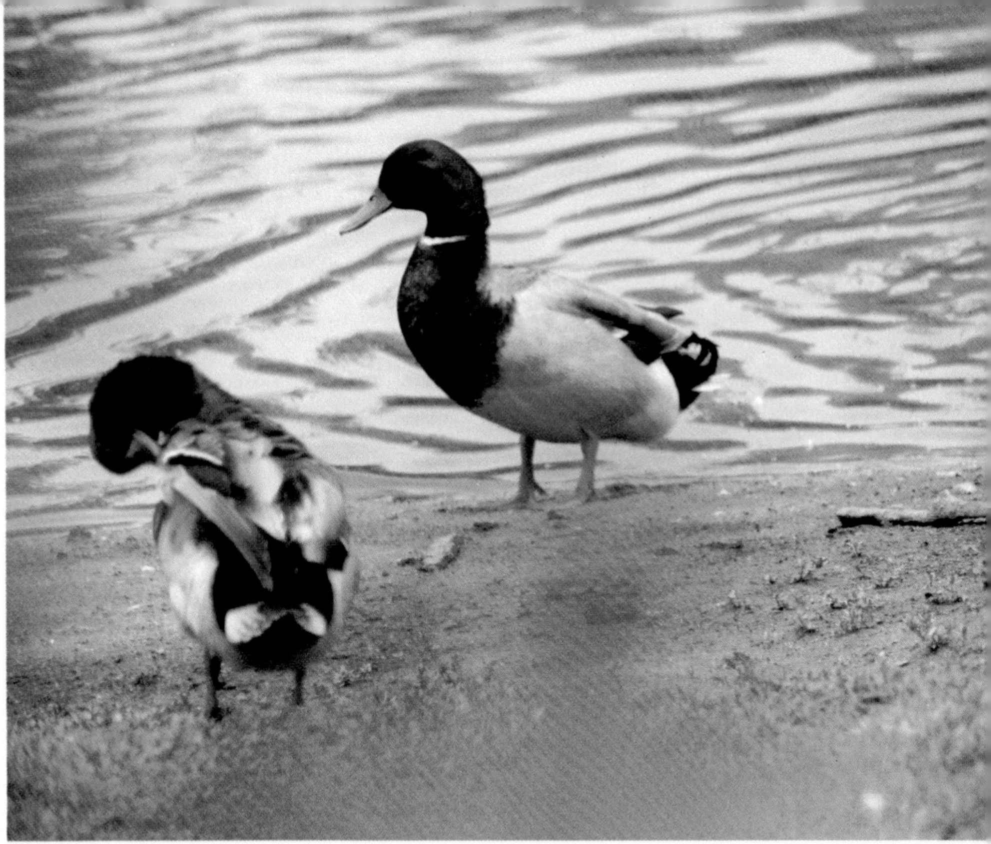

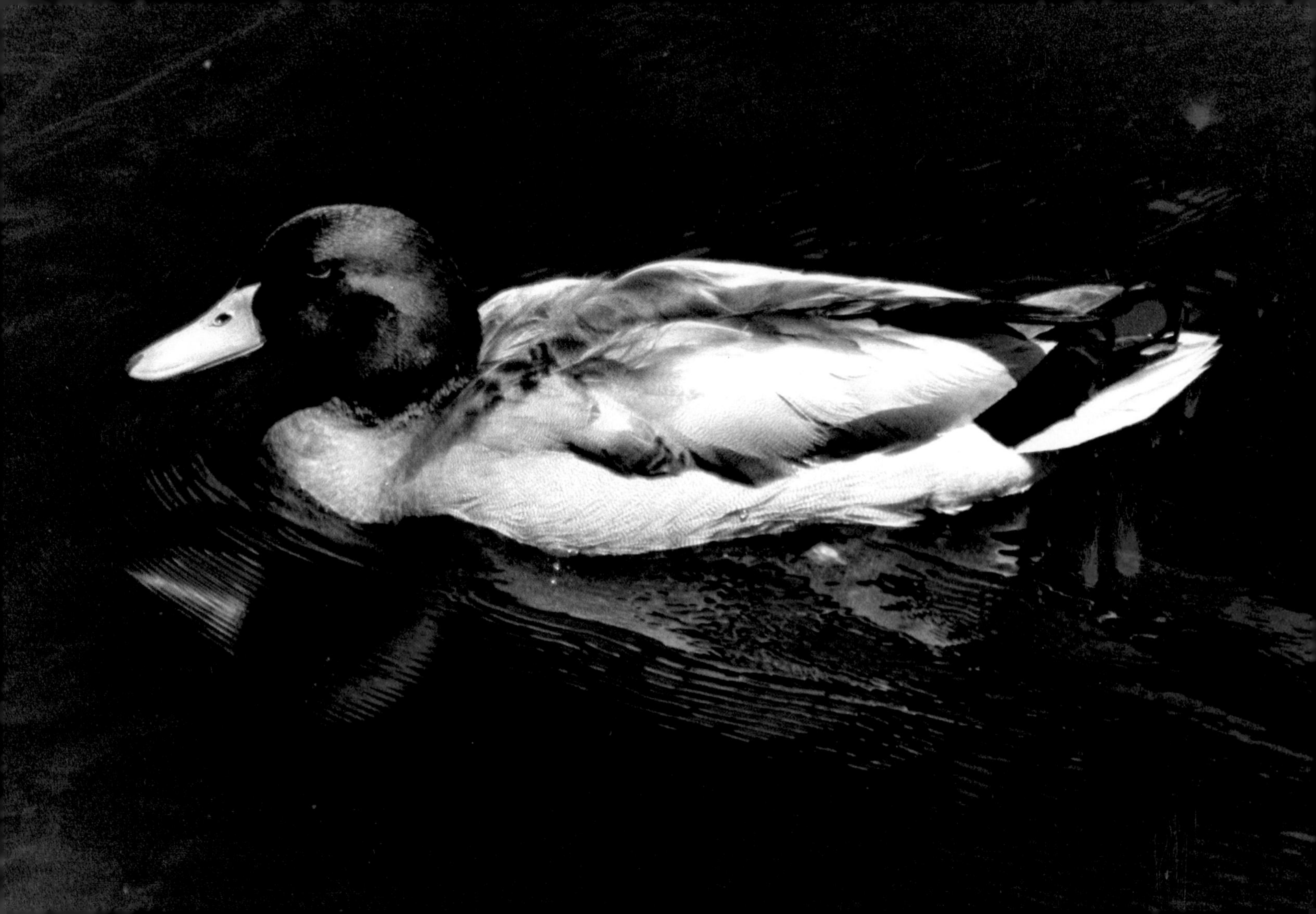

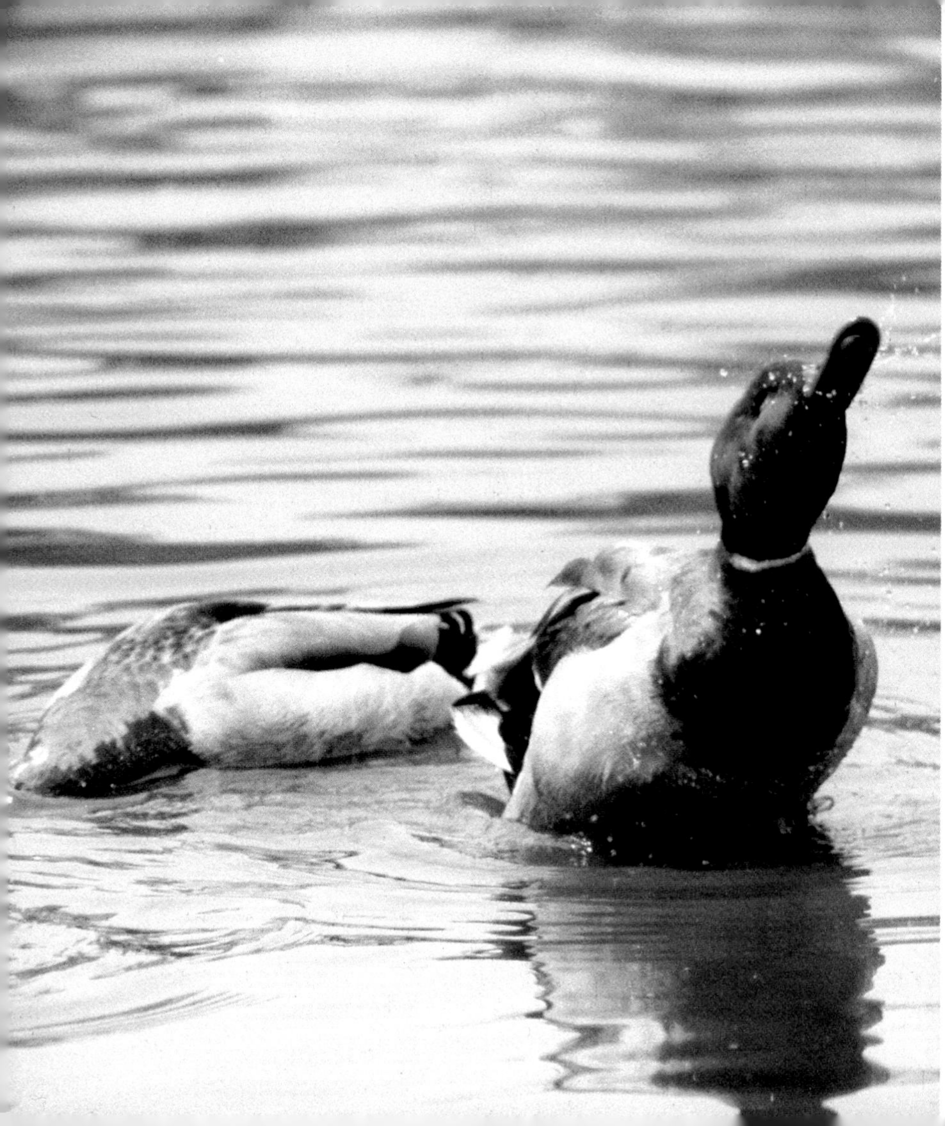
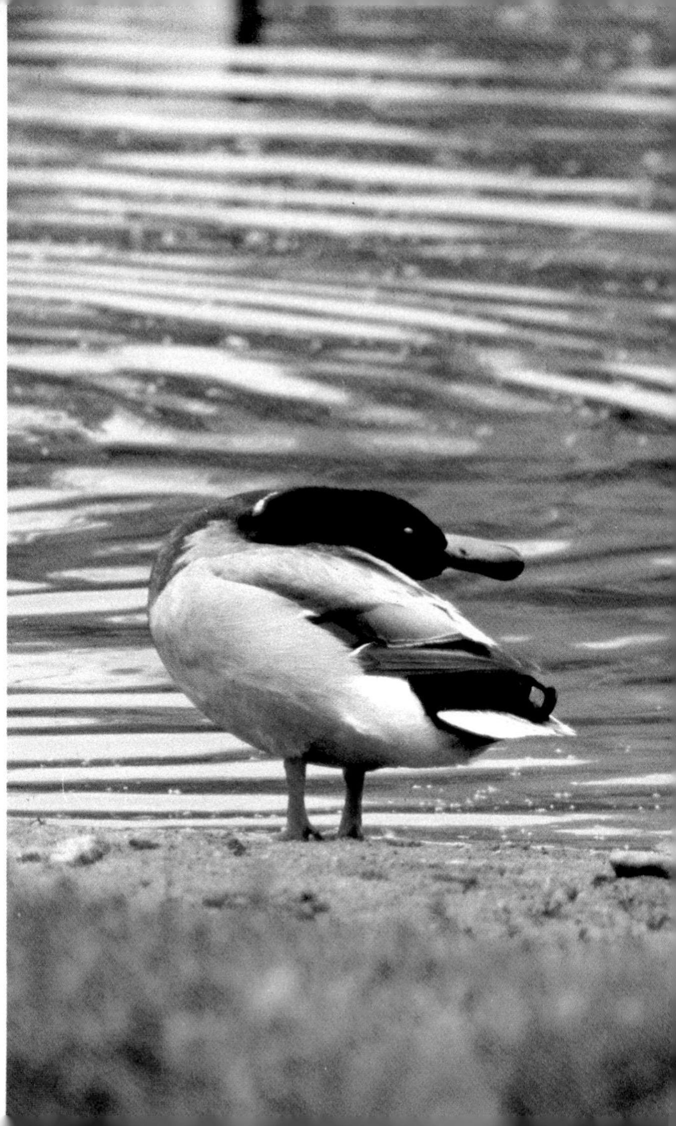

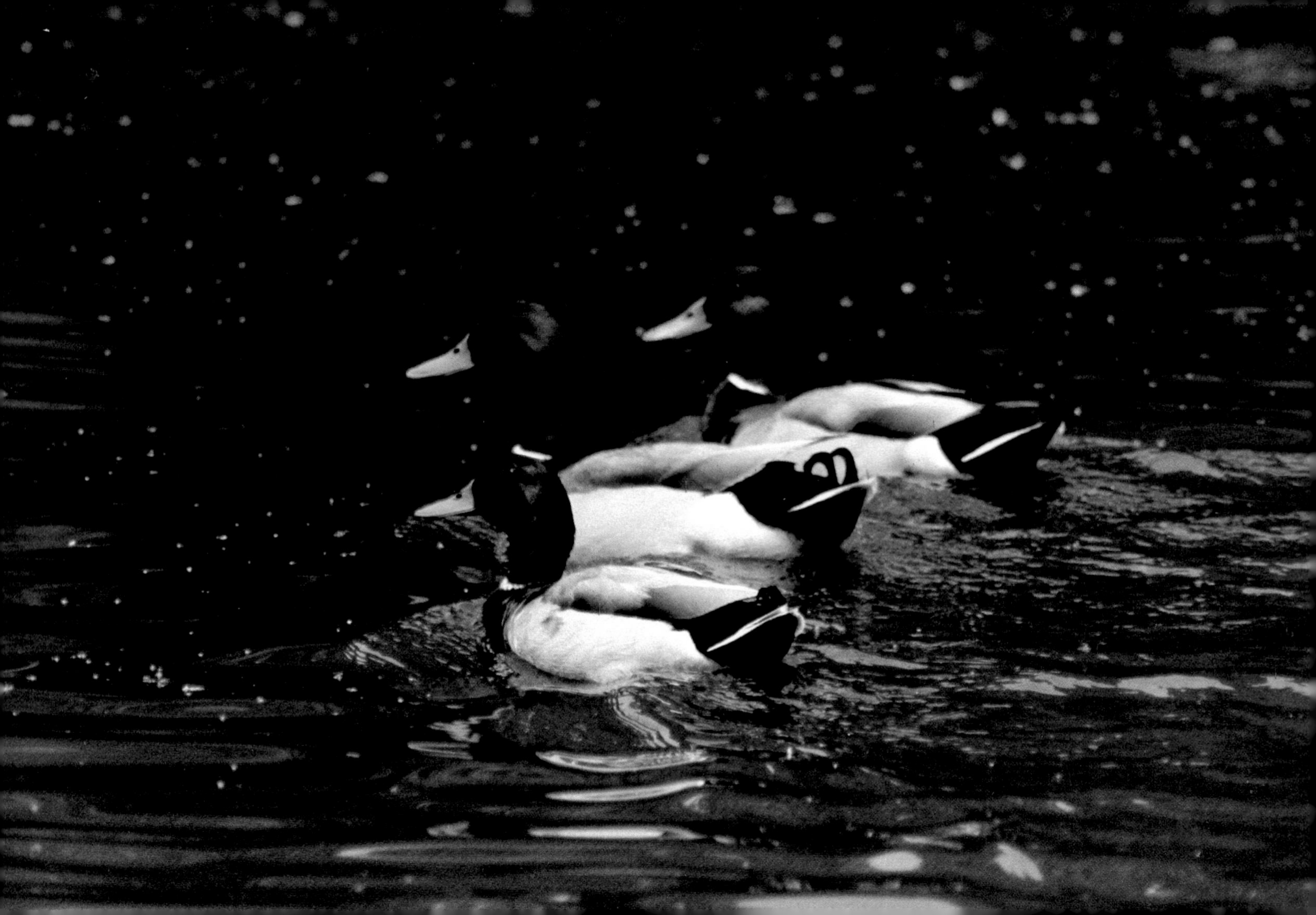

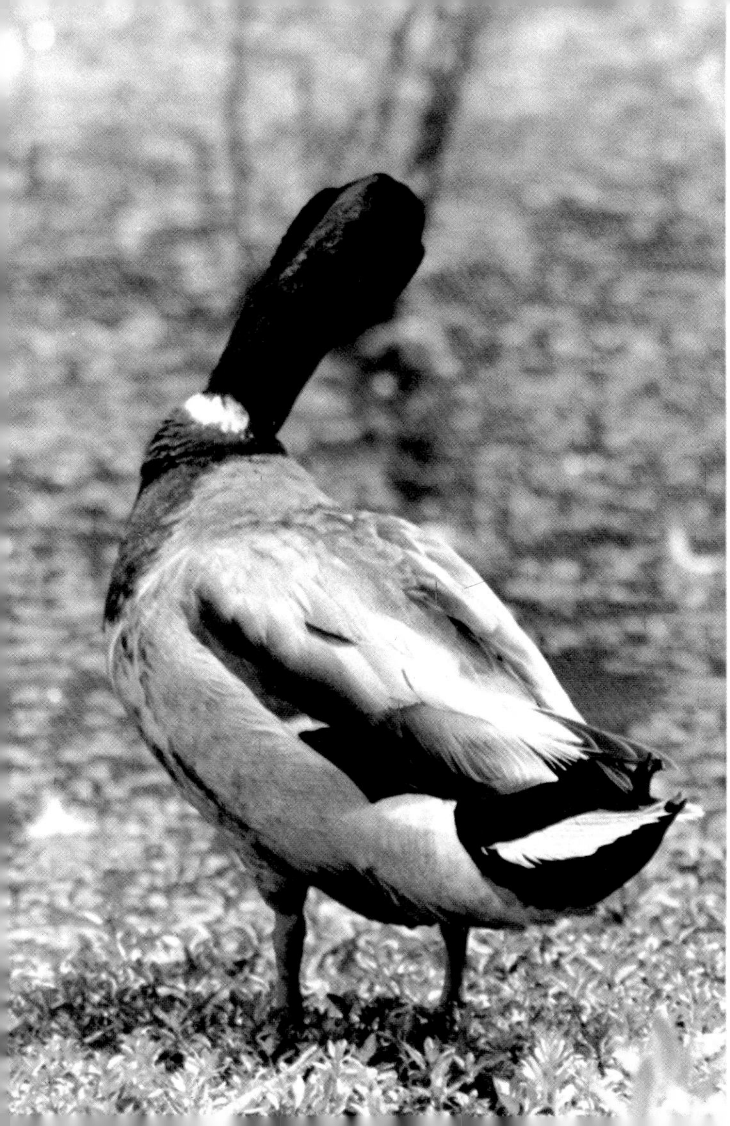

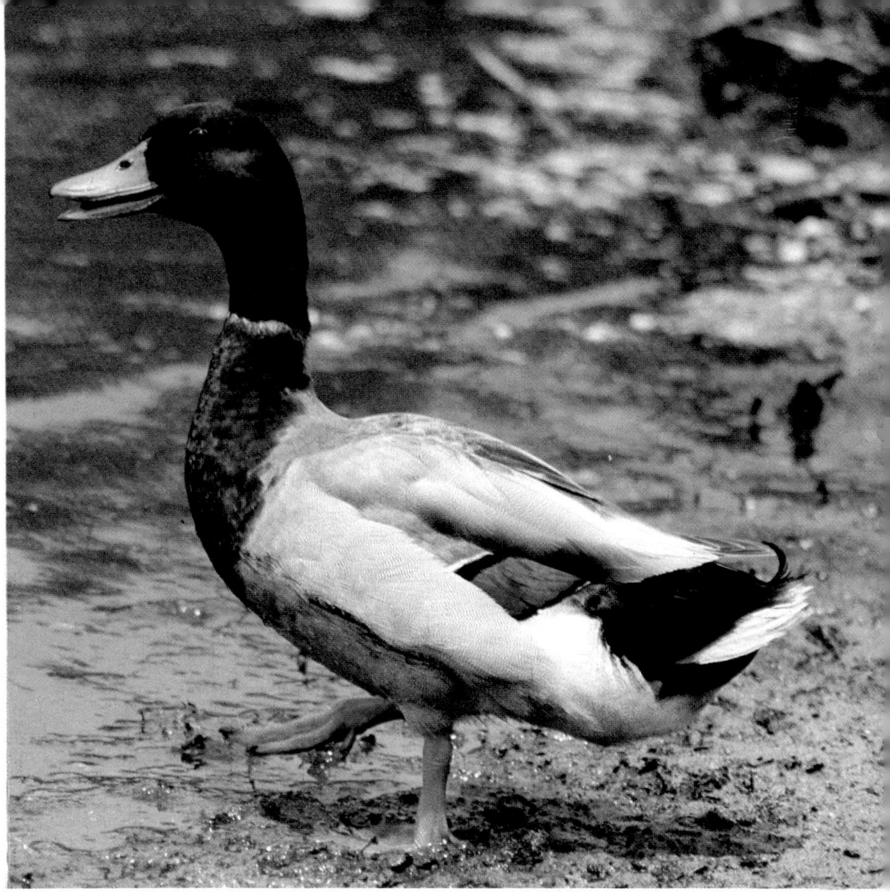

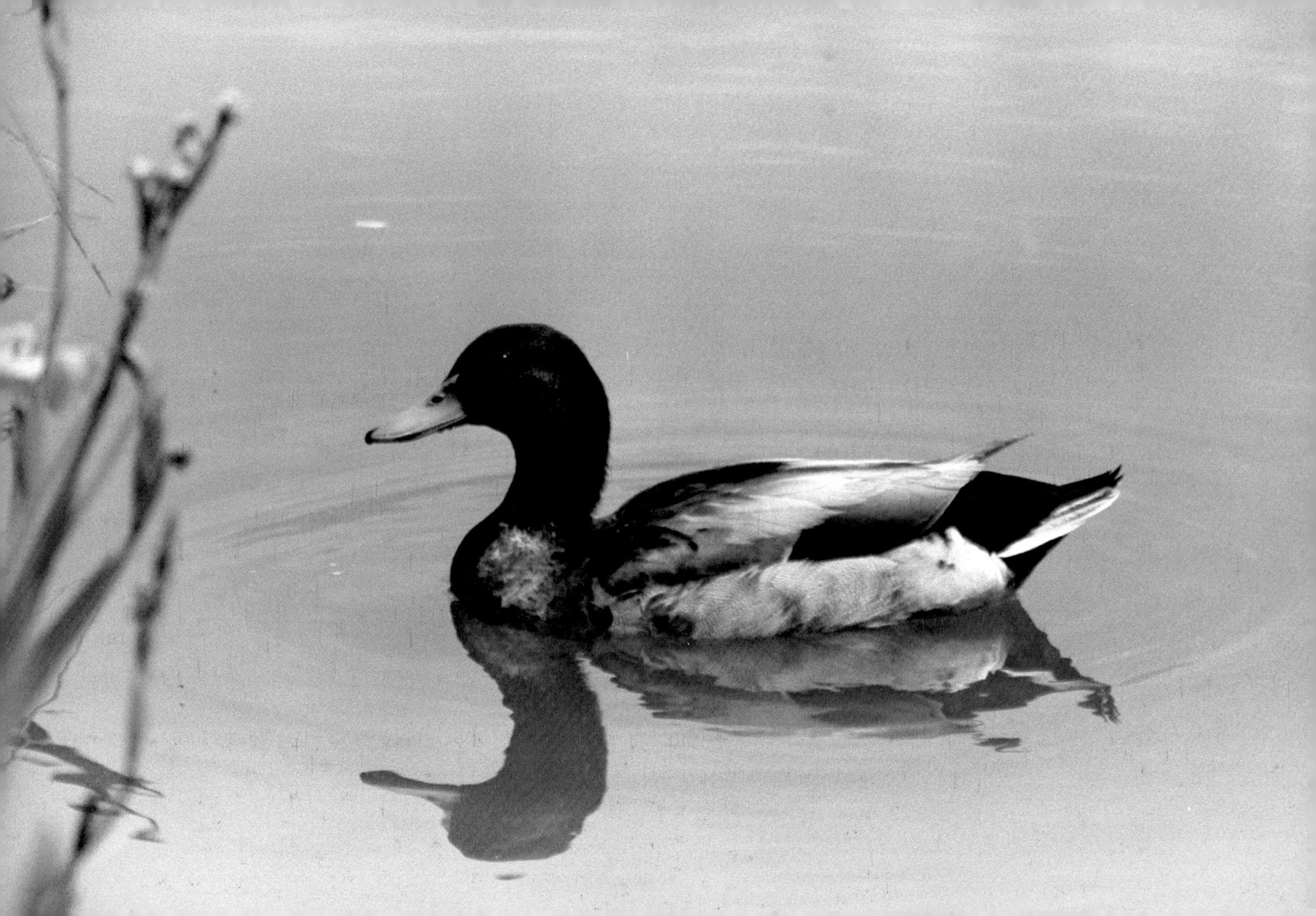

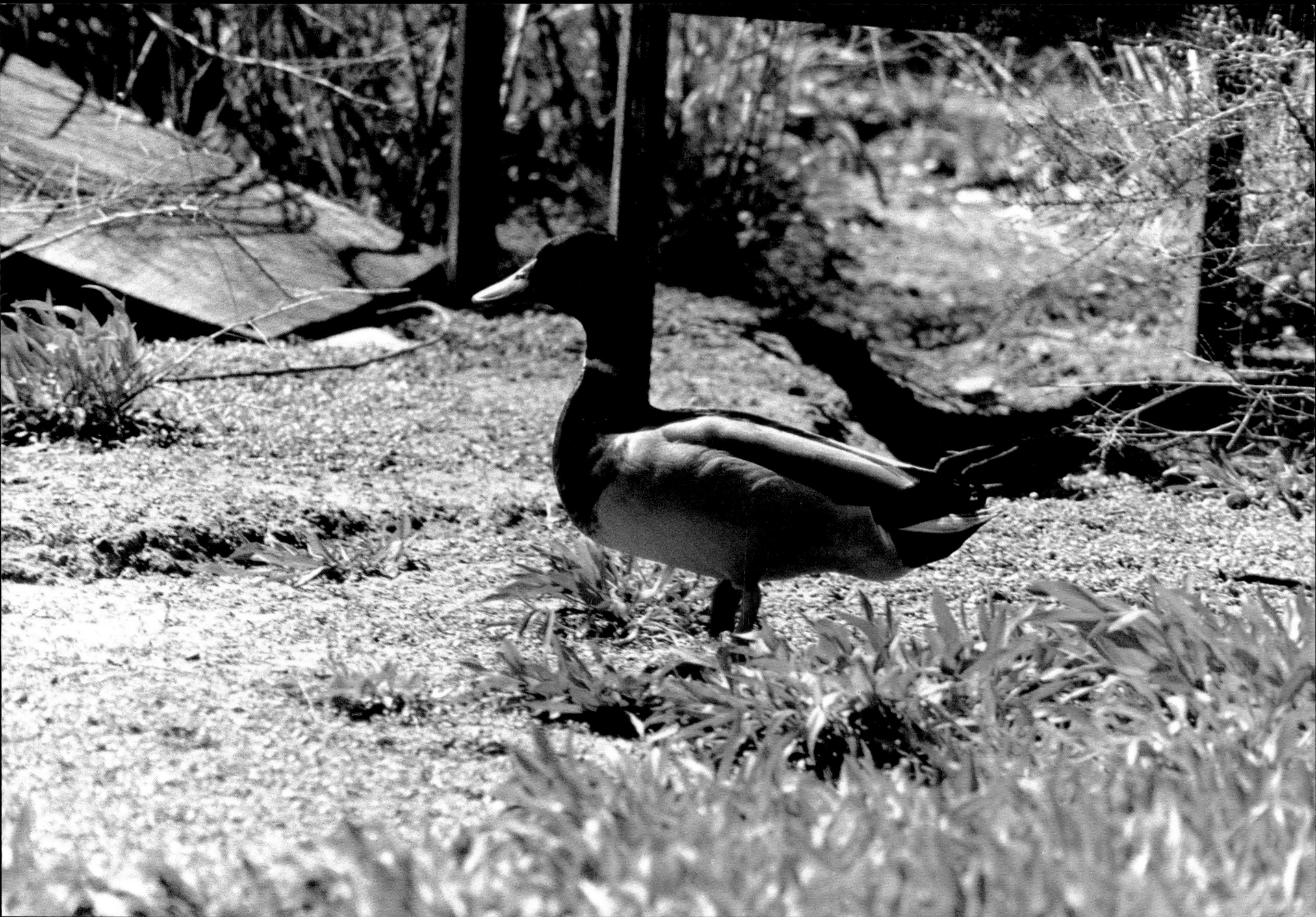

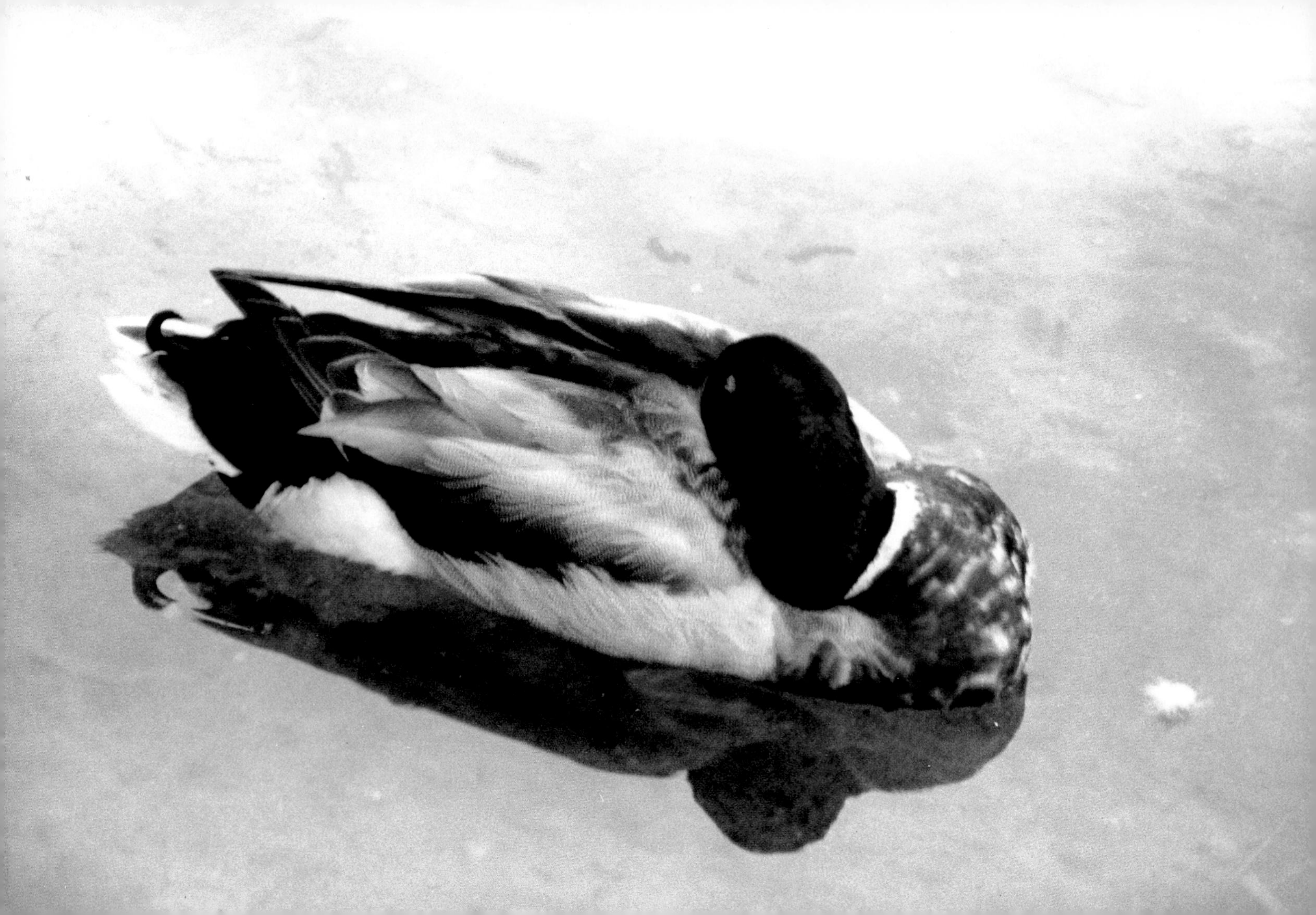

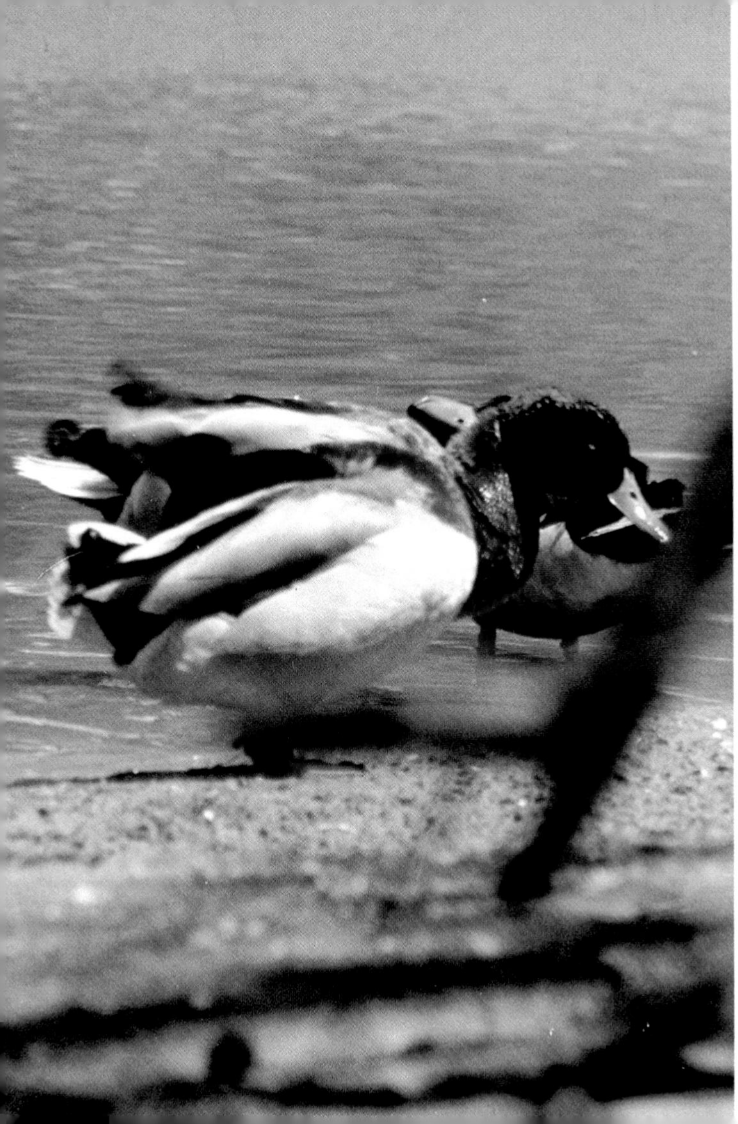

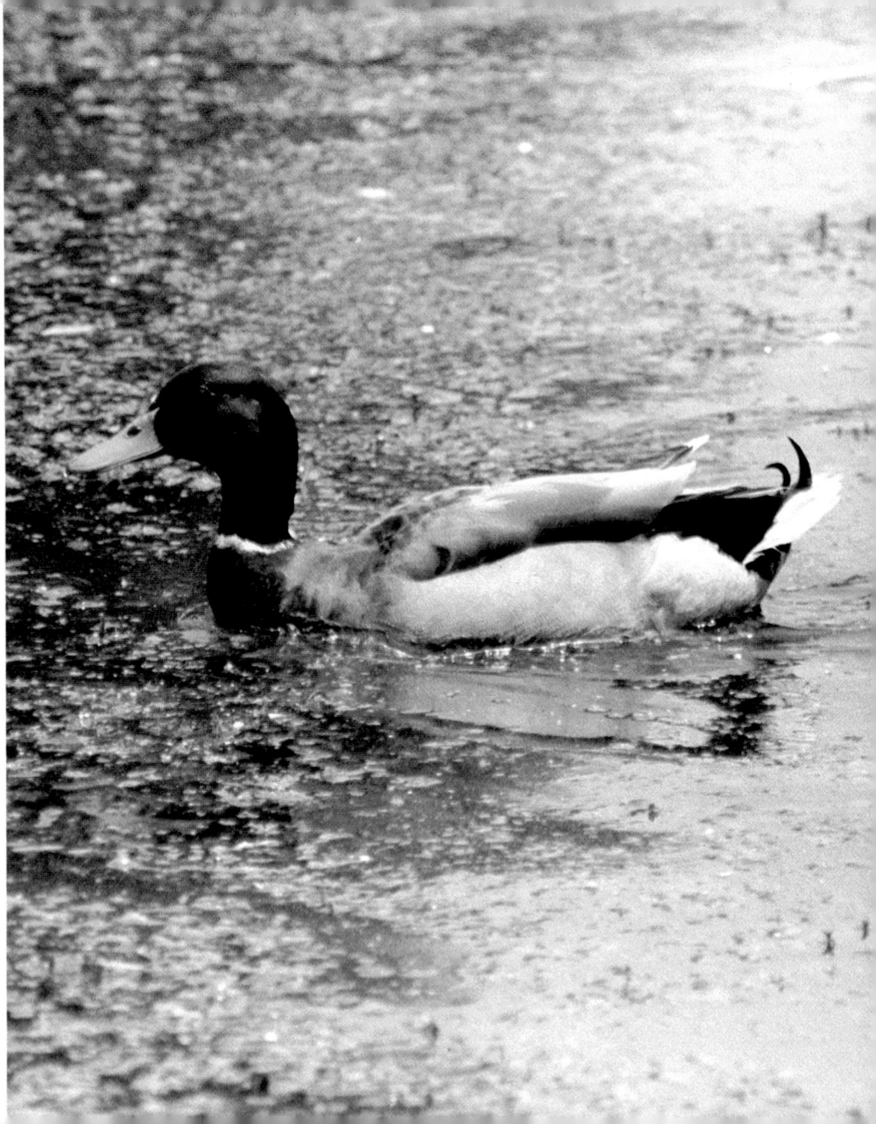

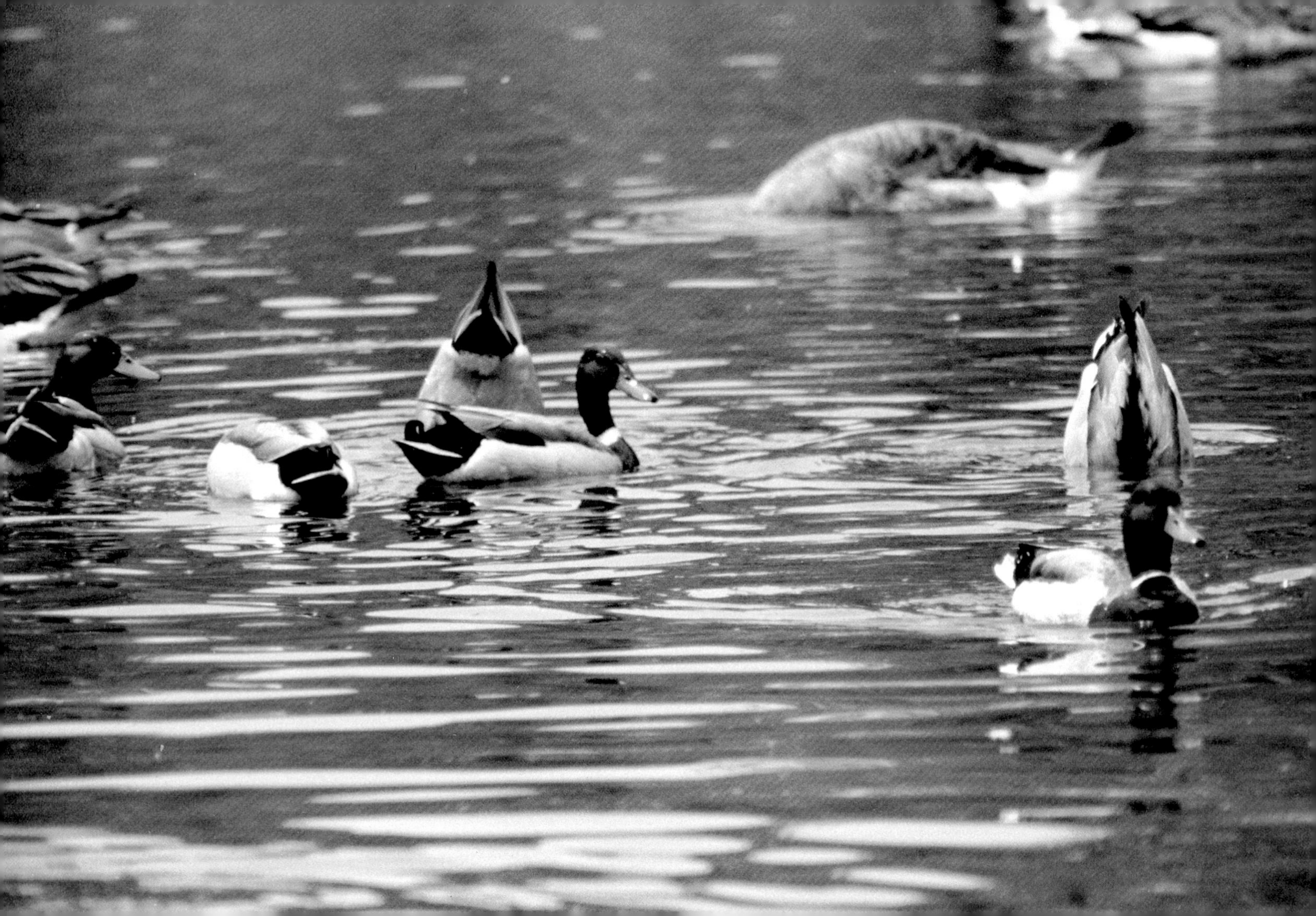

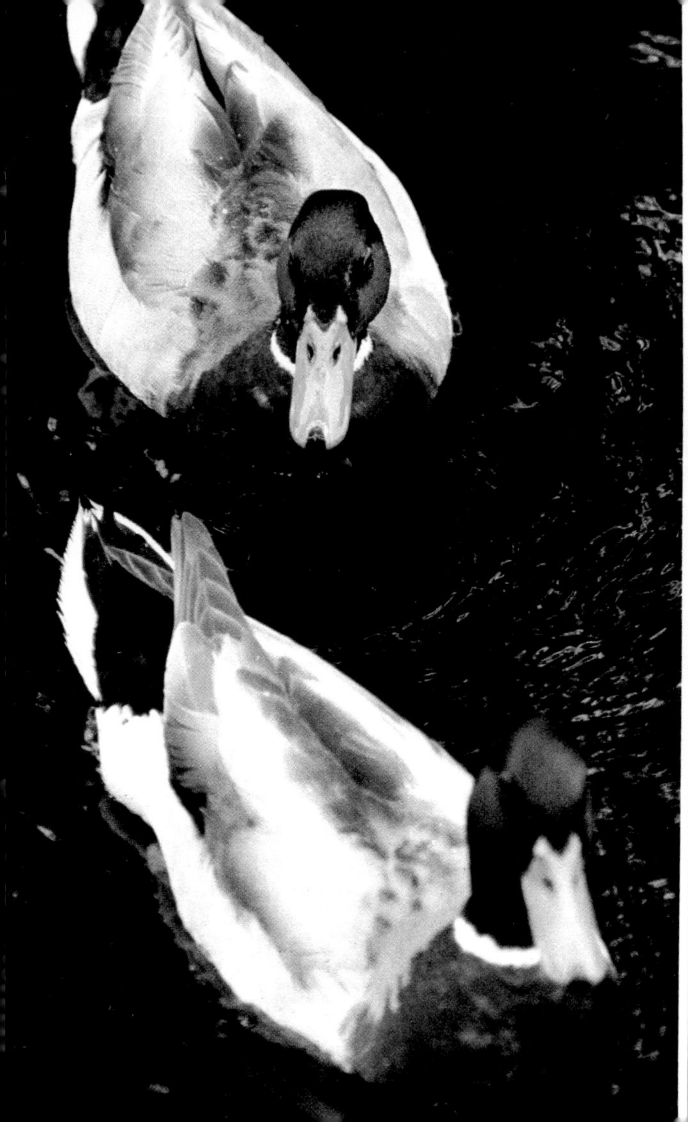

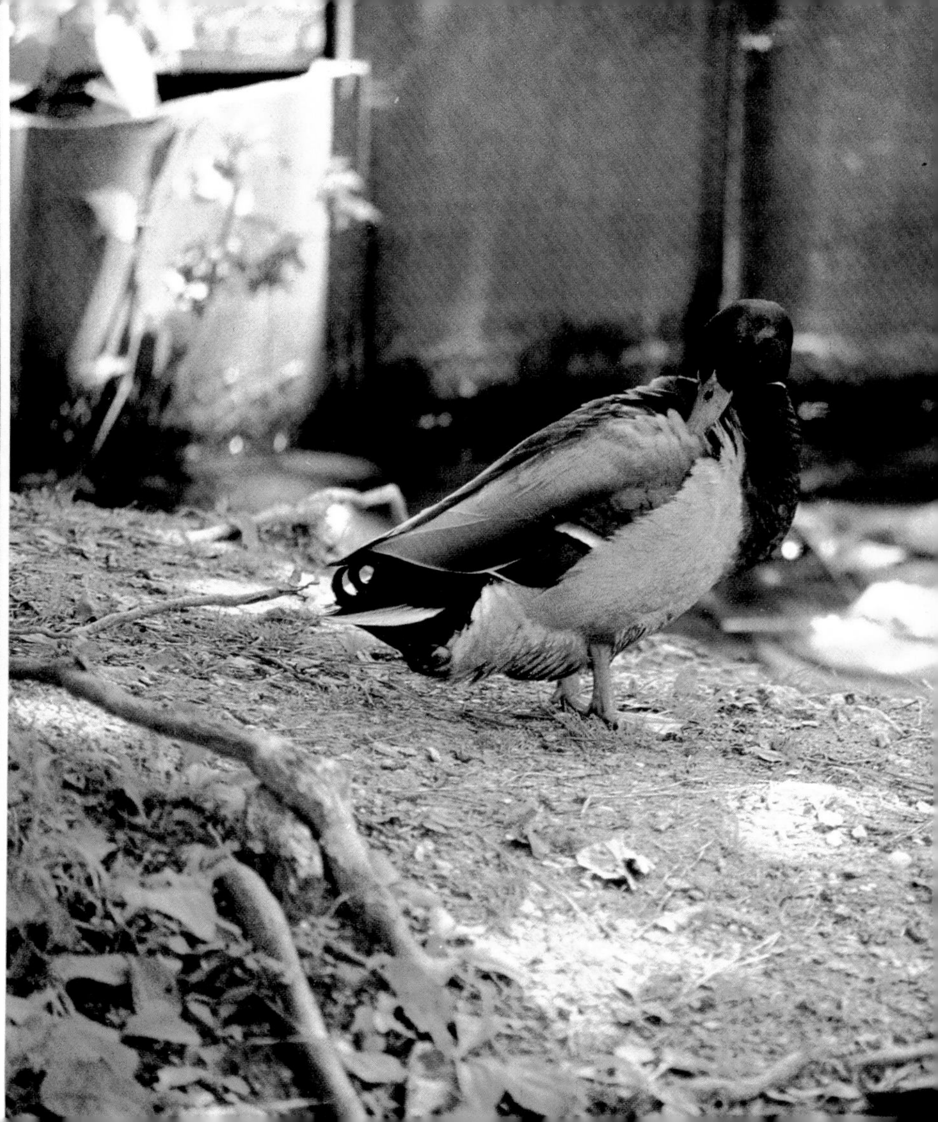

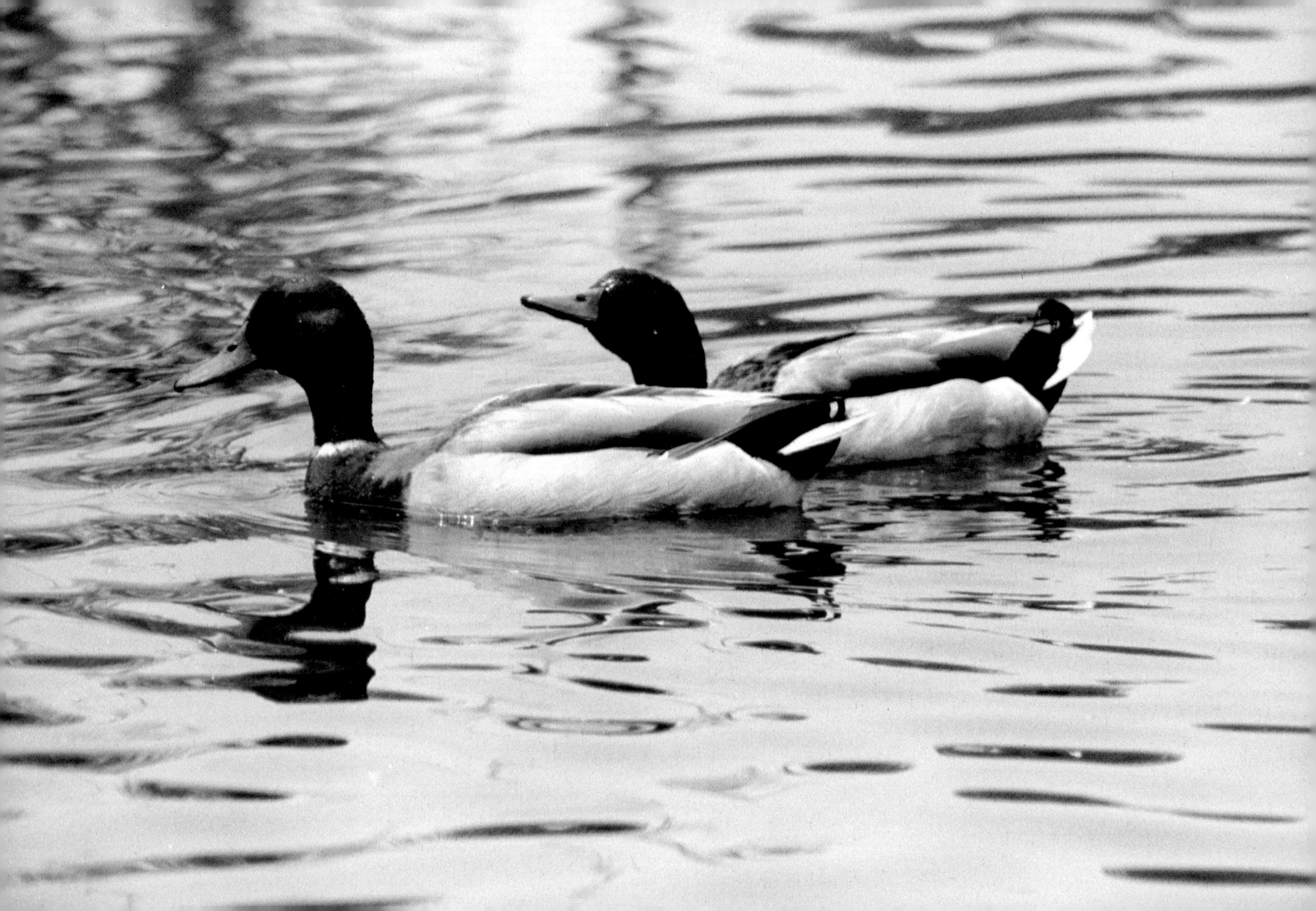

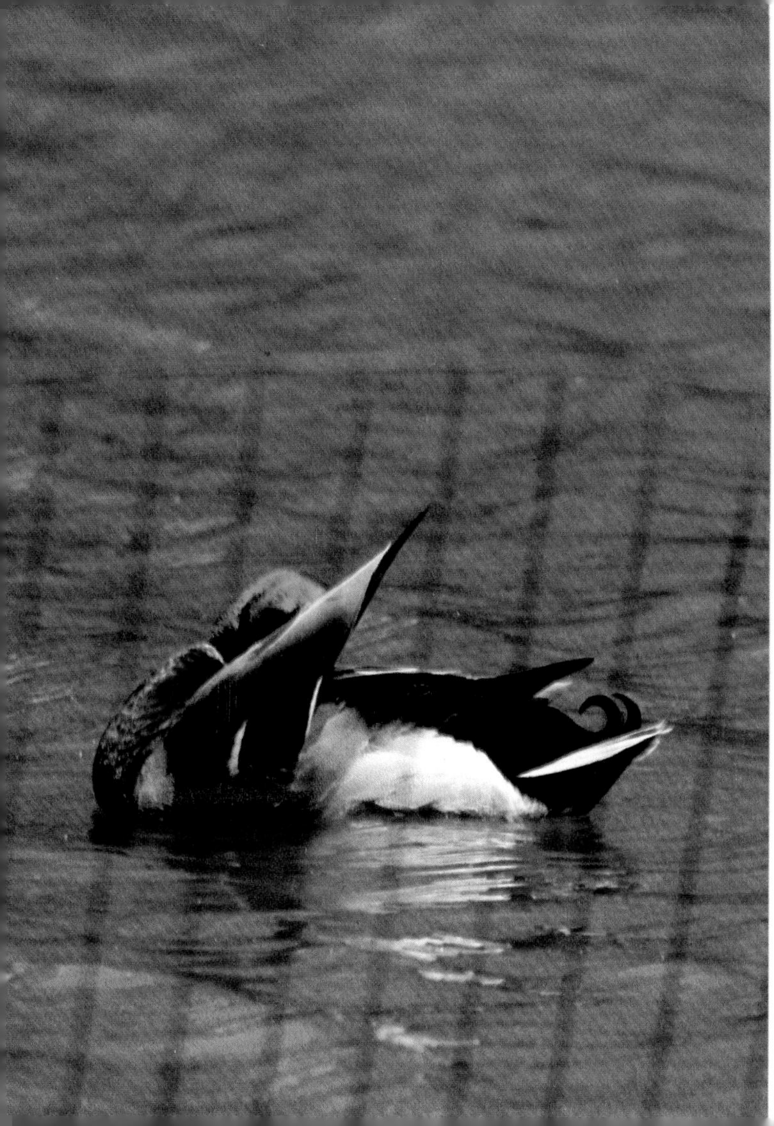
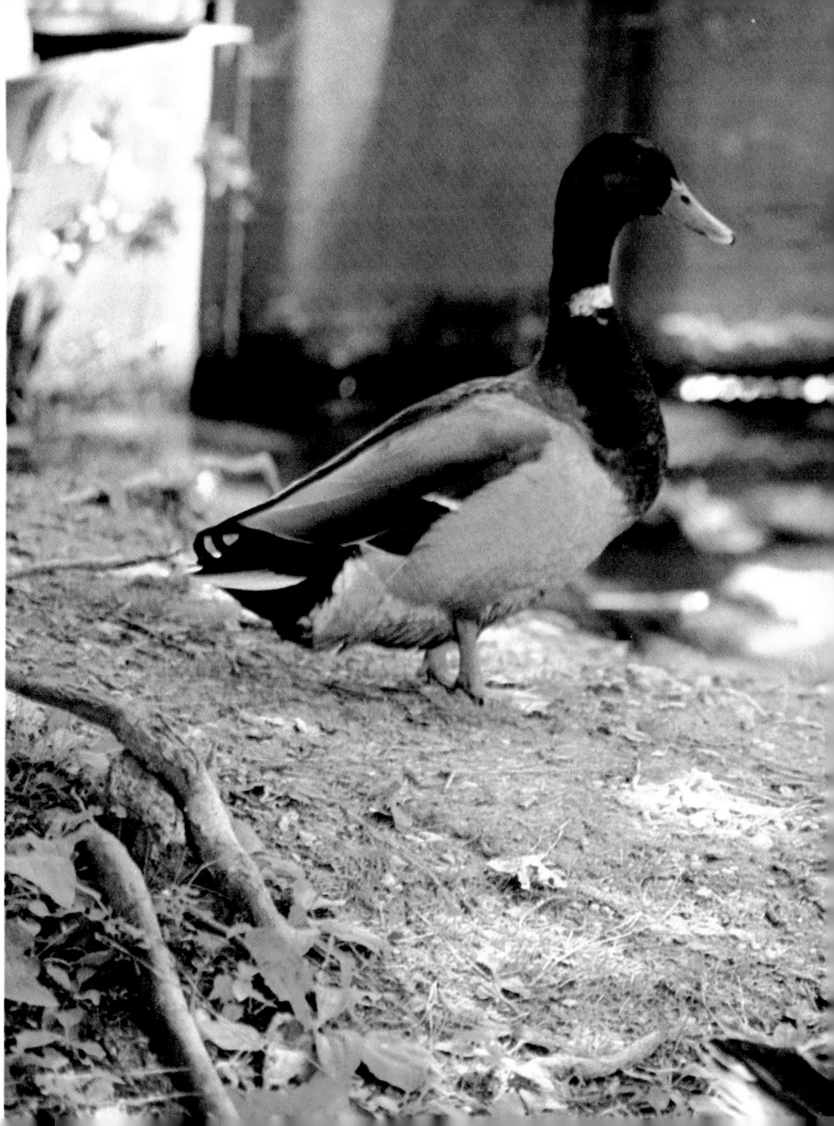

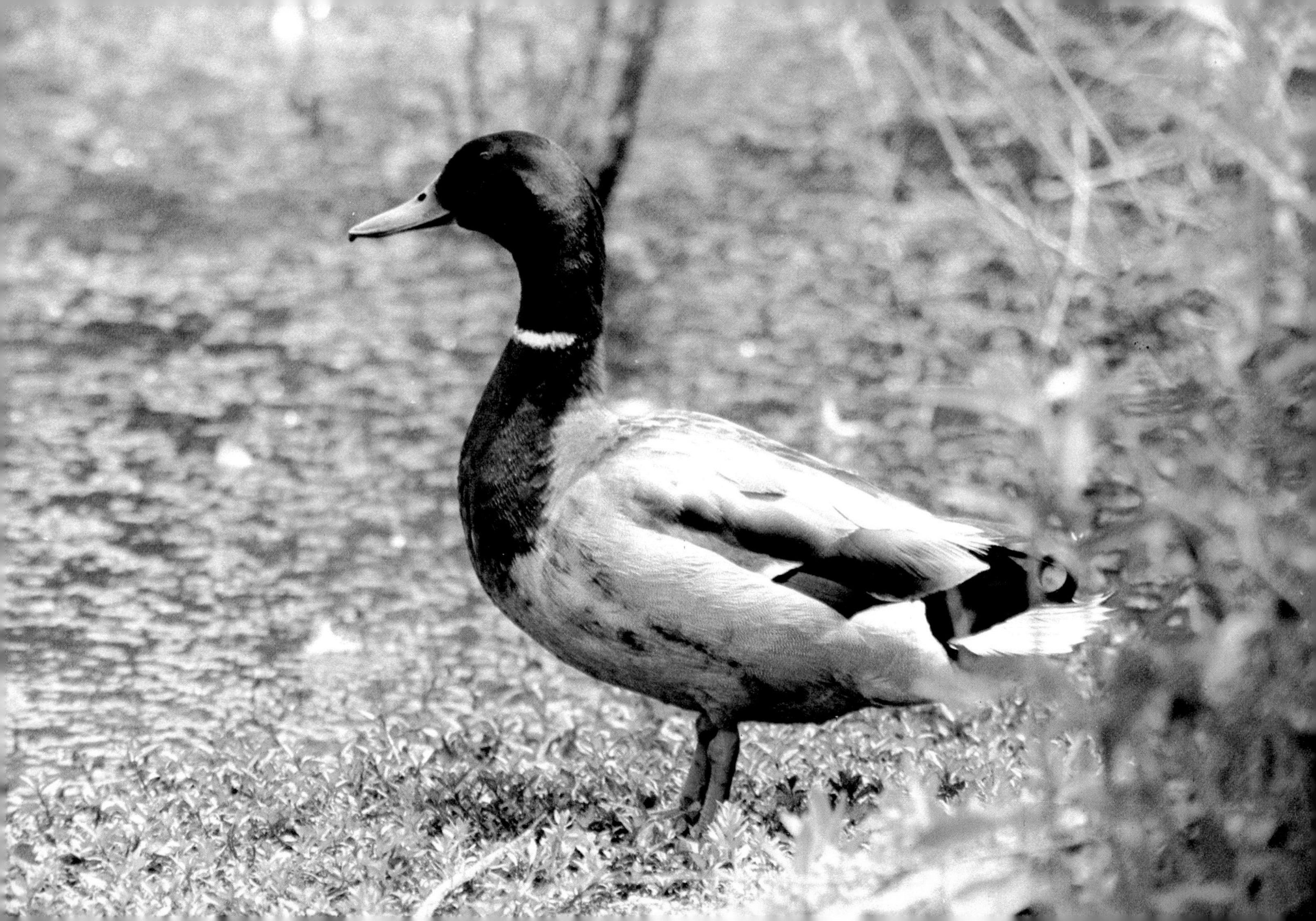

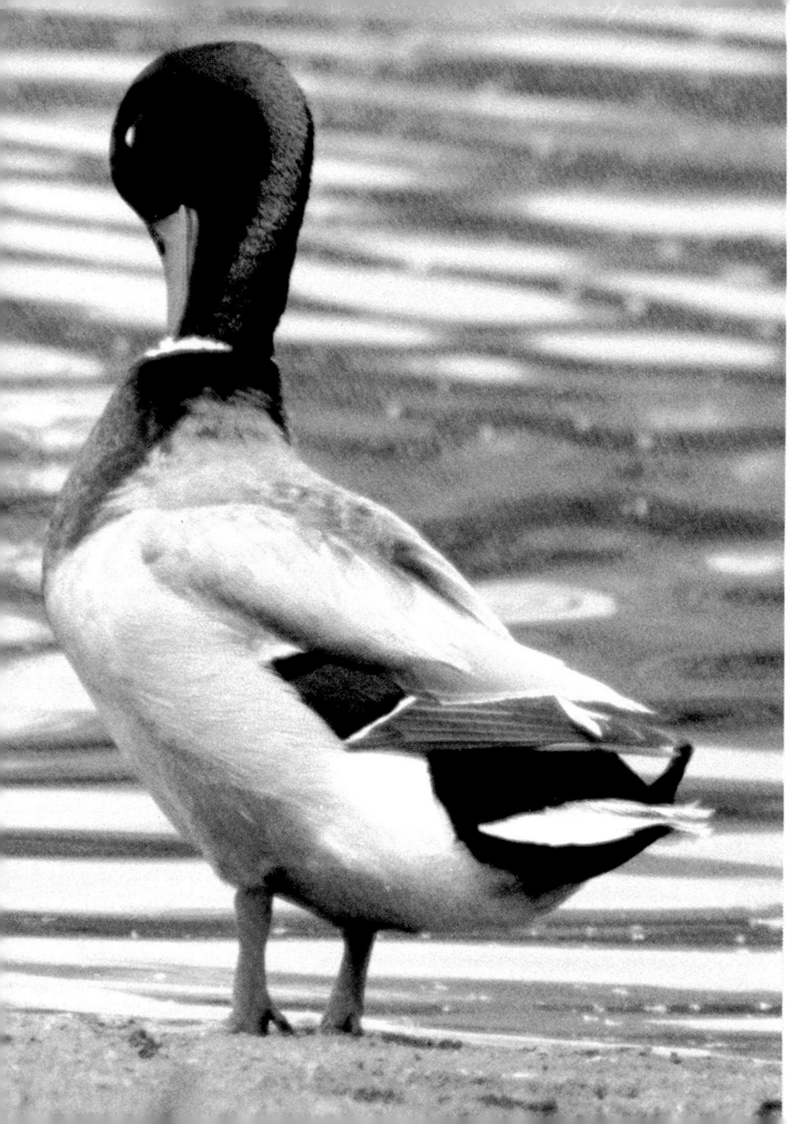

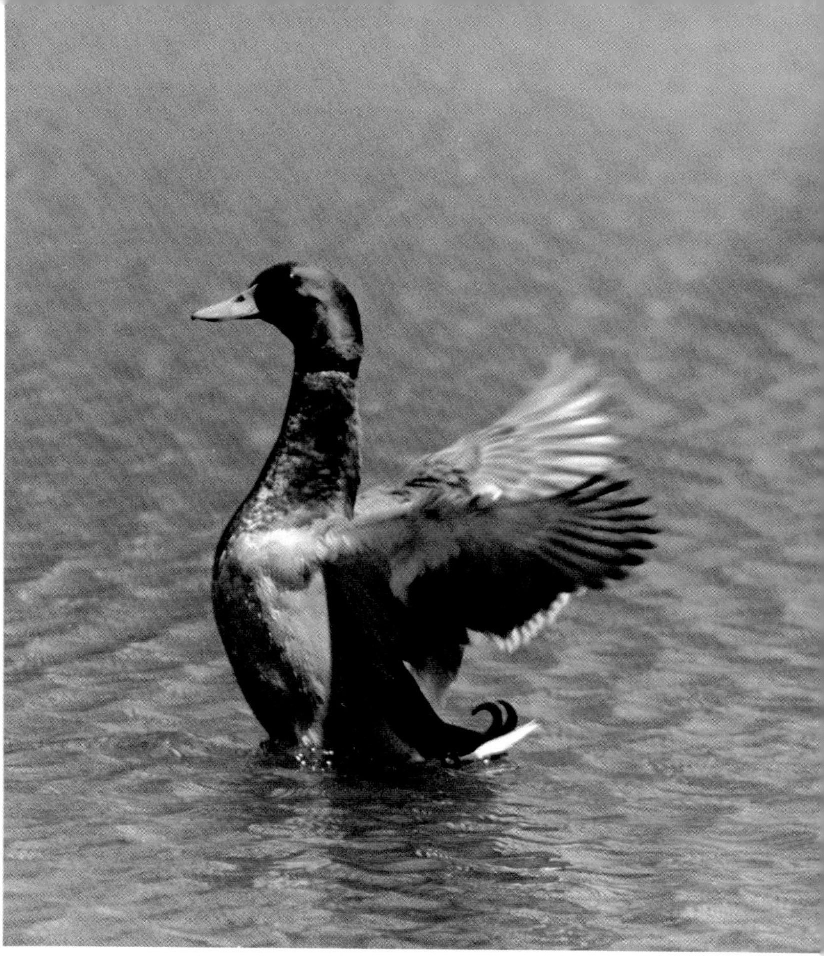

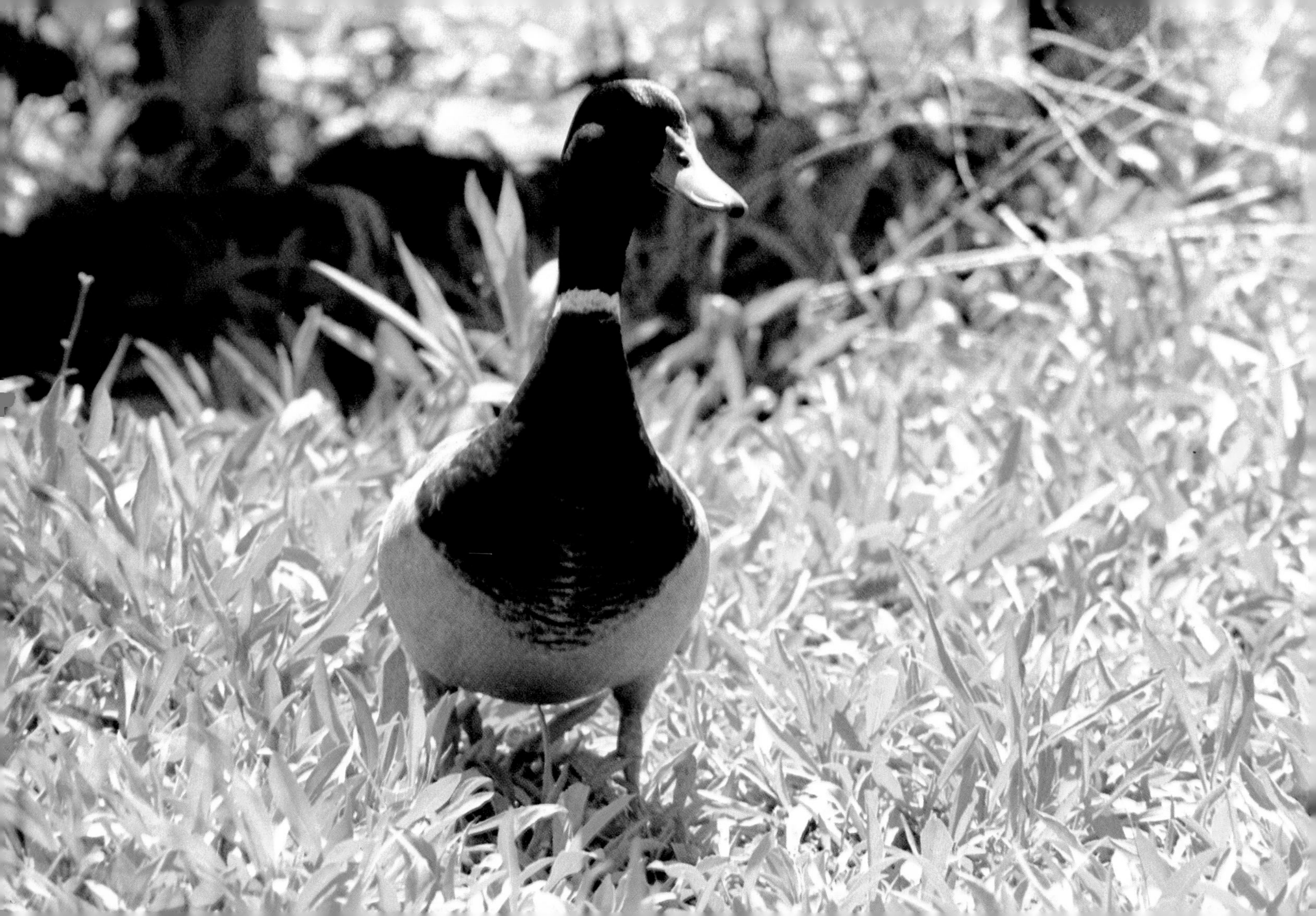

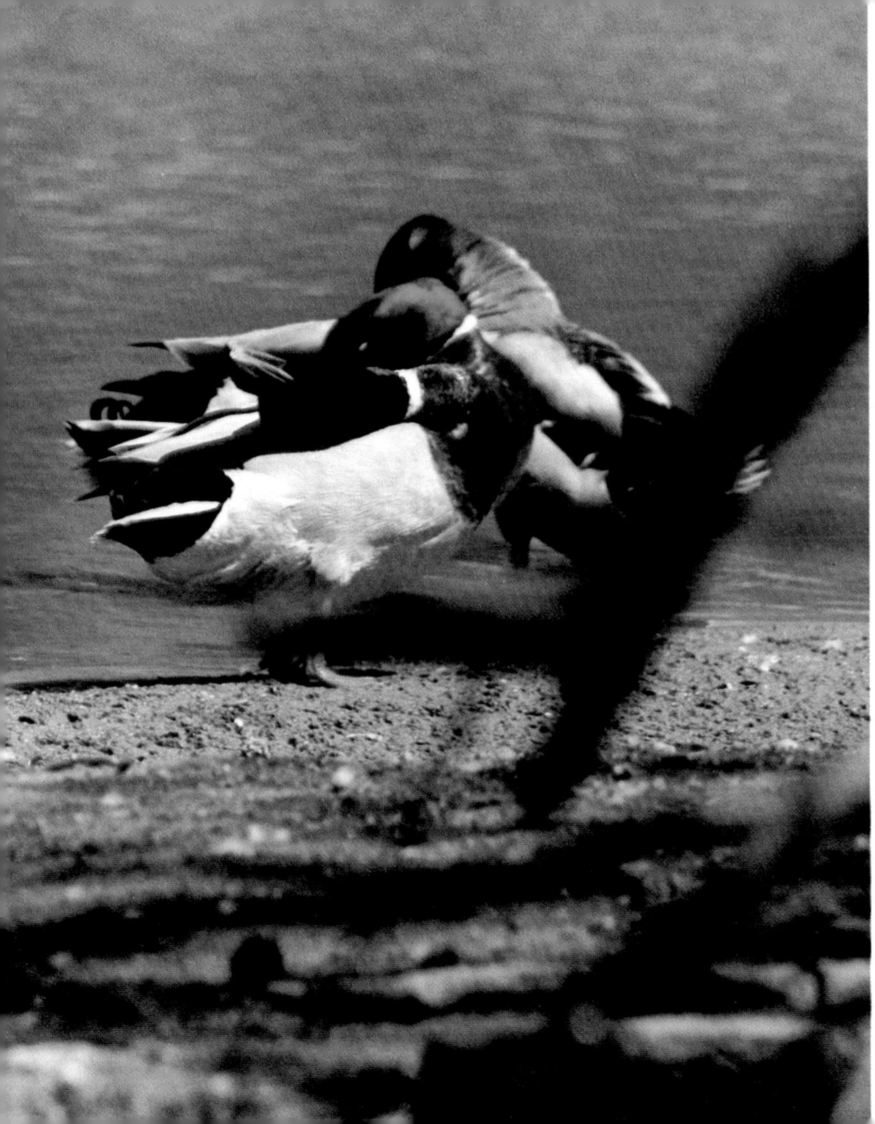
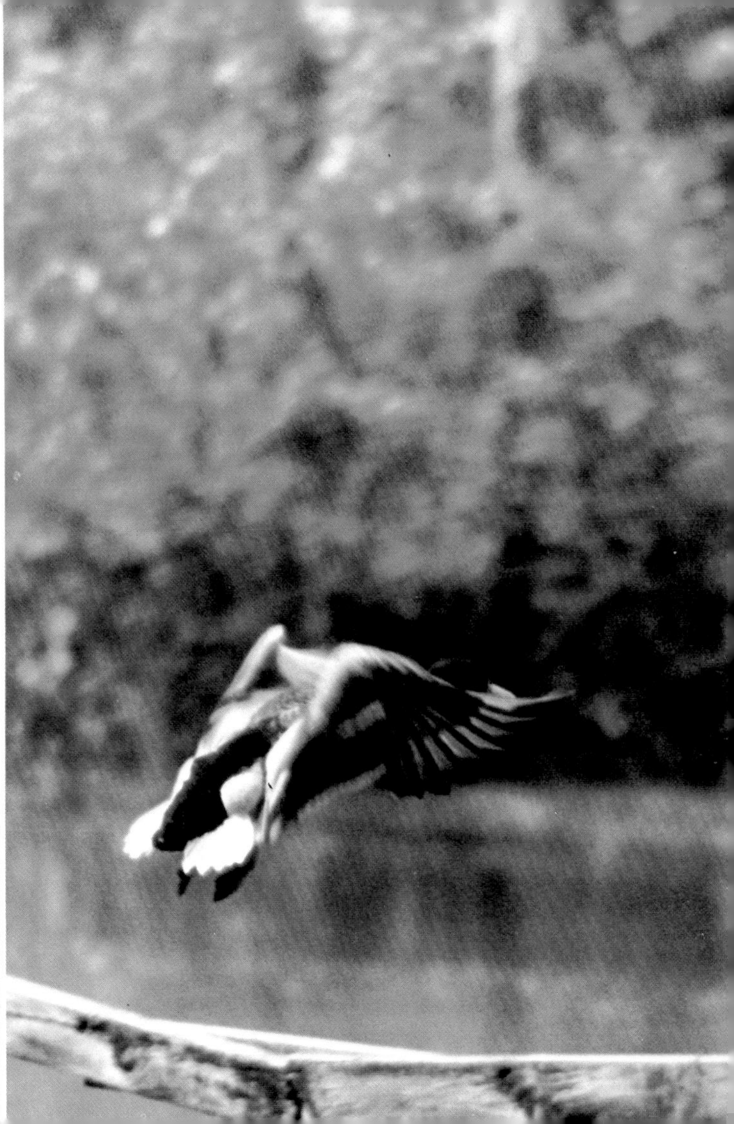

Pairs

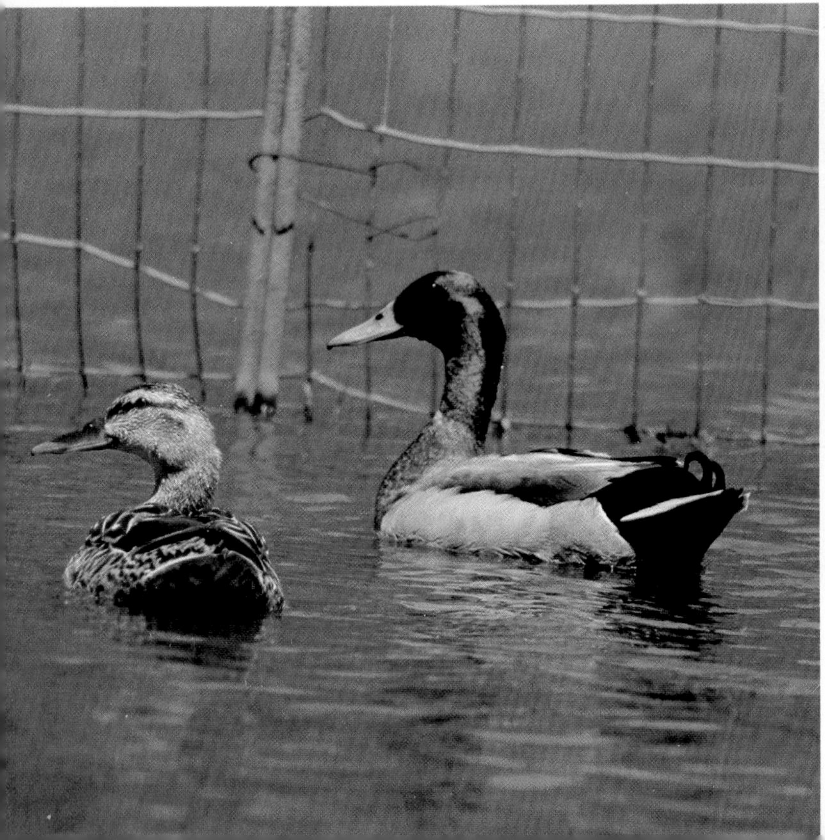

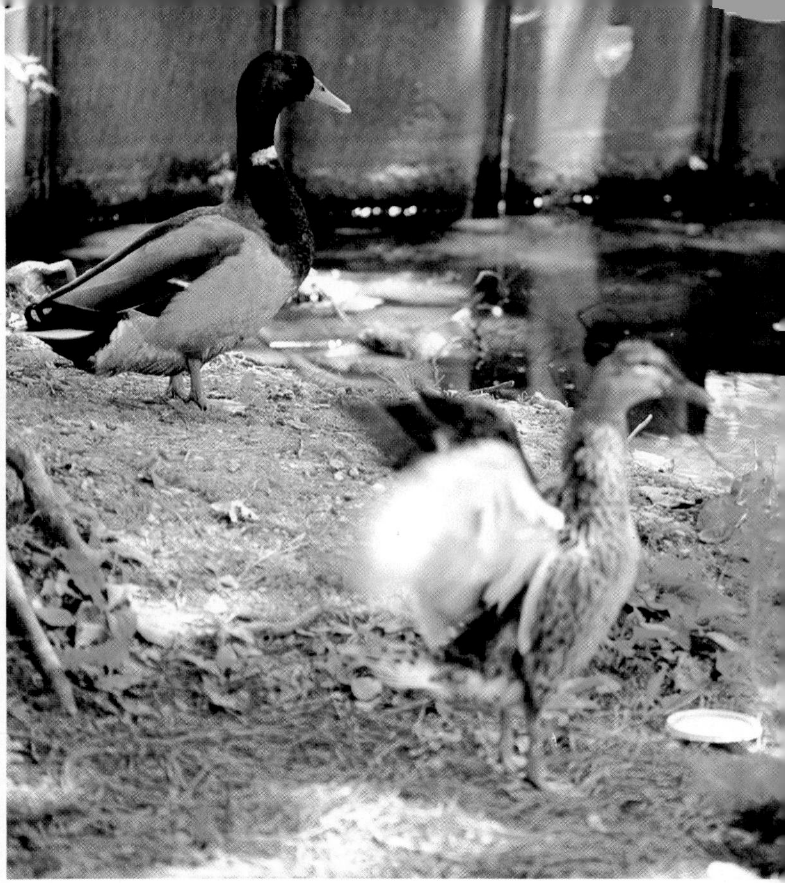

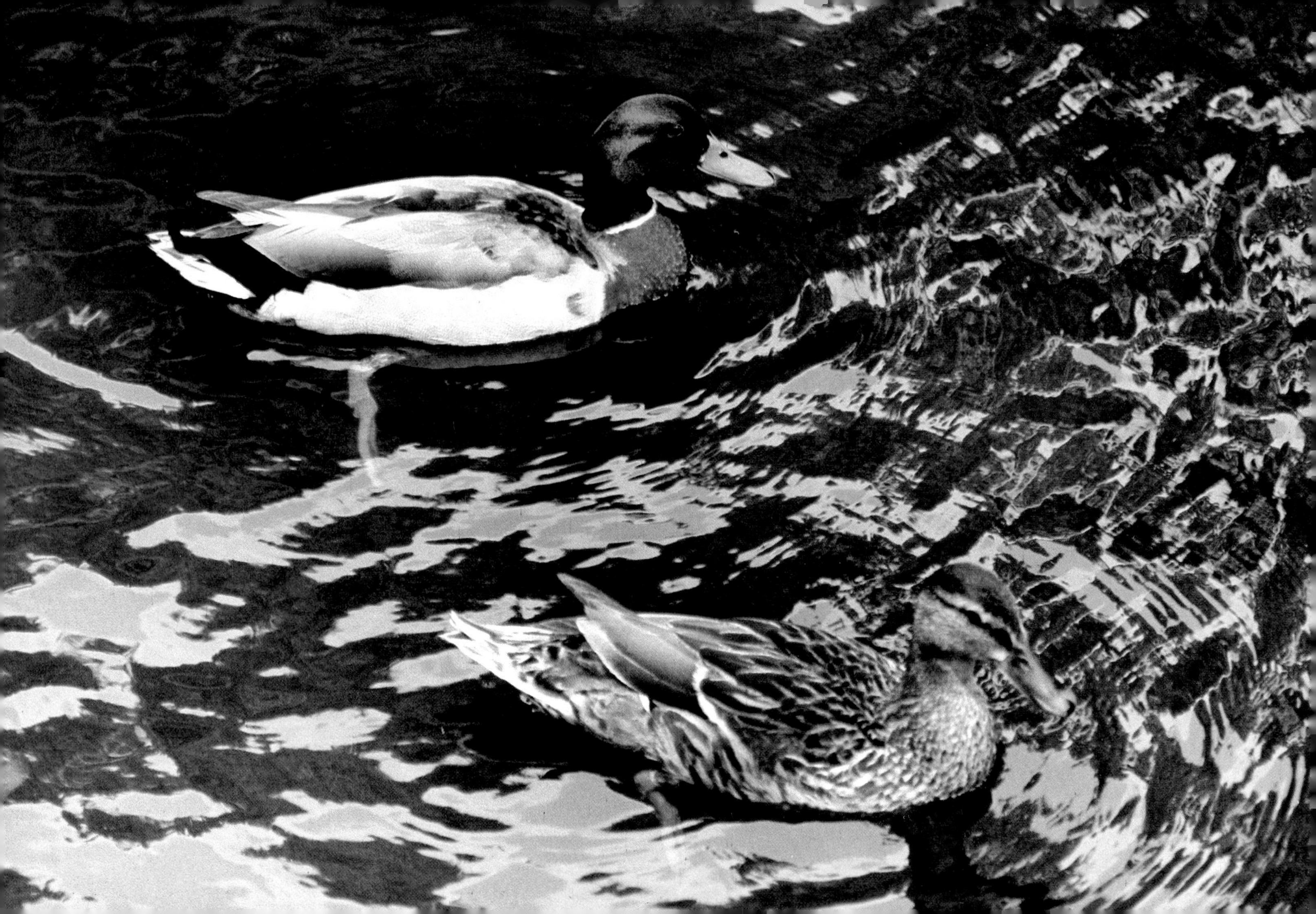

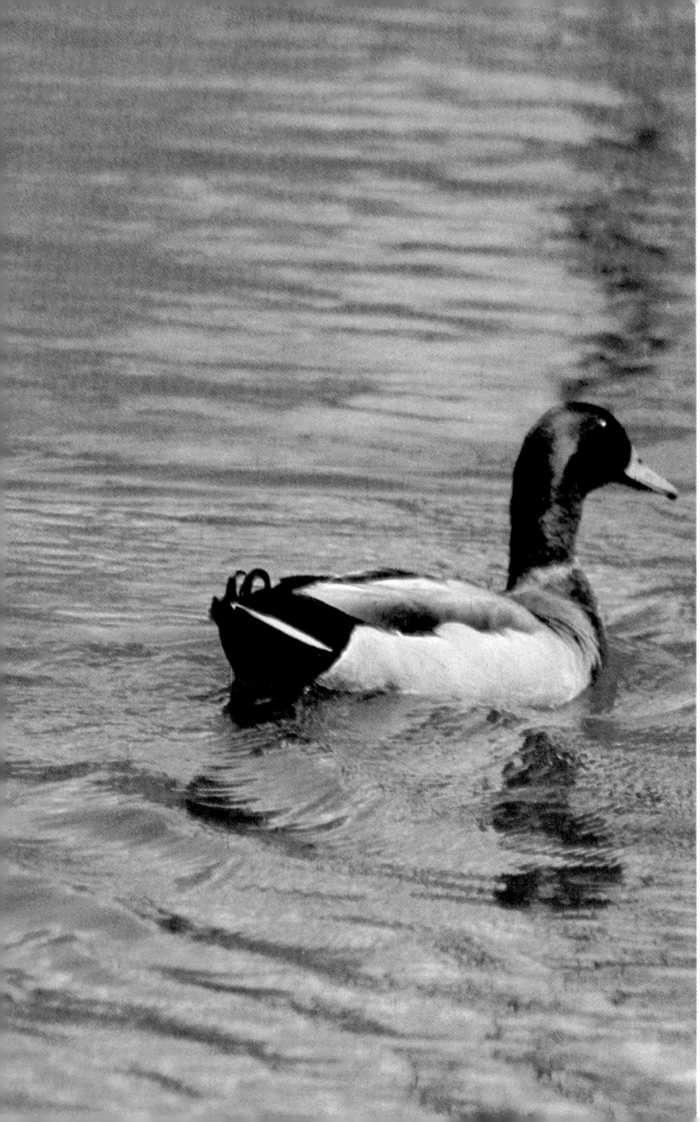
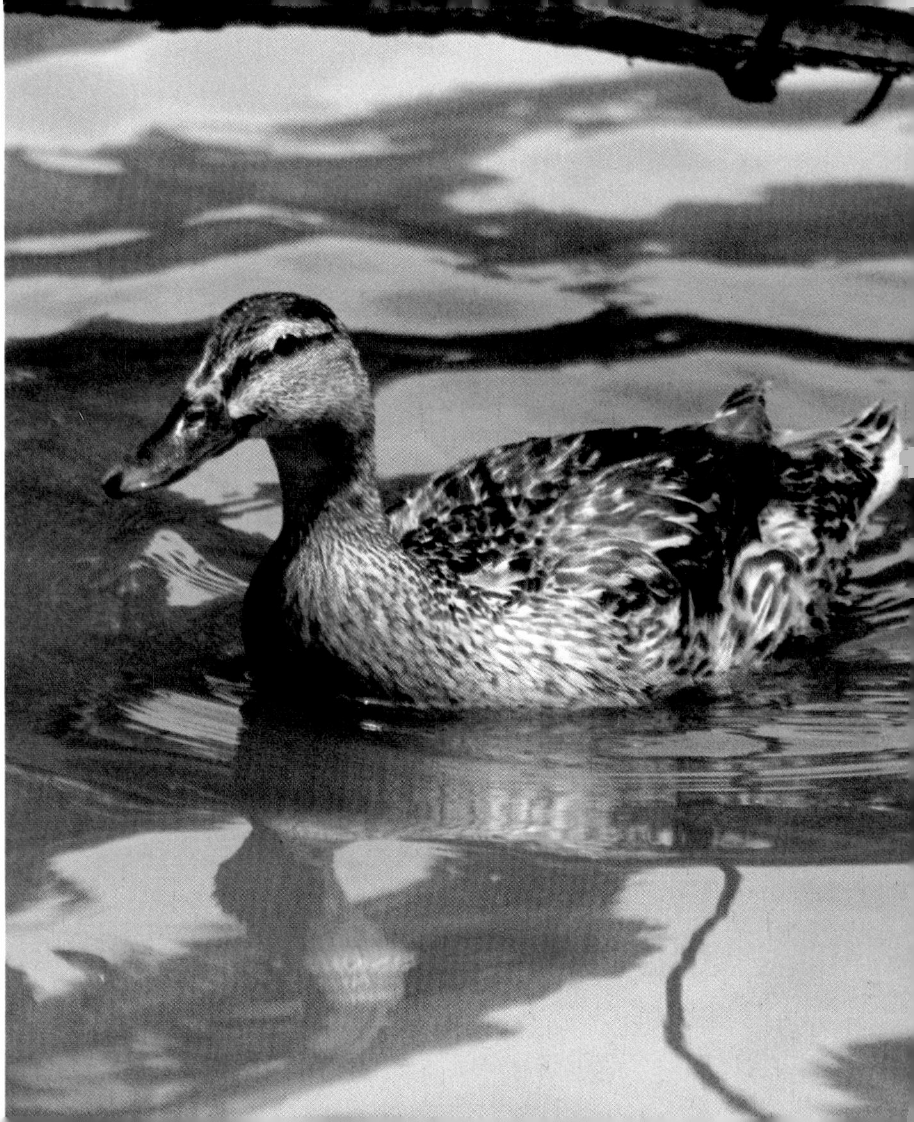

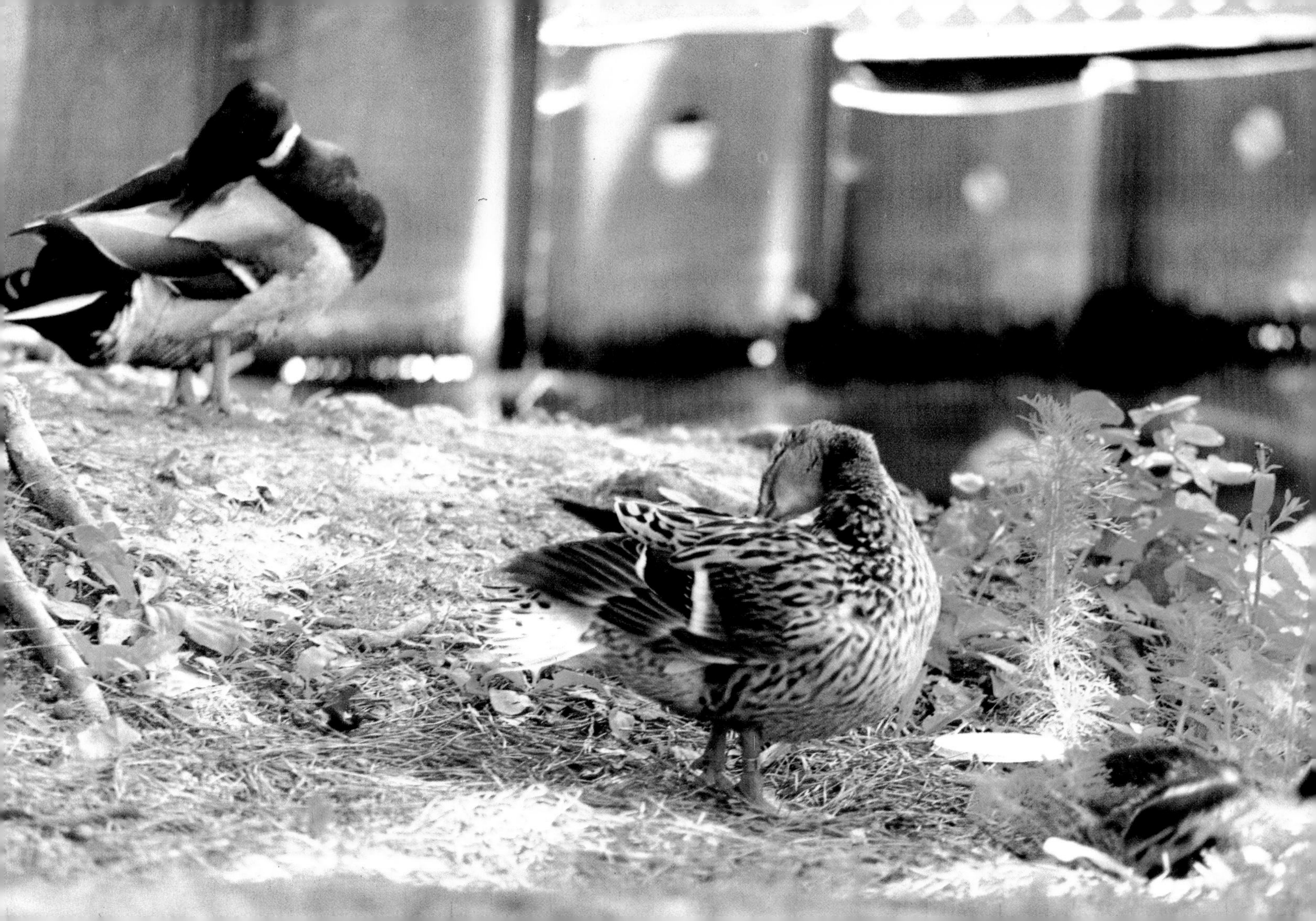

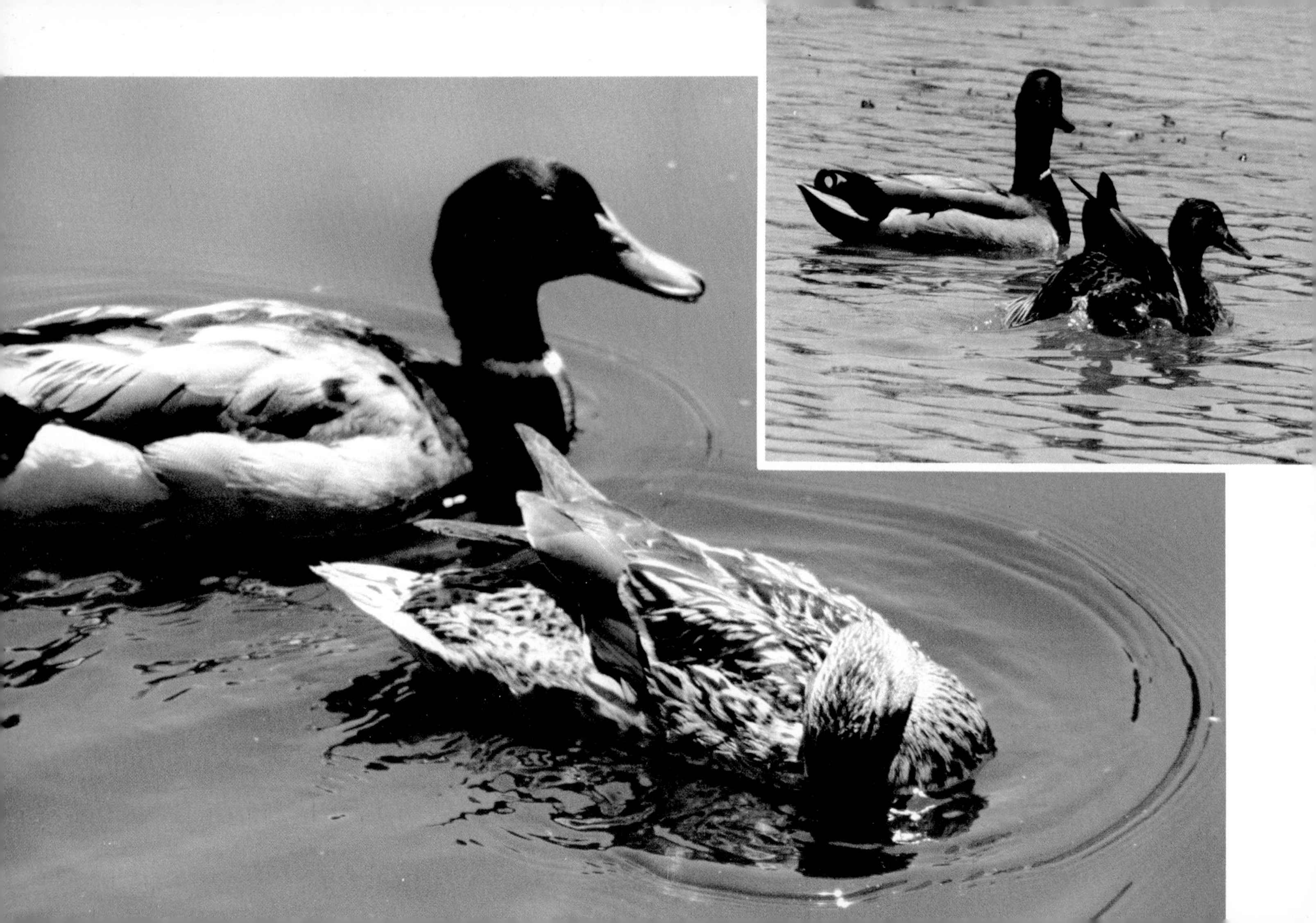

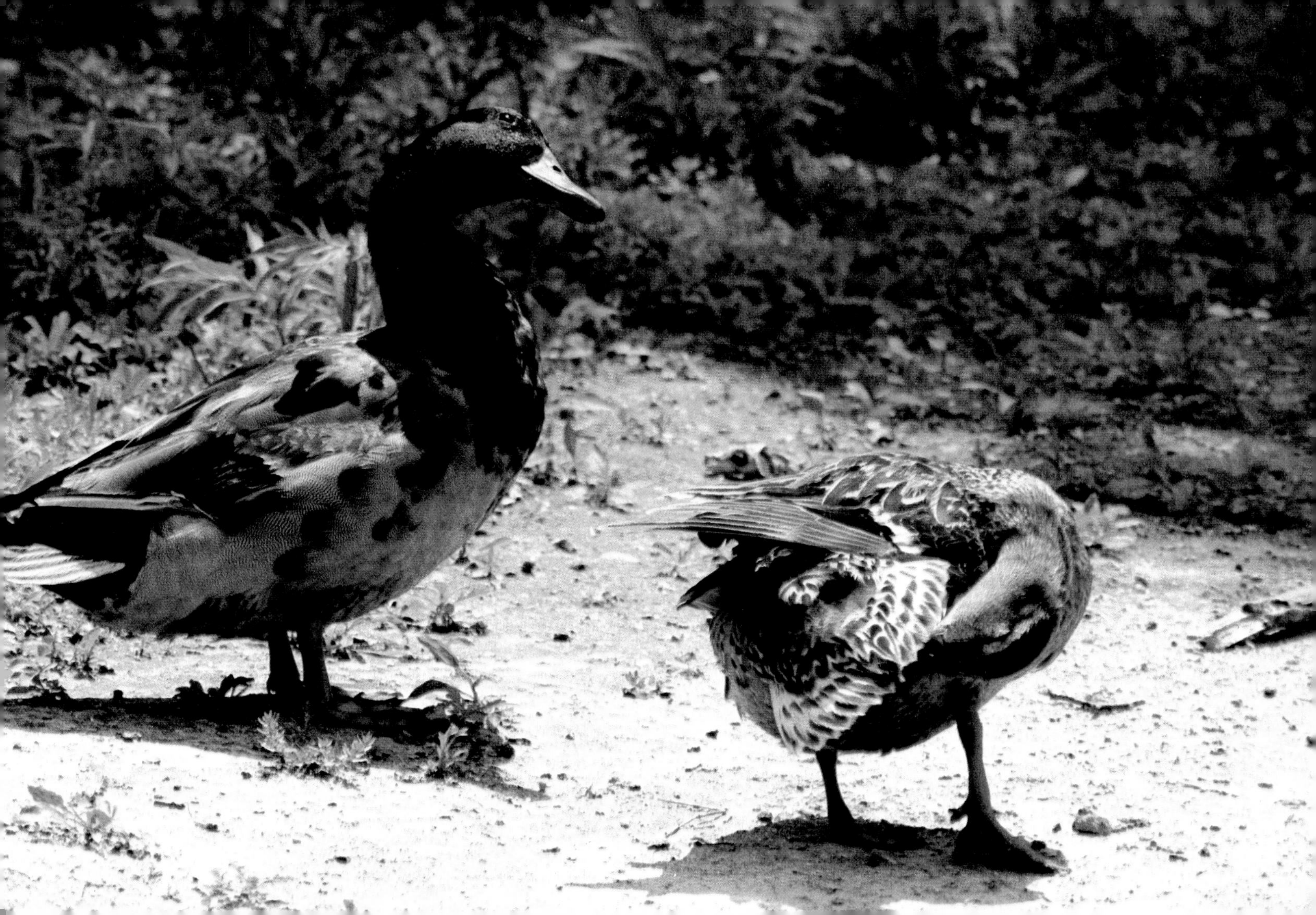

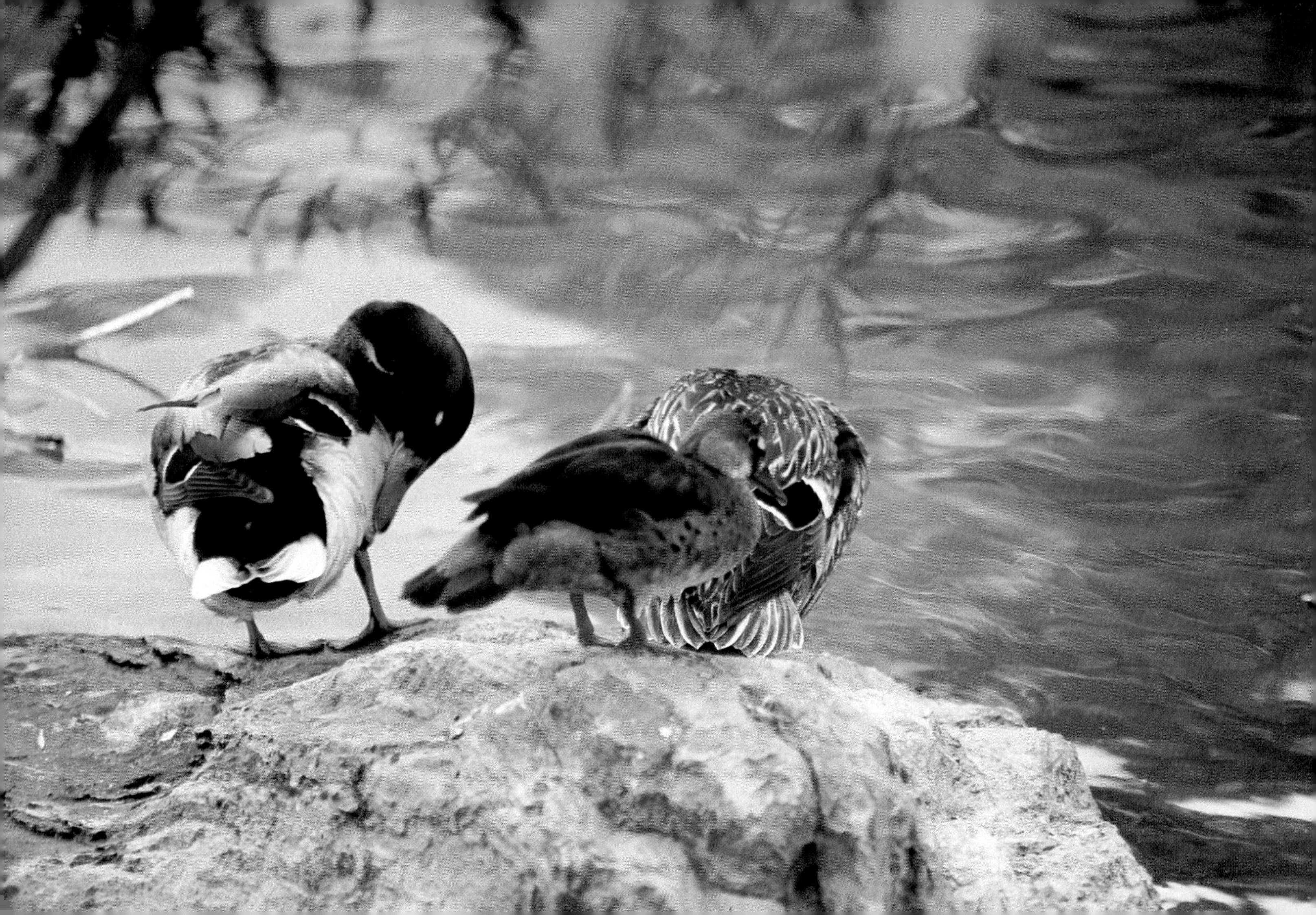

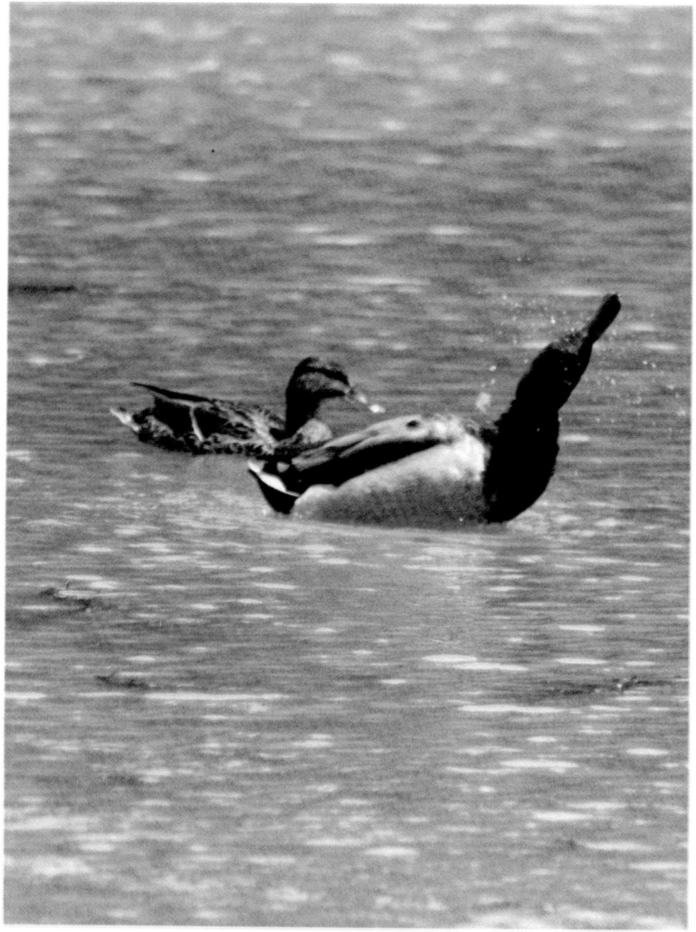
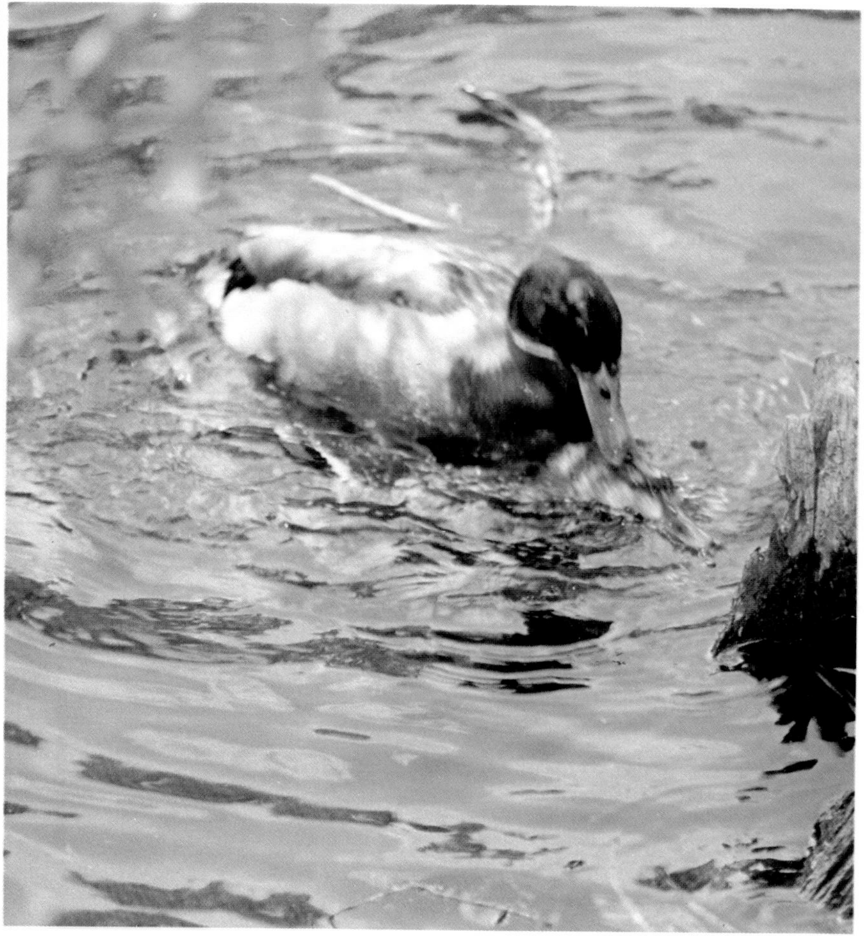

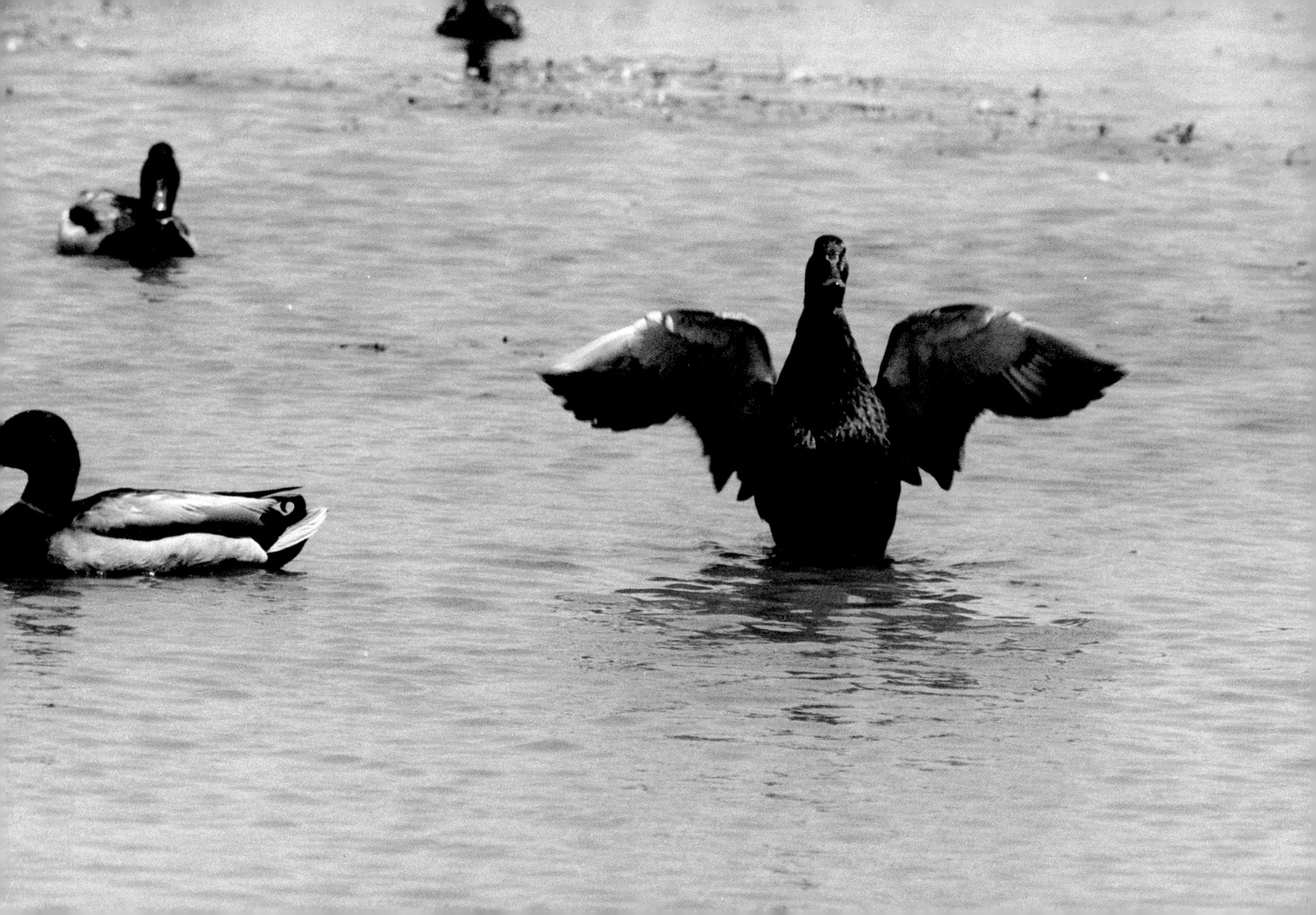

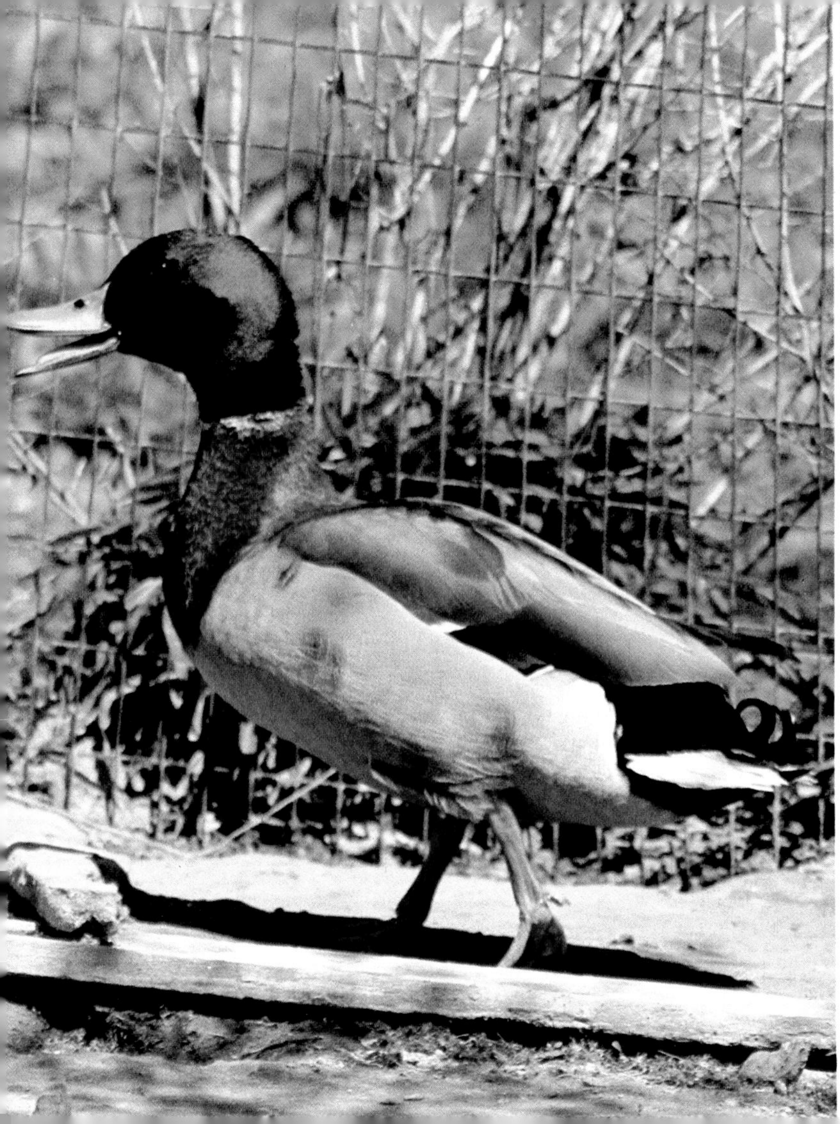

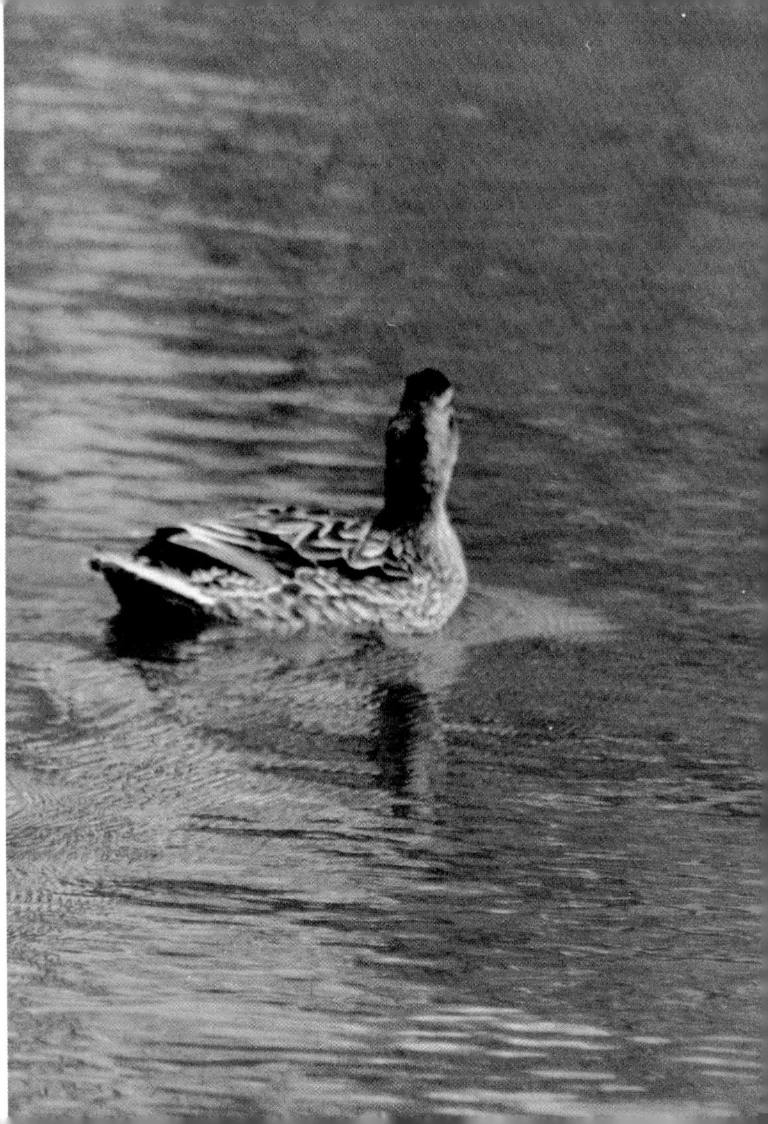

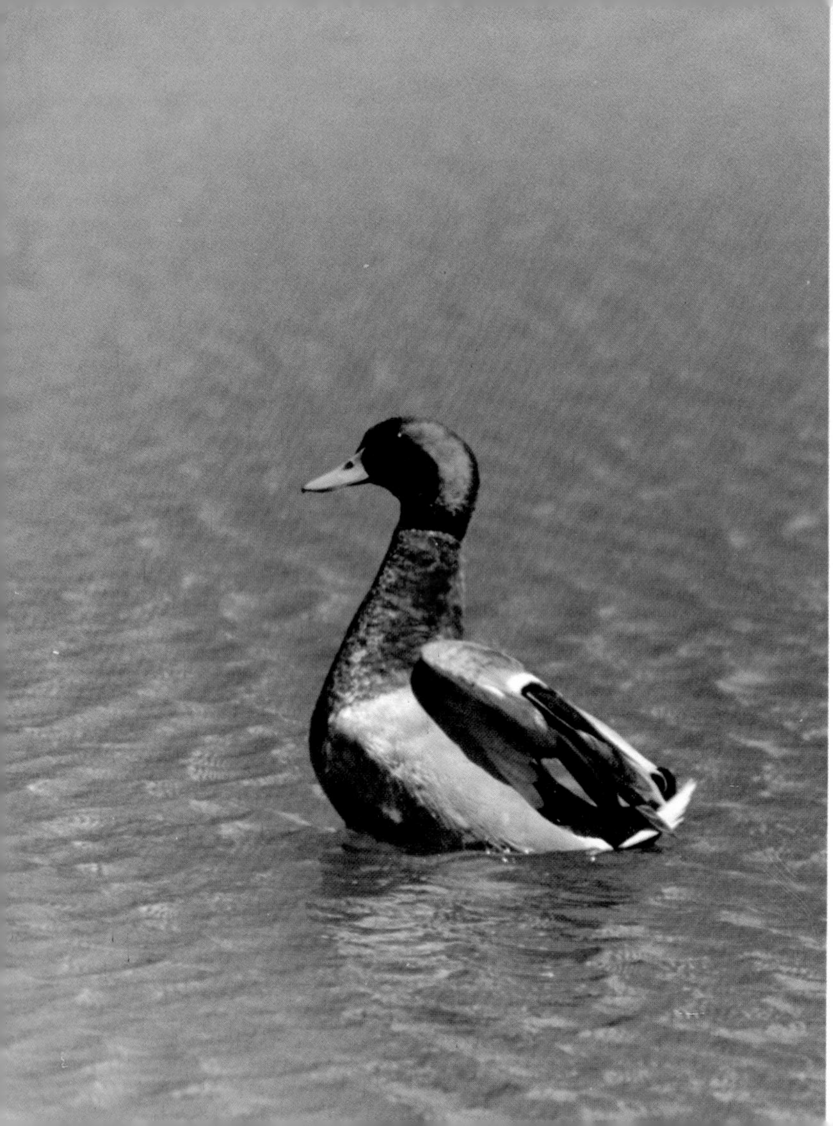

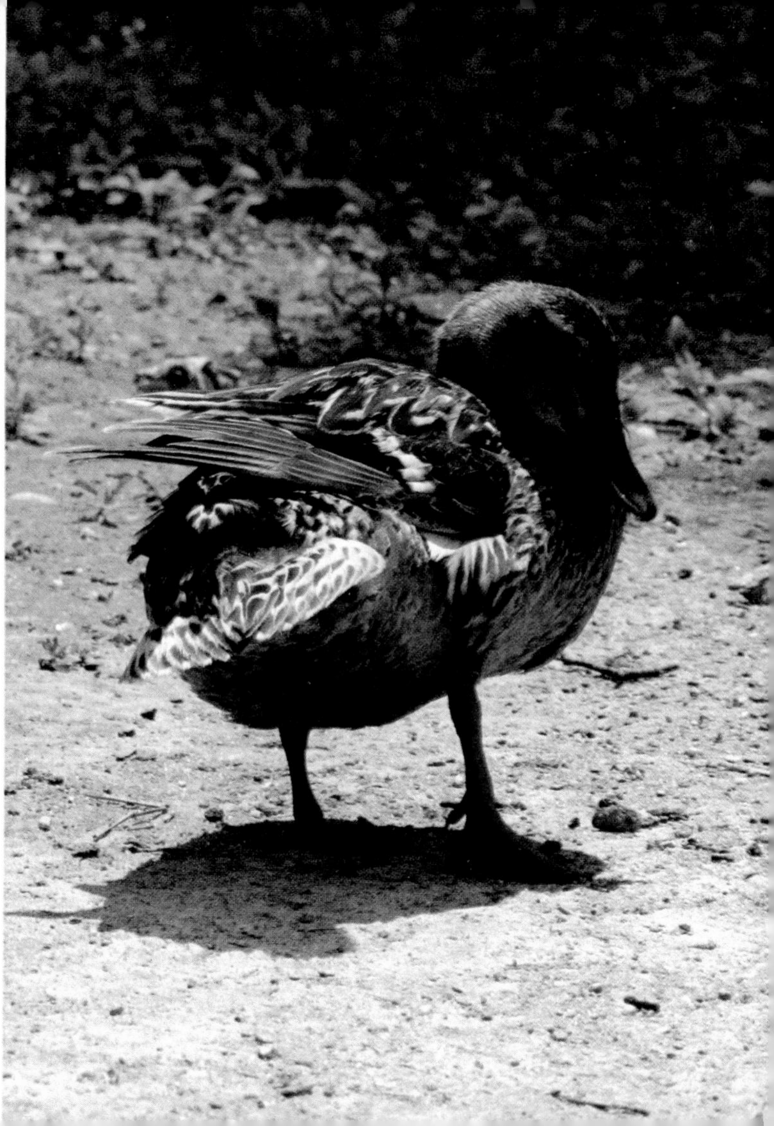

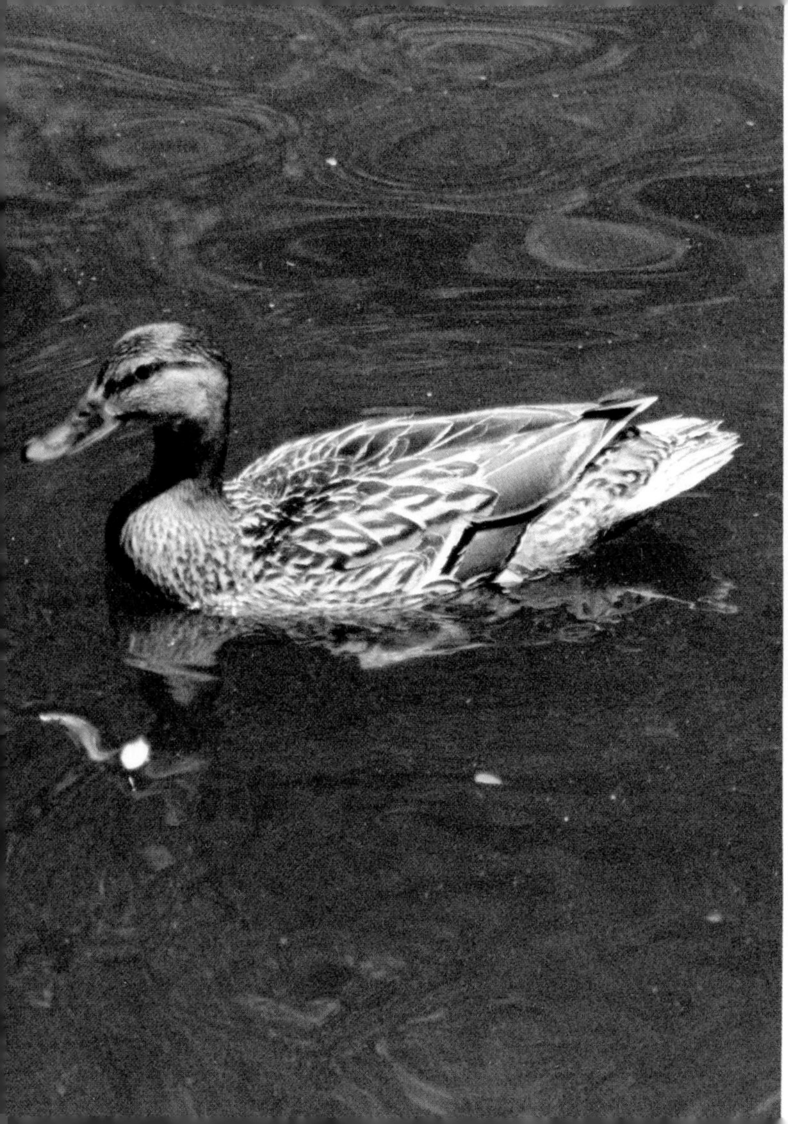

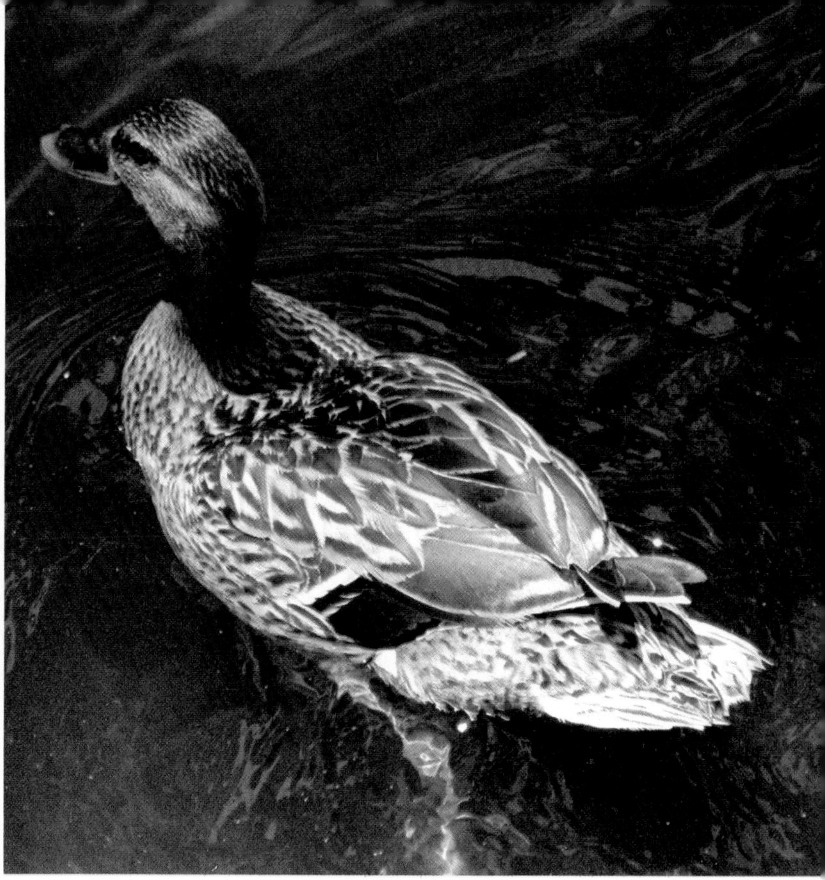

Hens

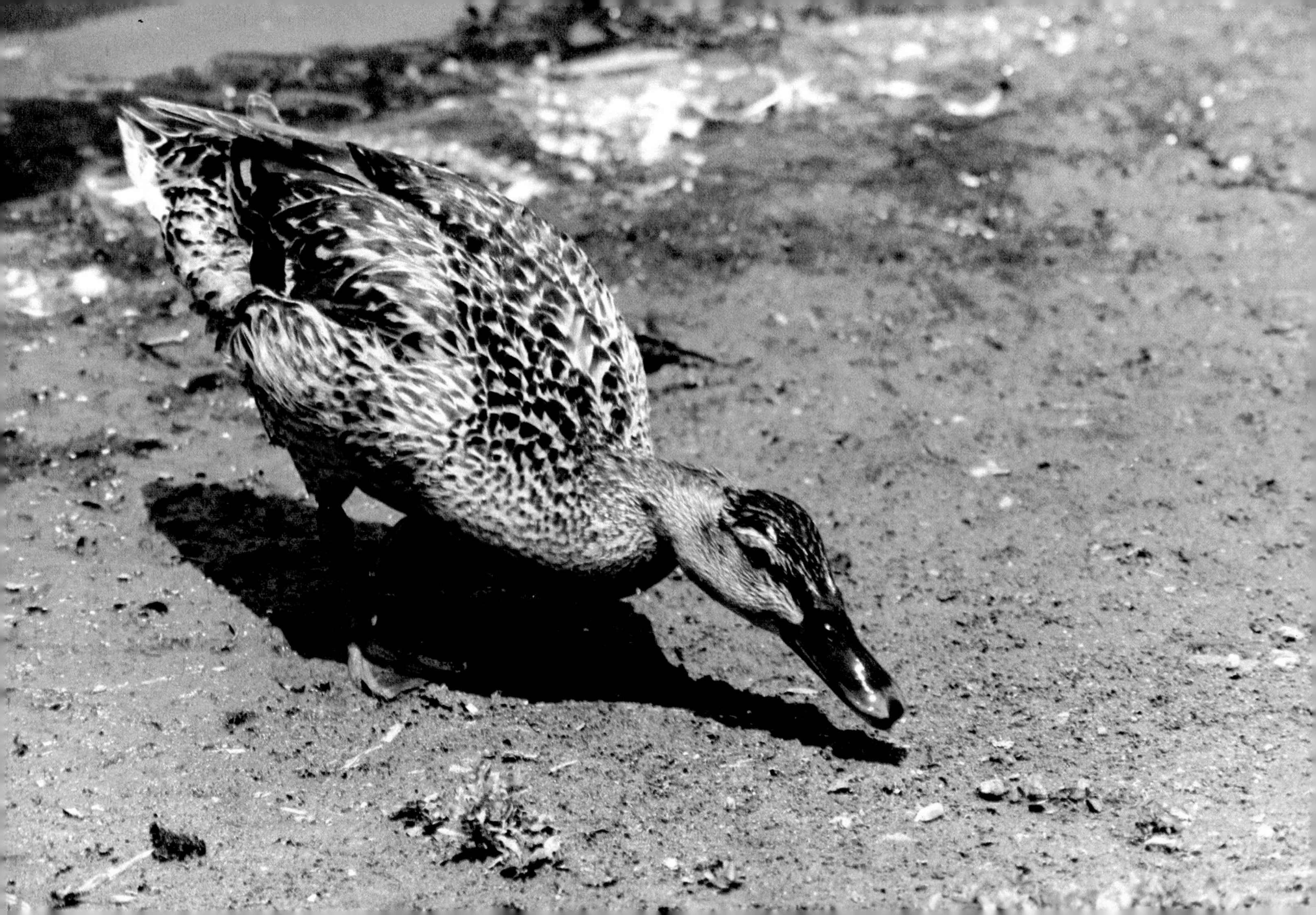

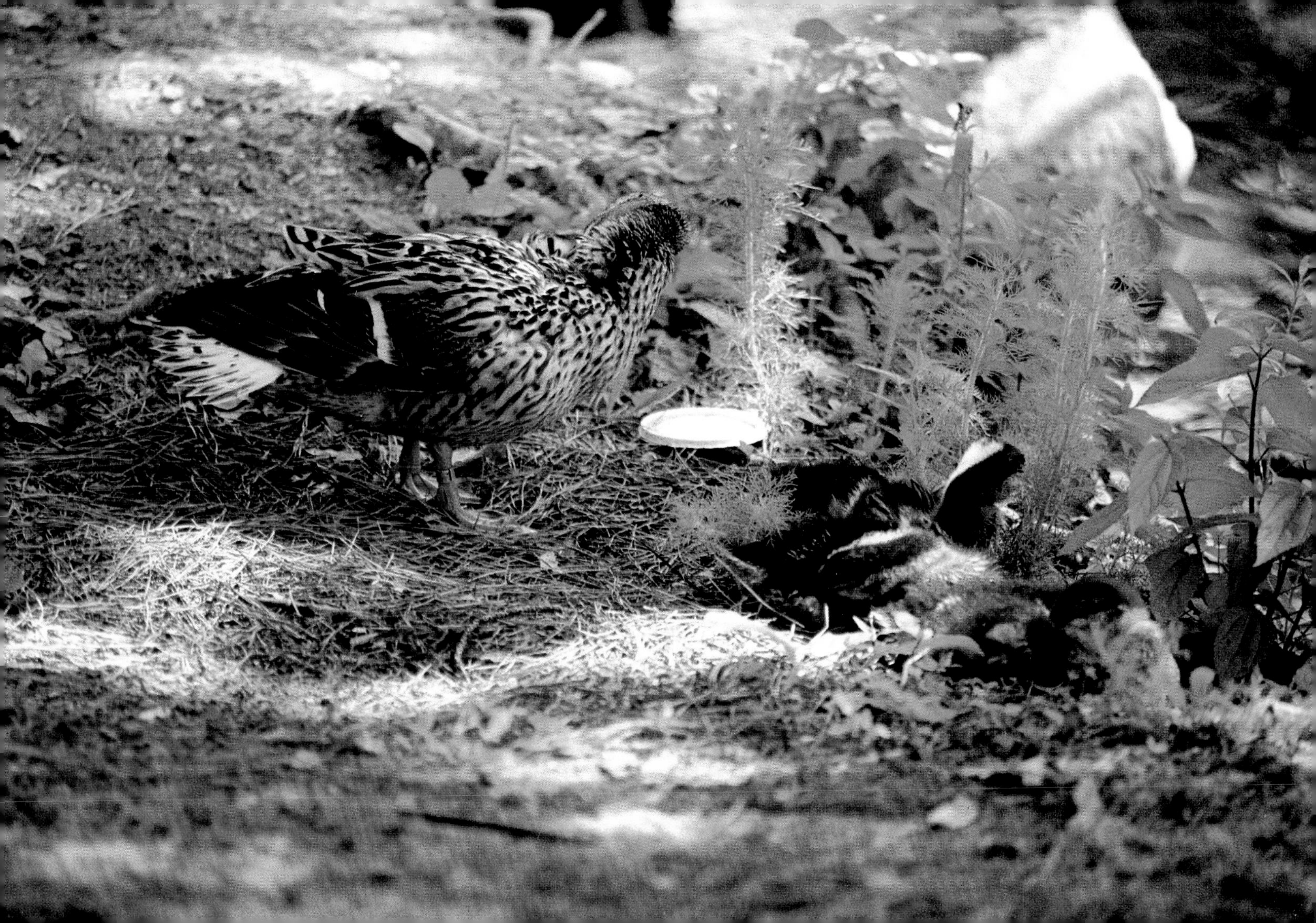

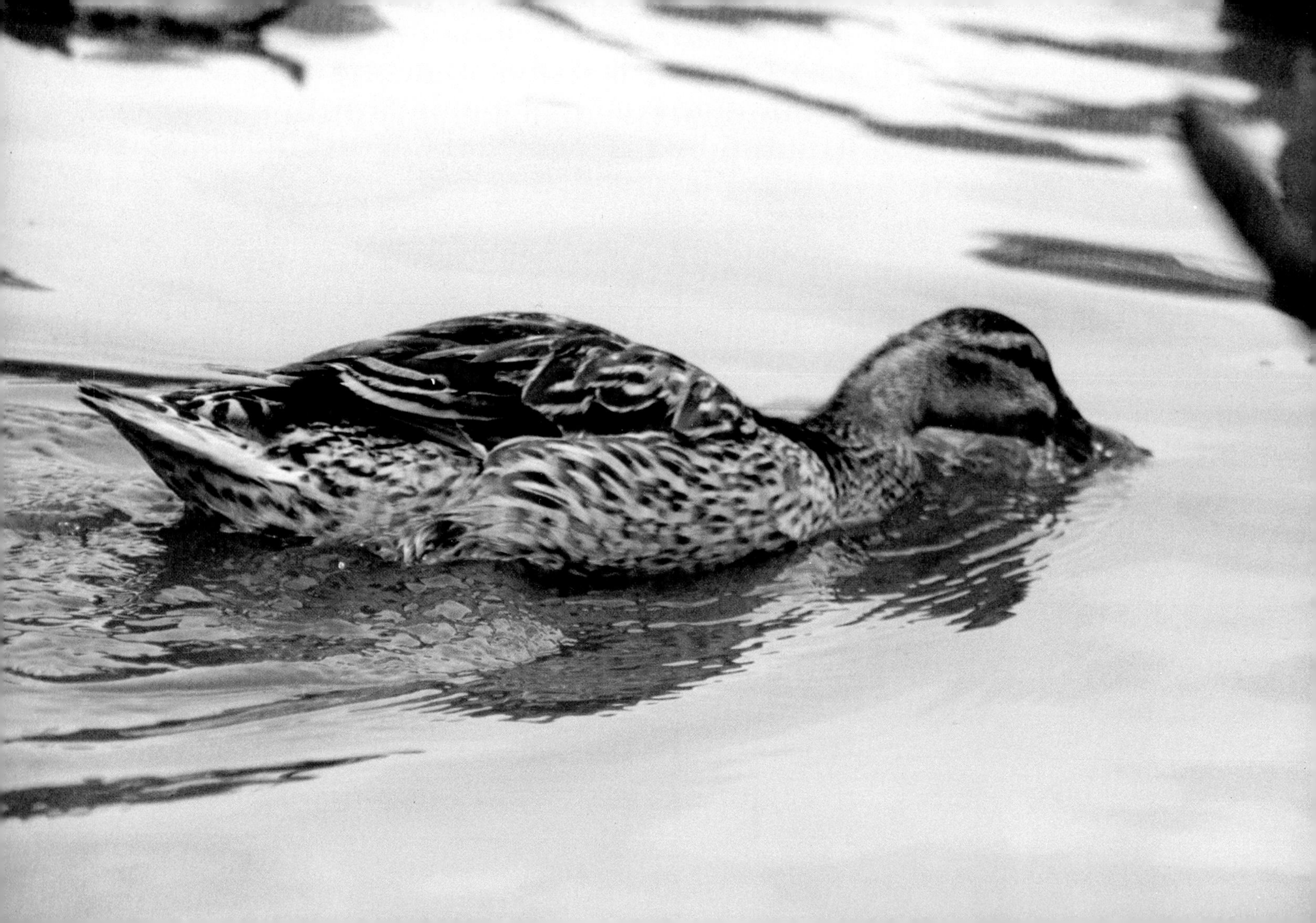

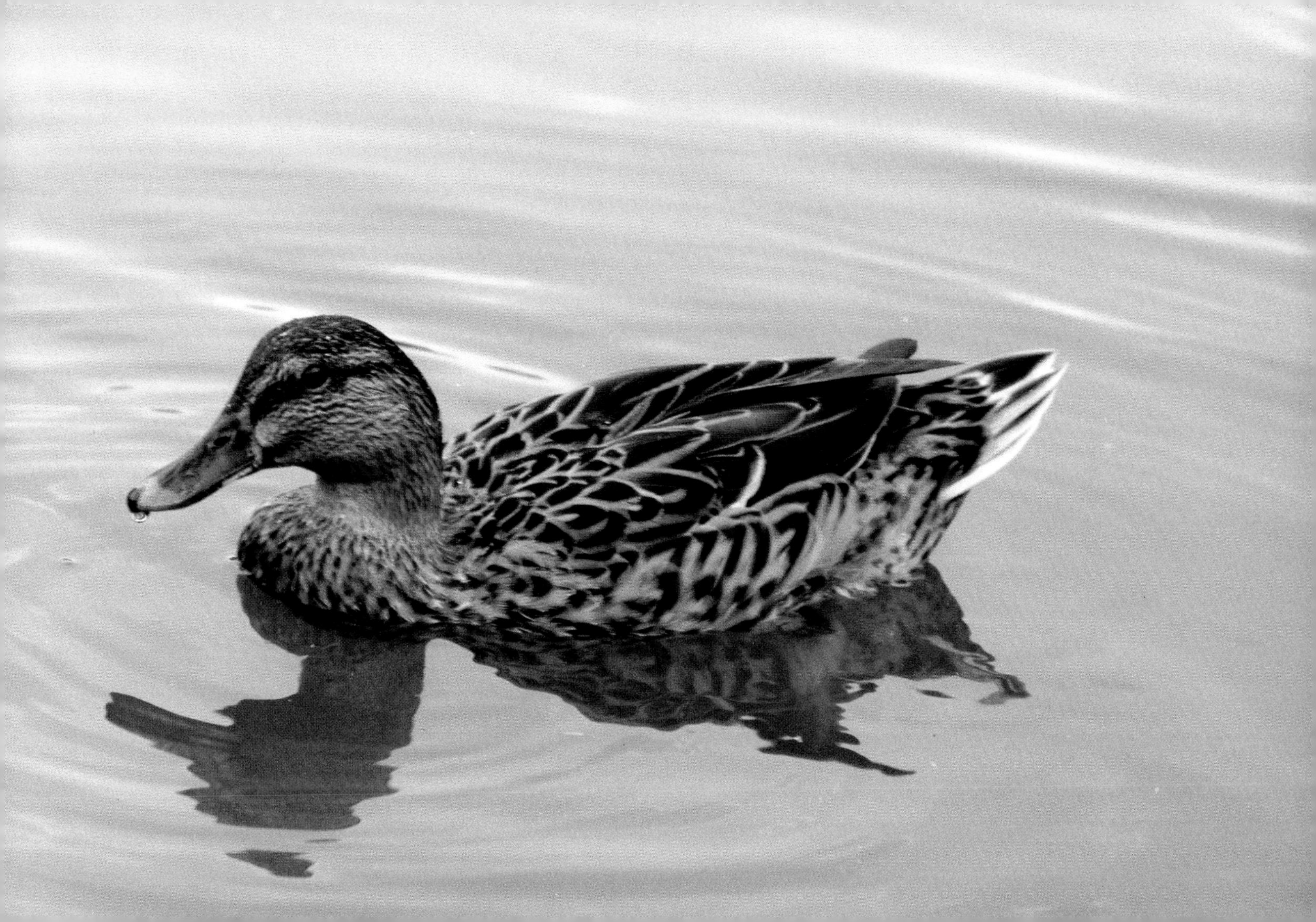

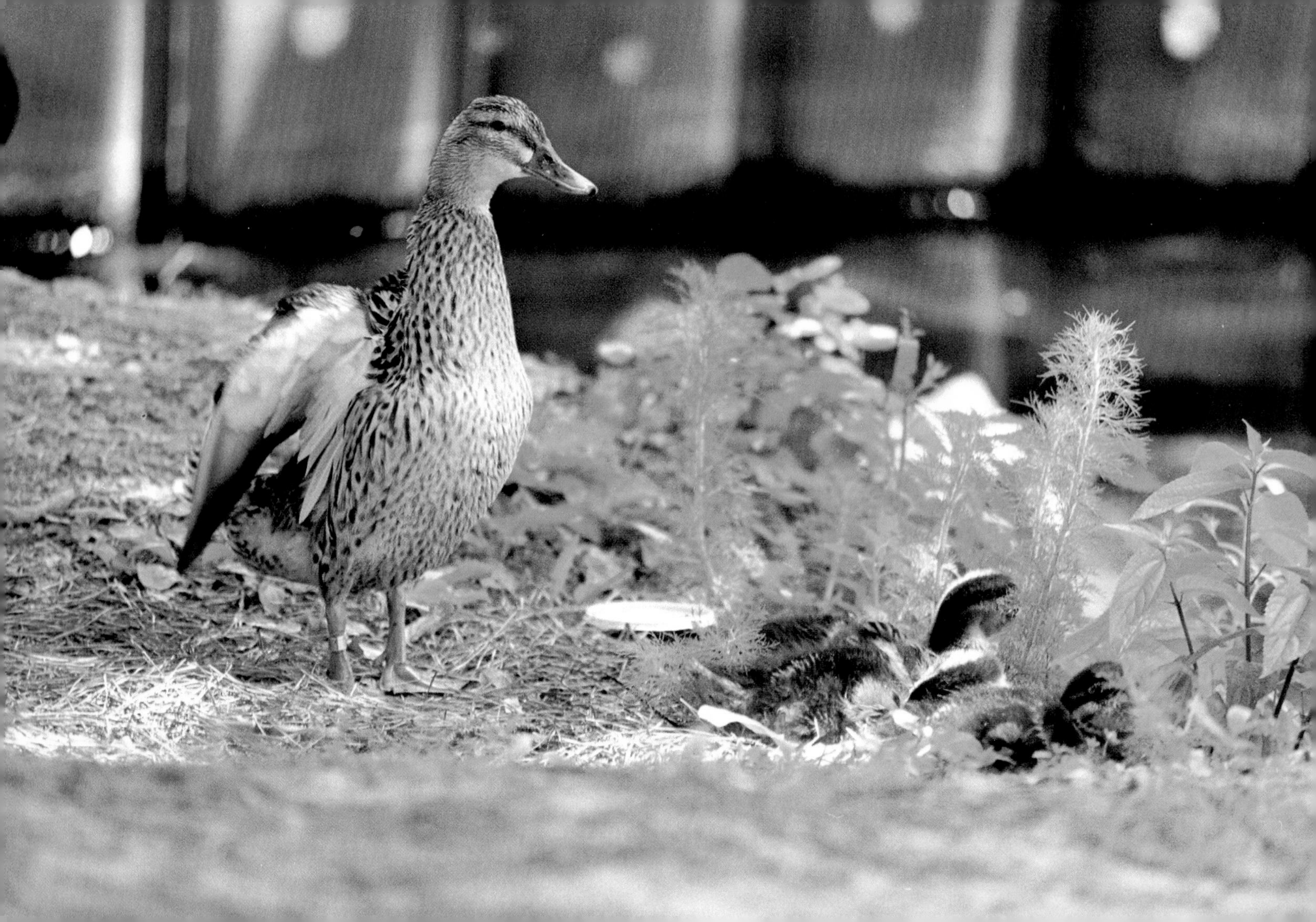

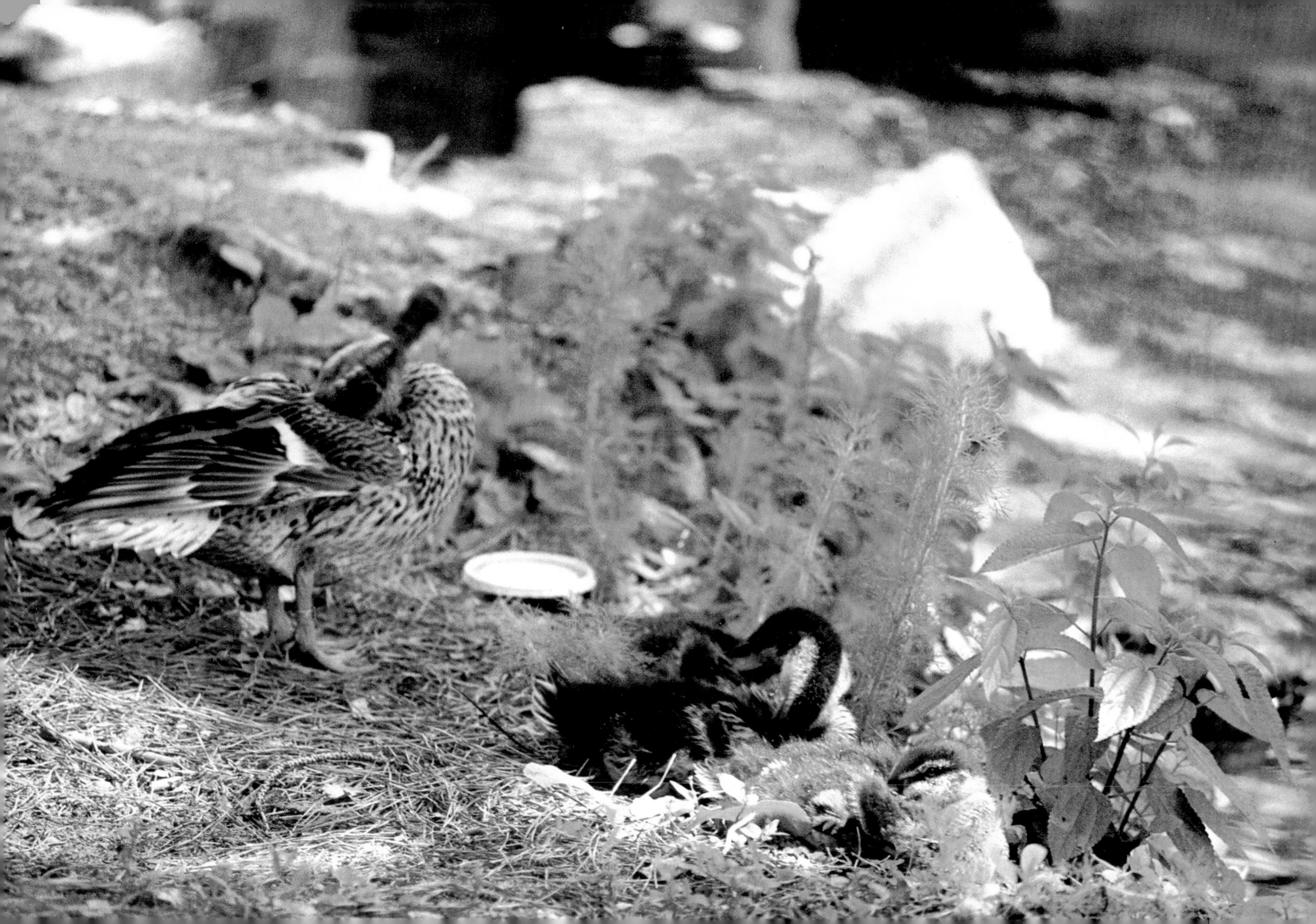

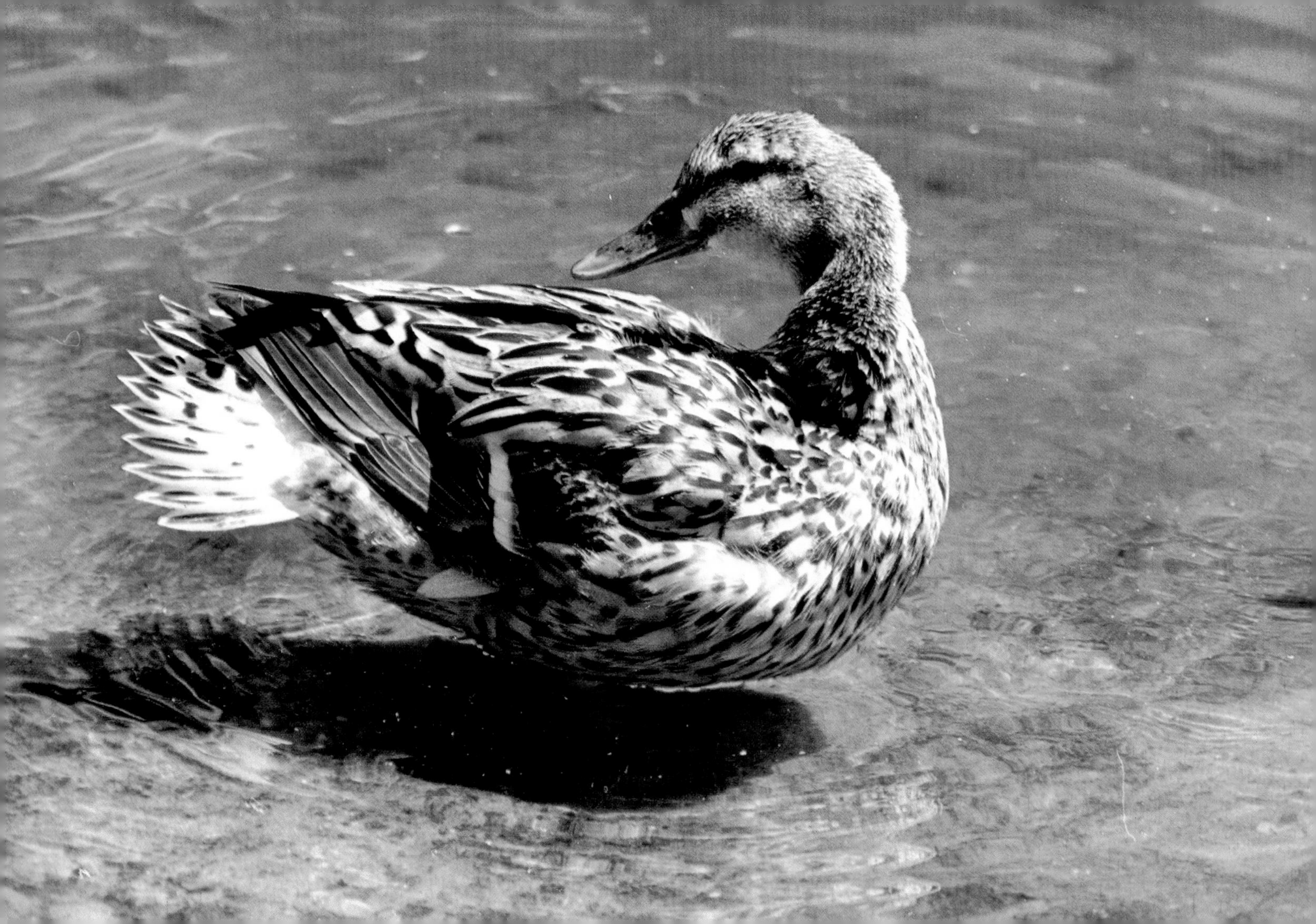

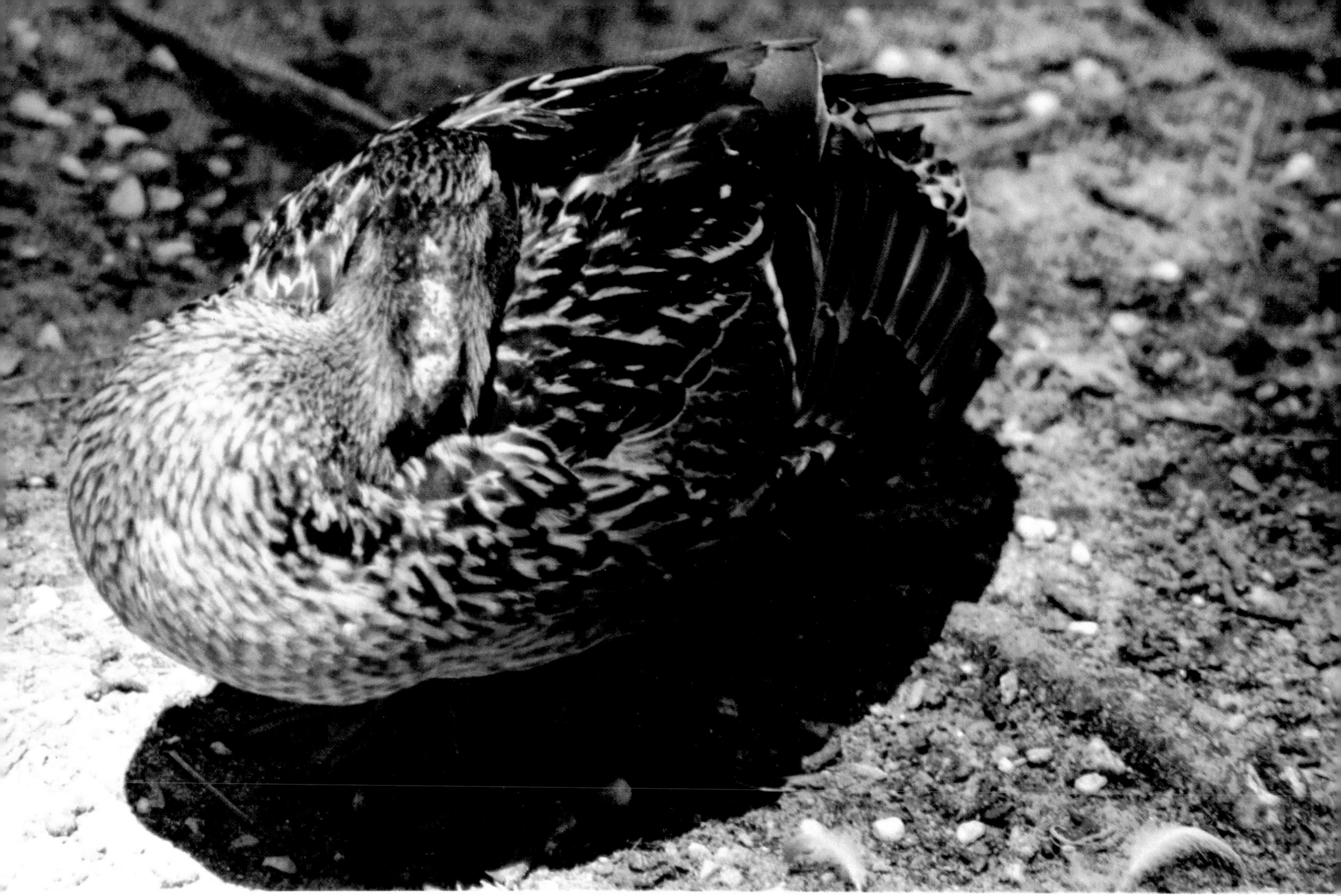

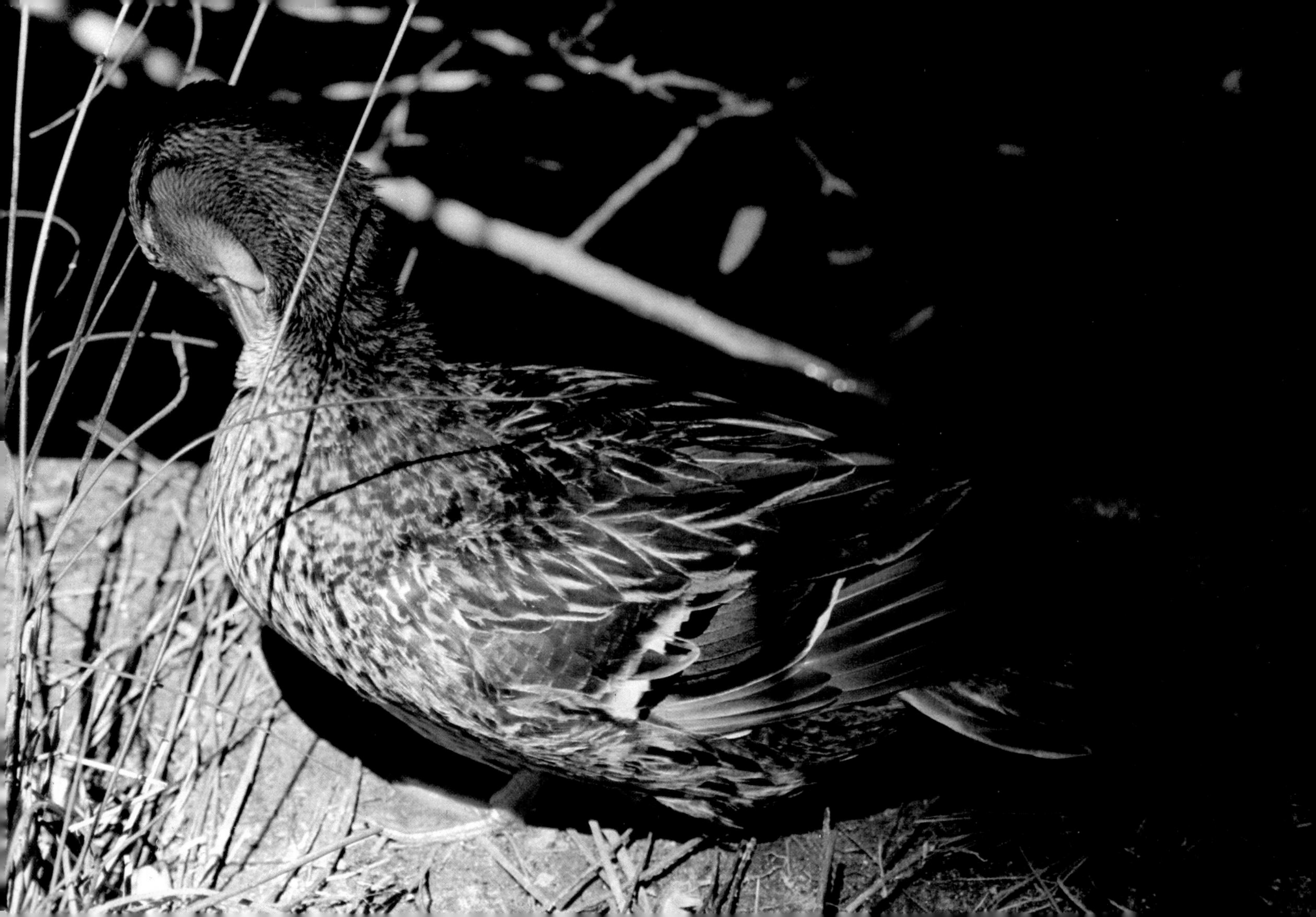

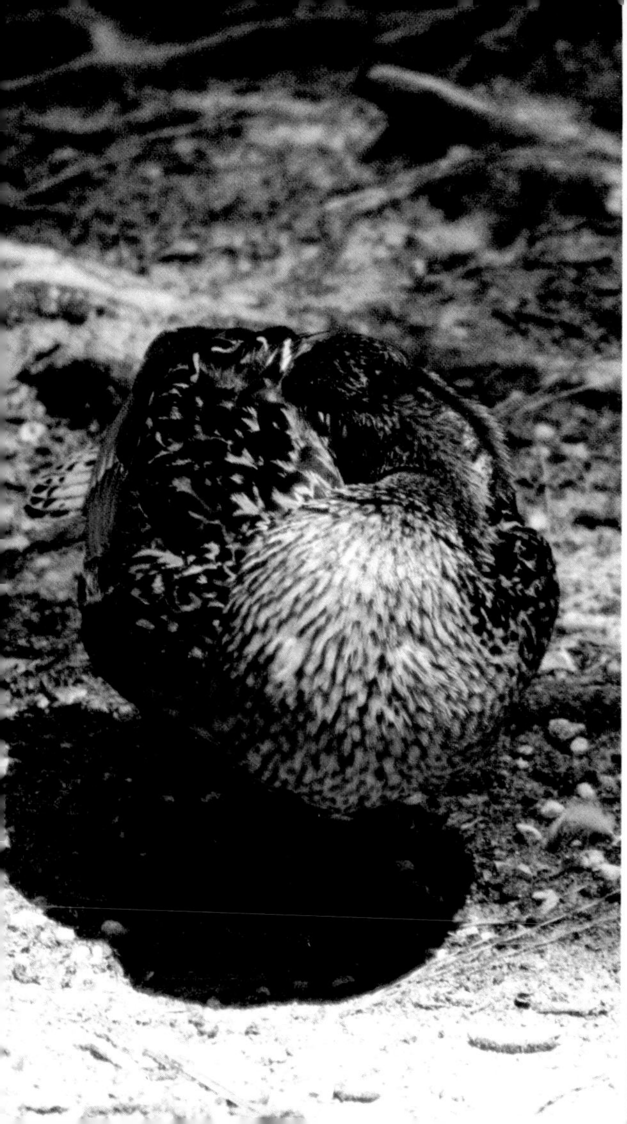
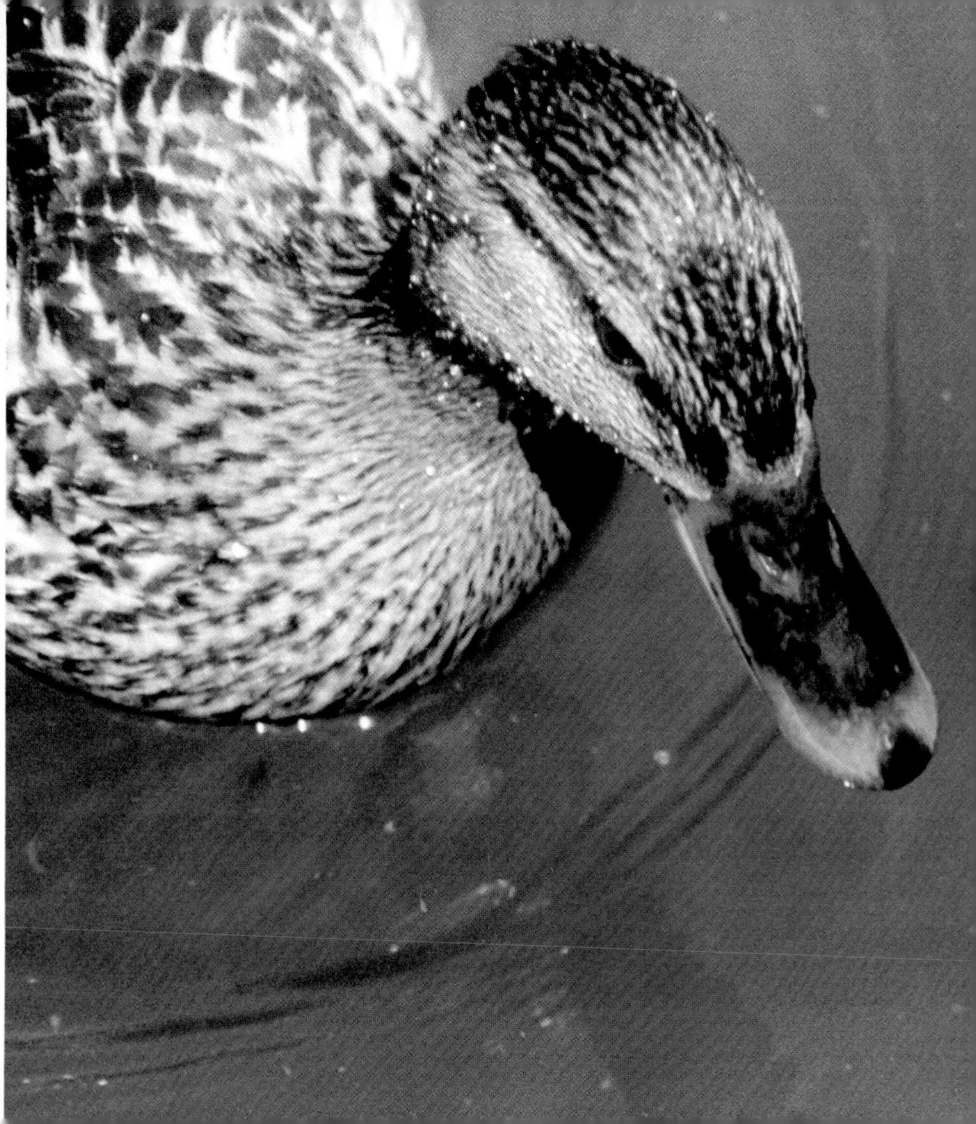

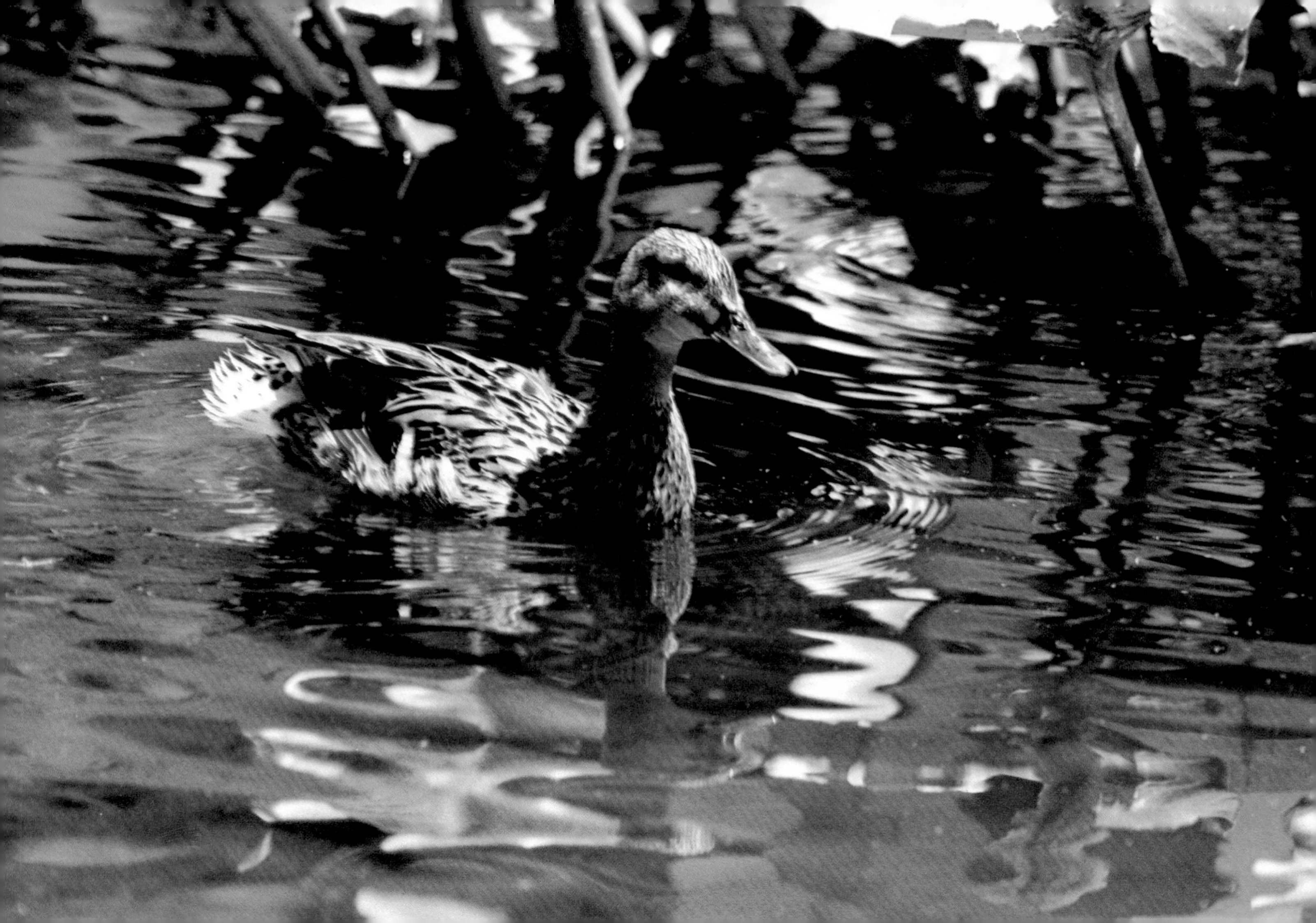

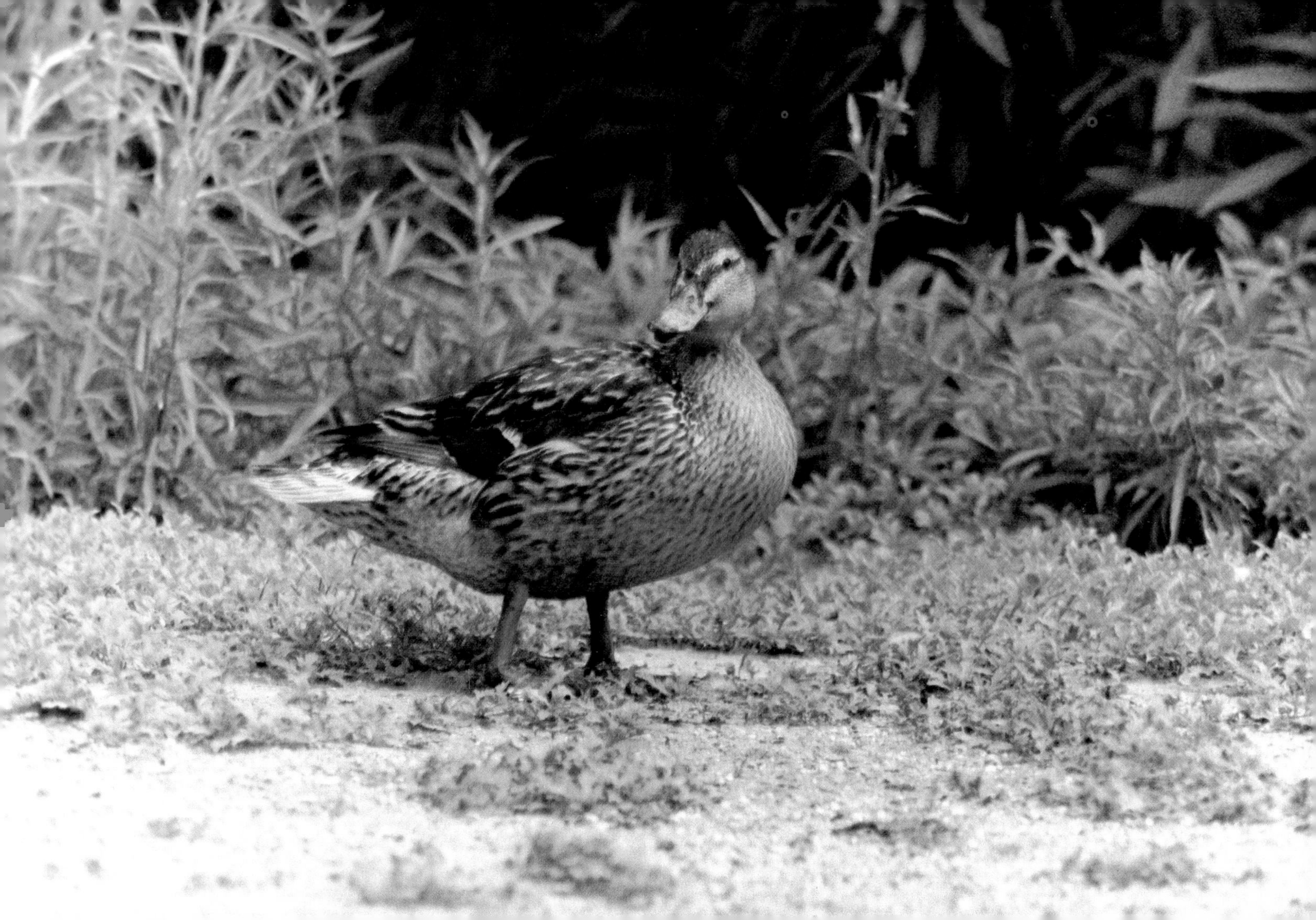

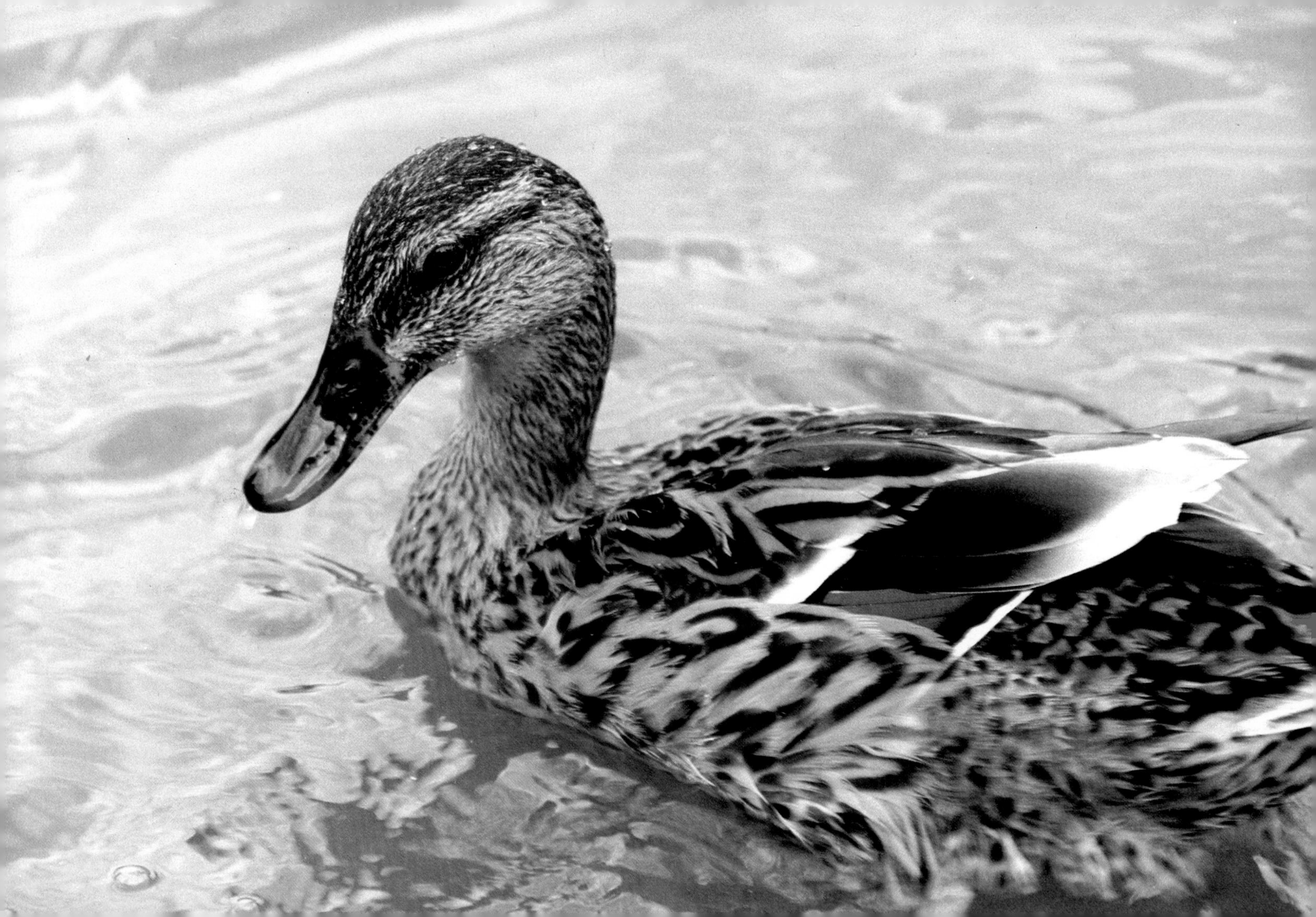

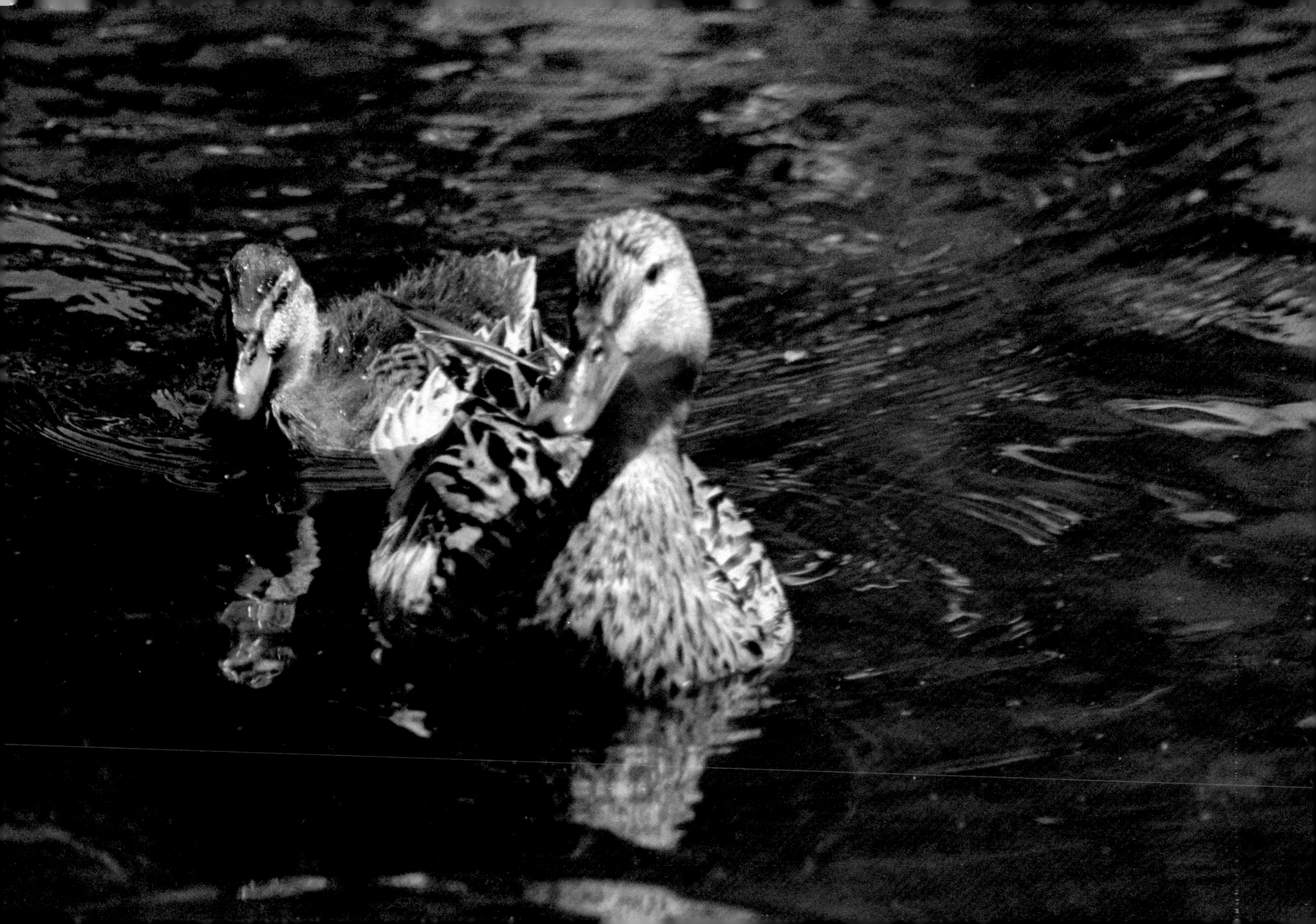

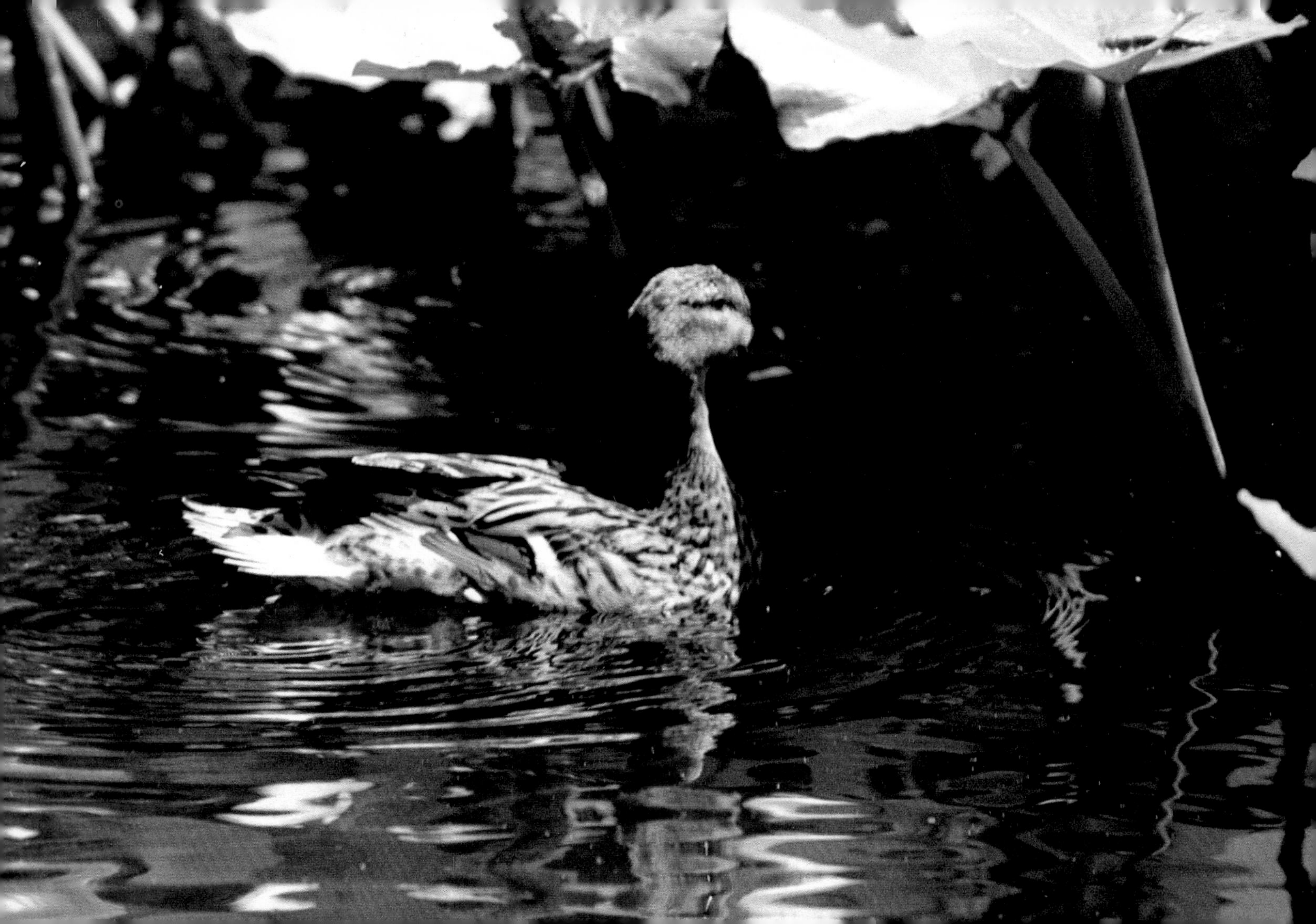

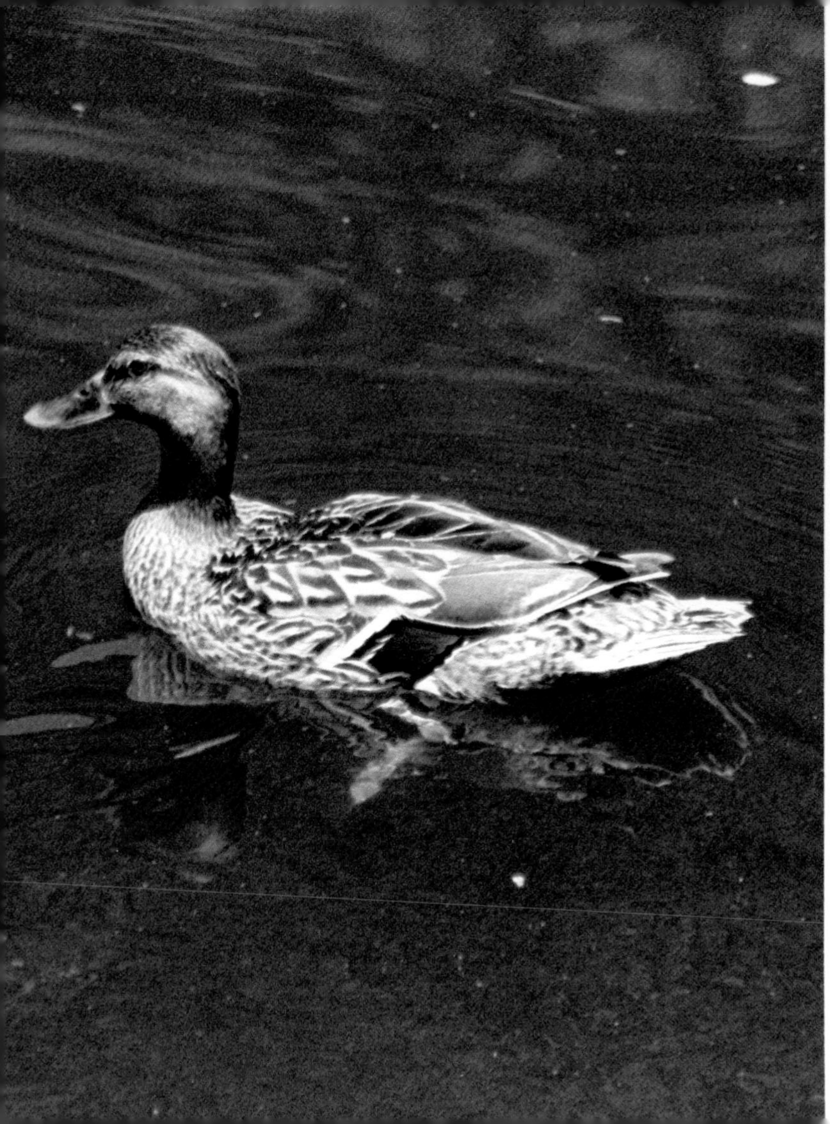
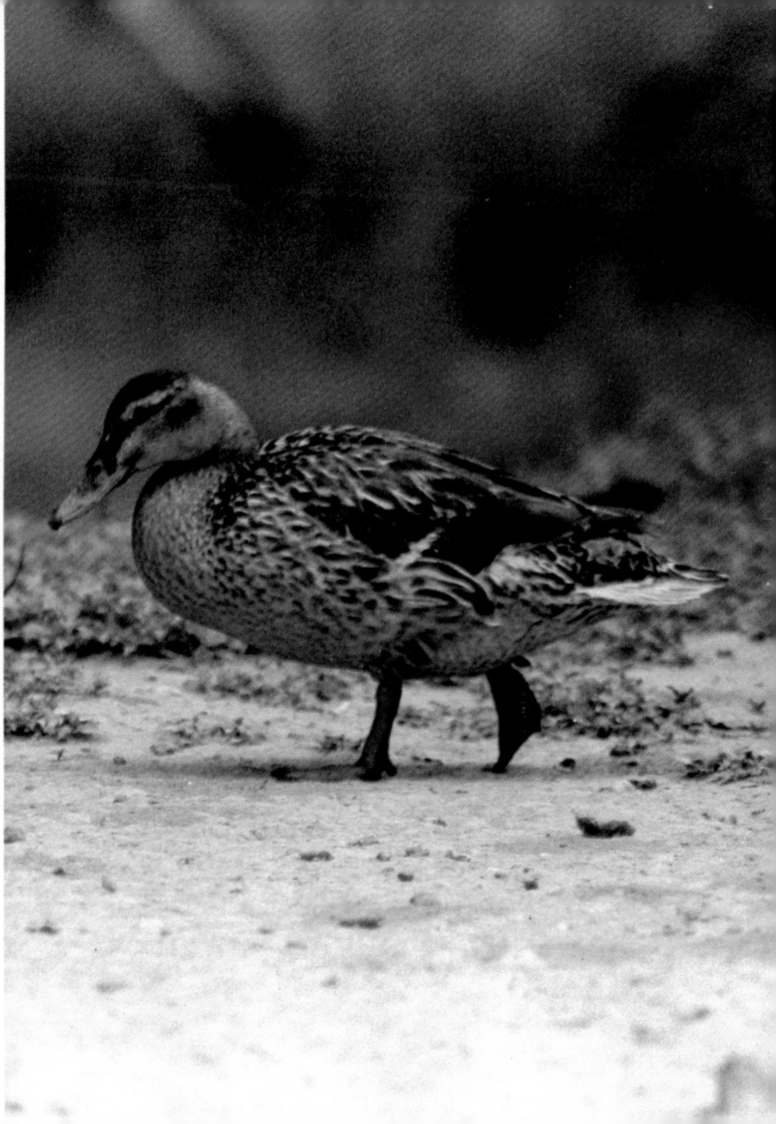

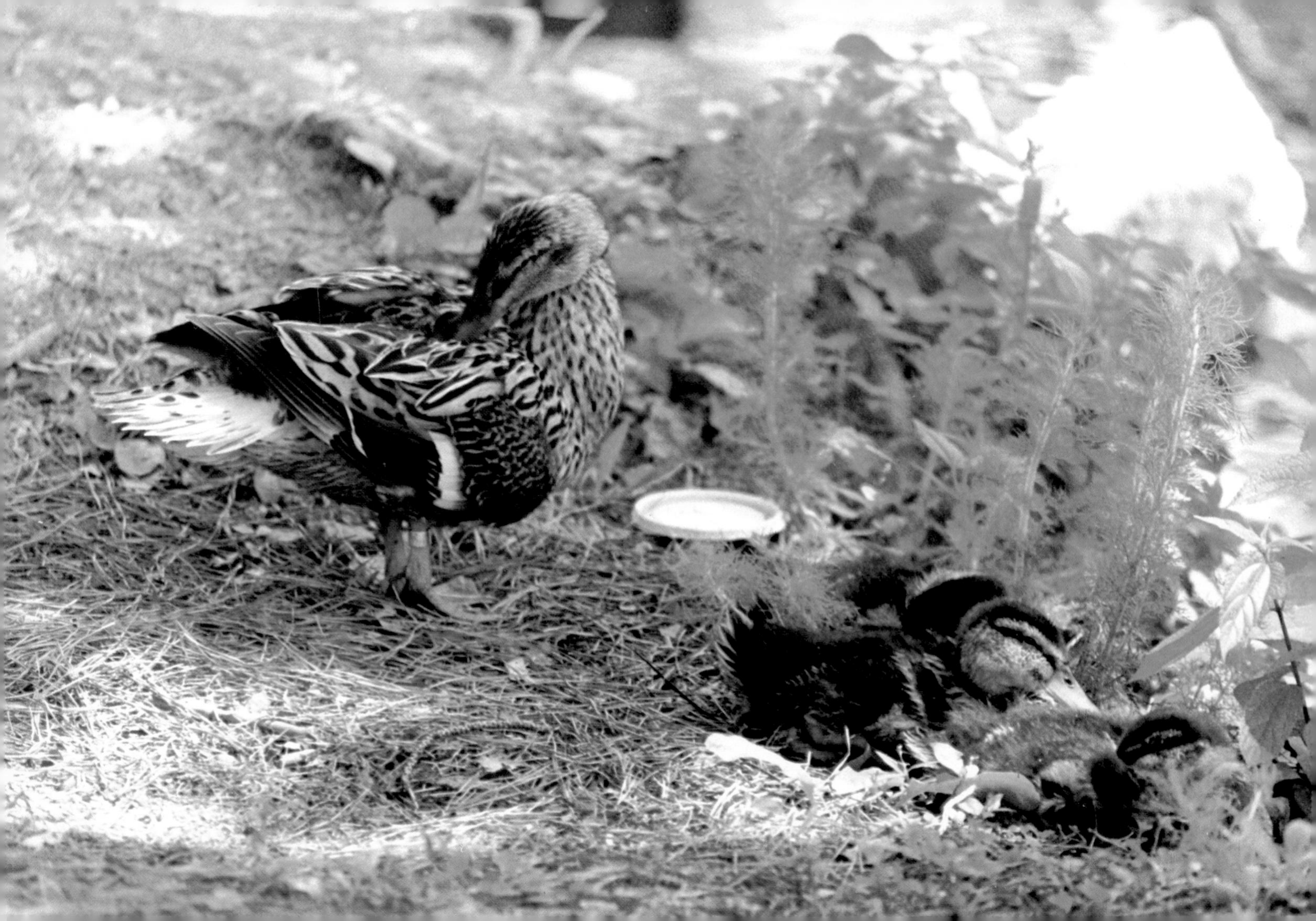

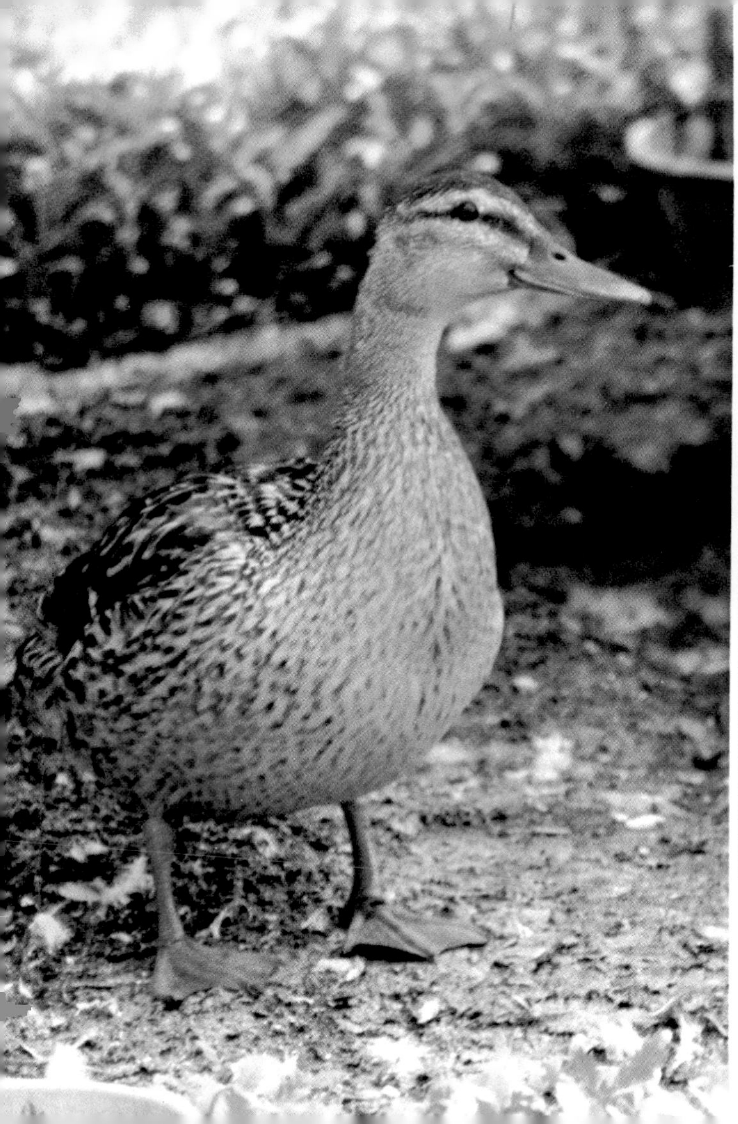
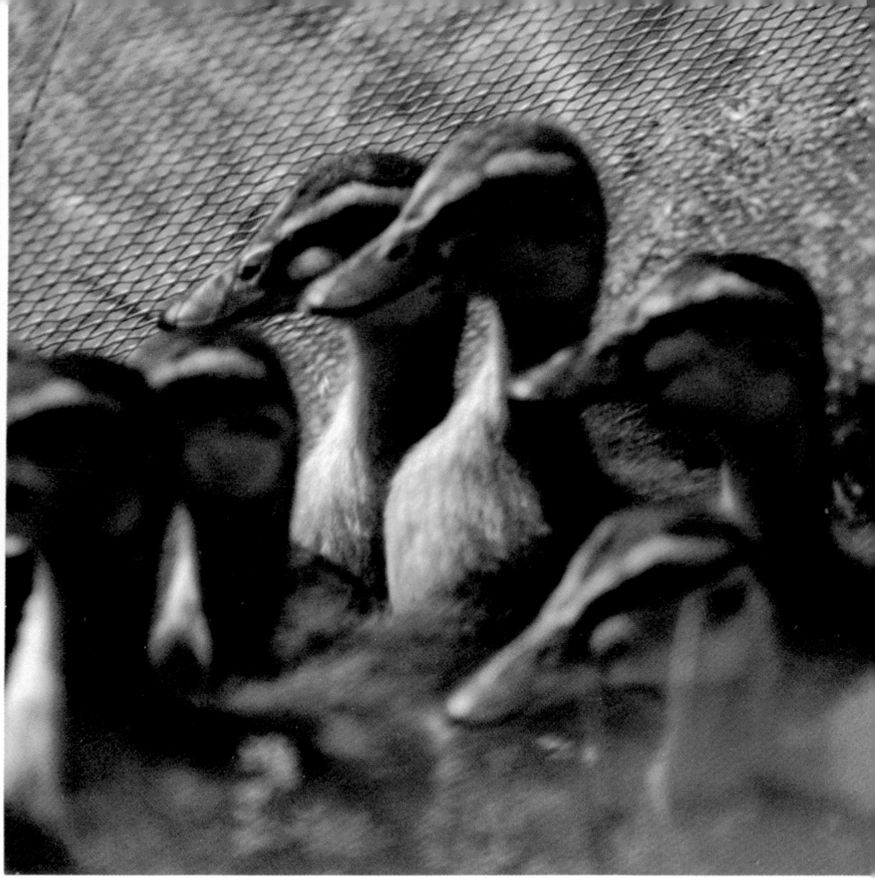

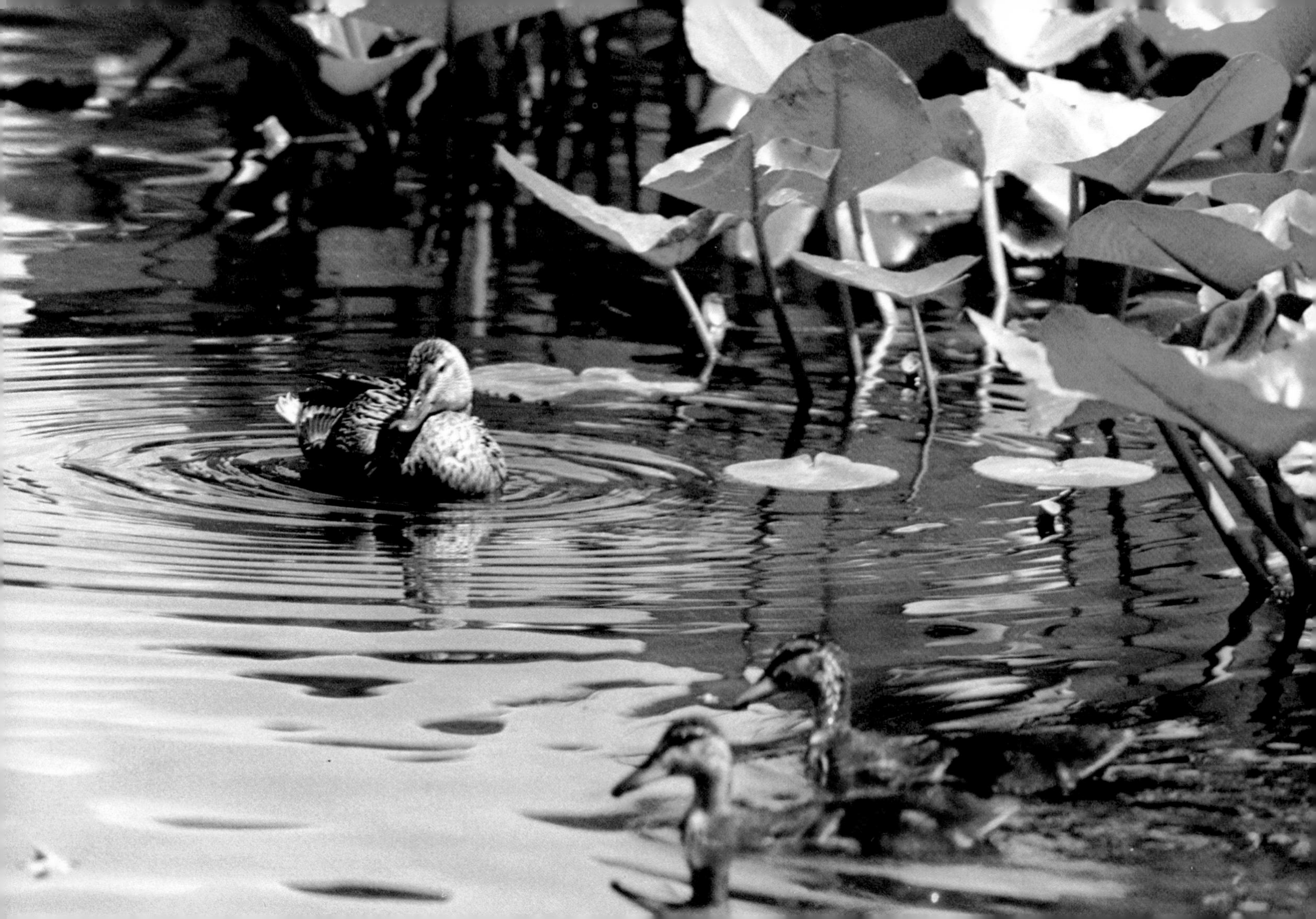

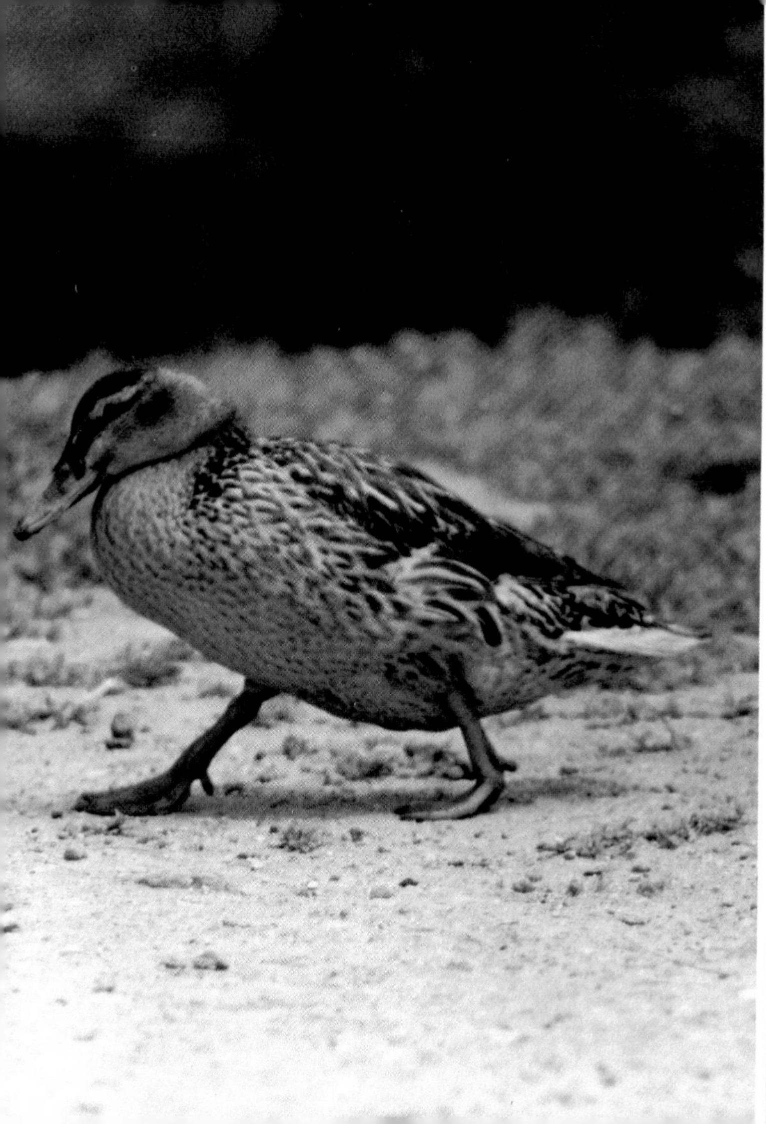
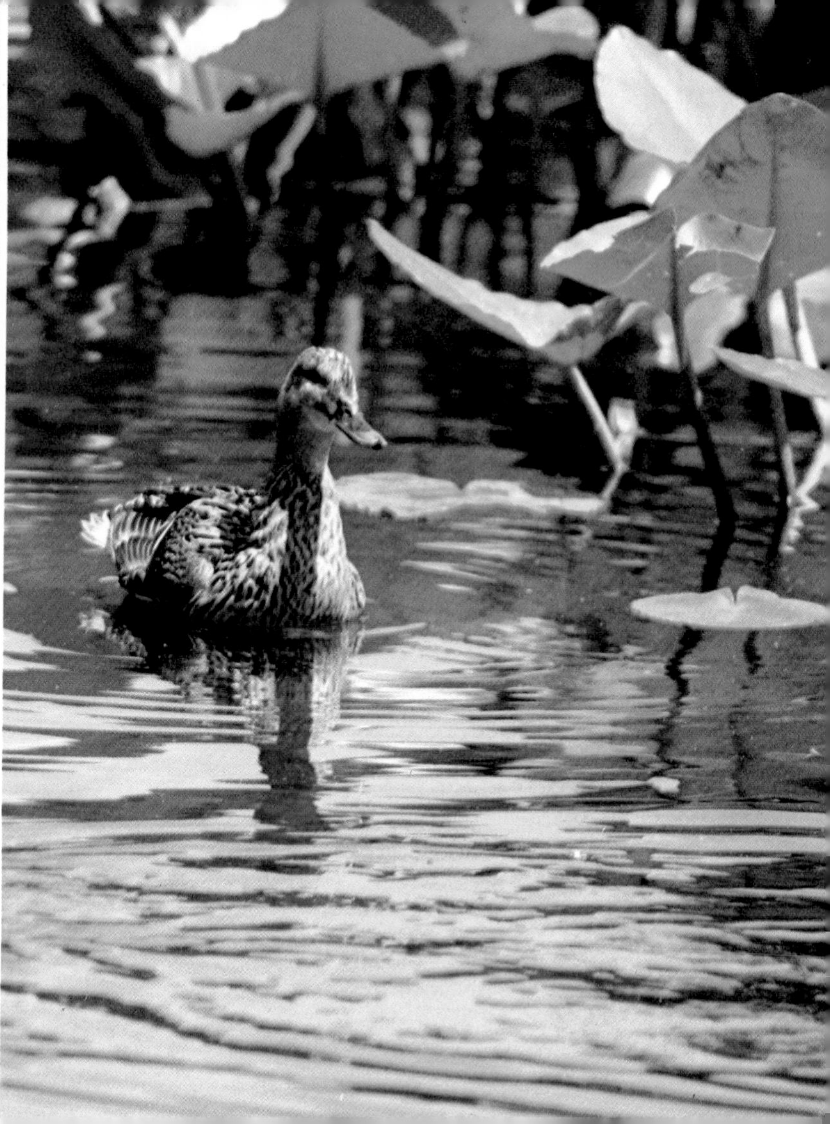

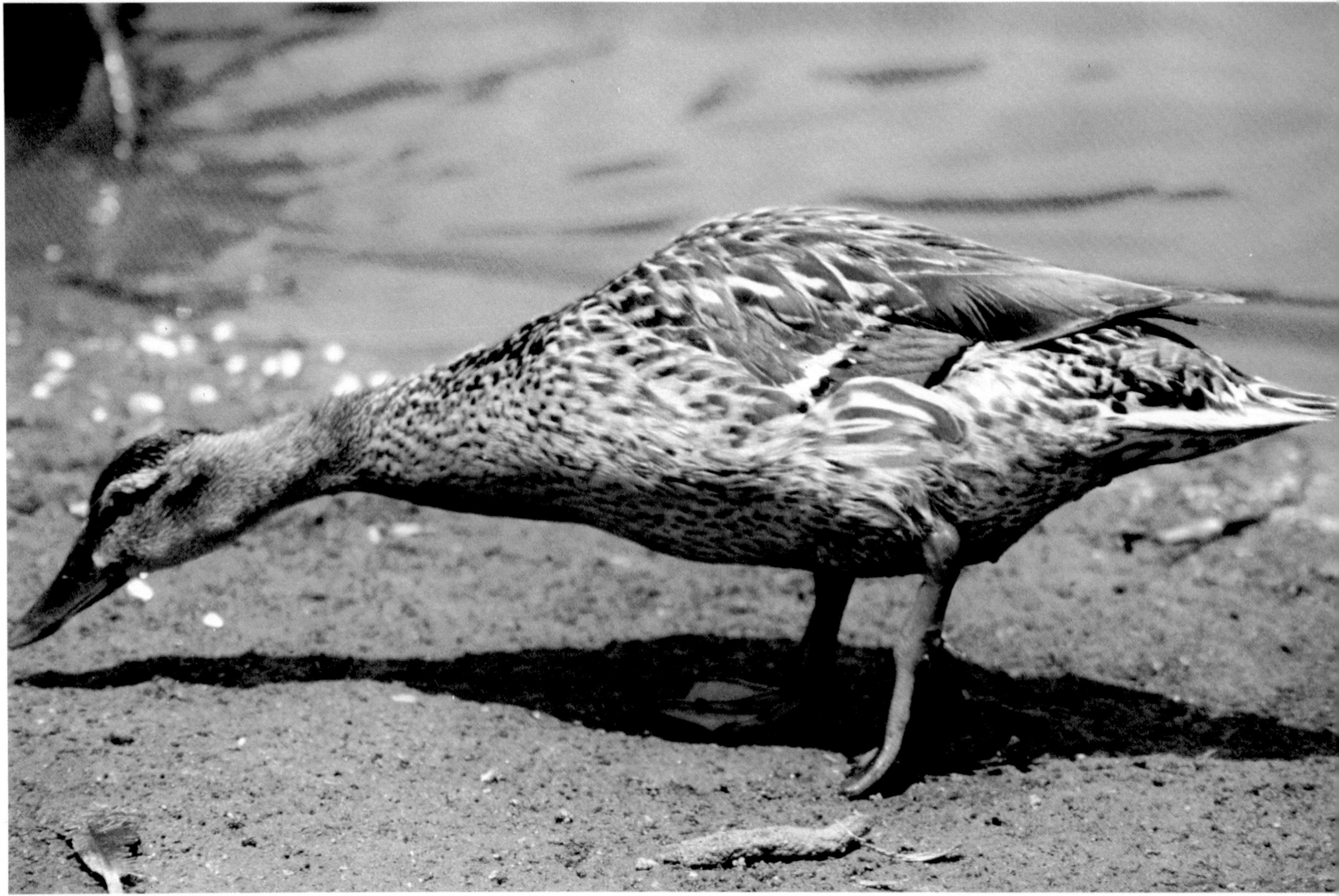

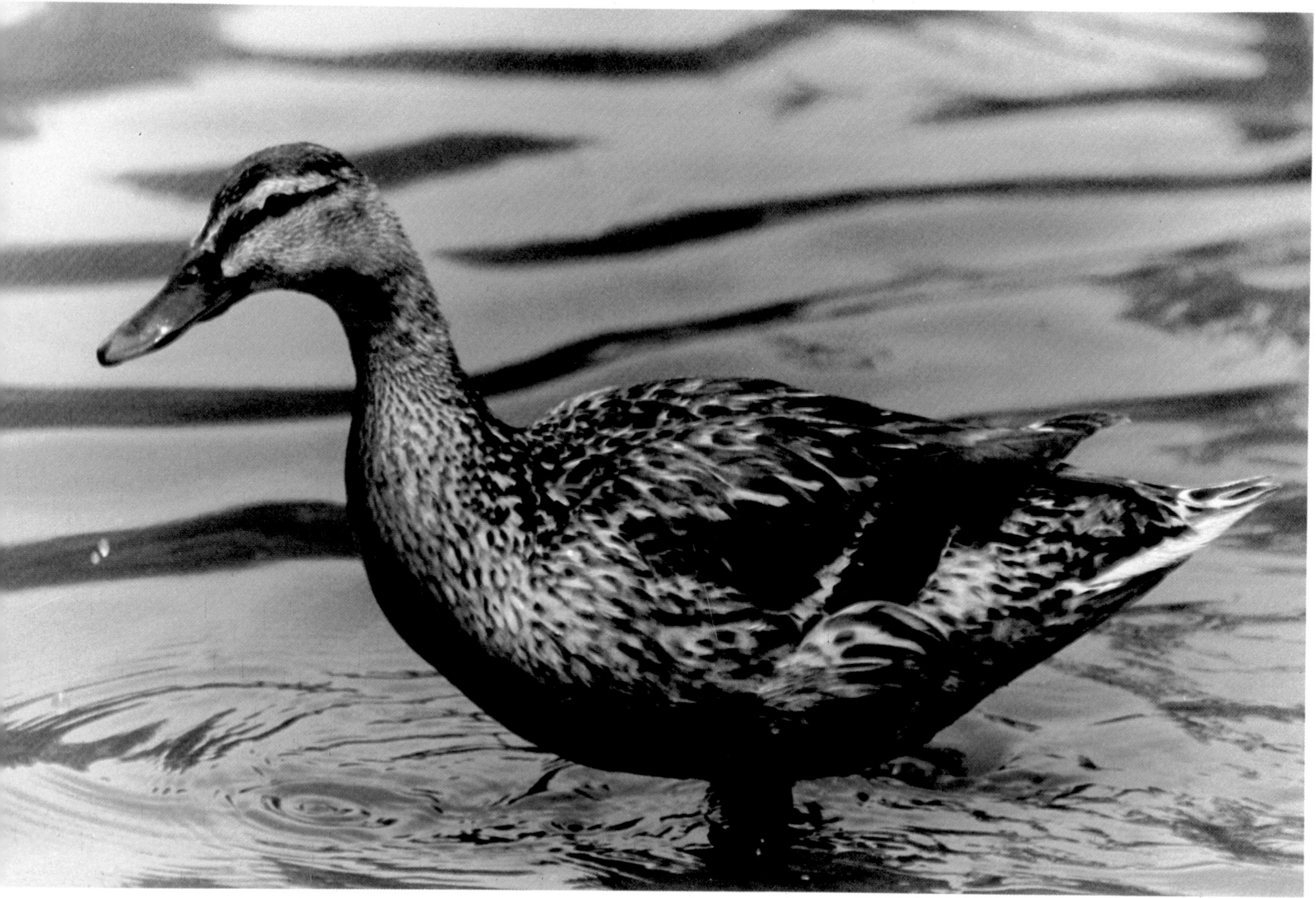

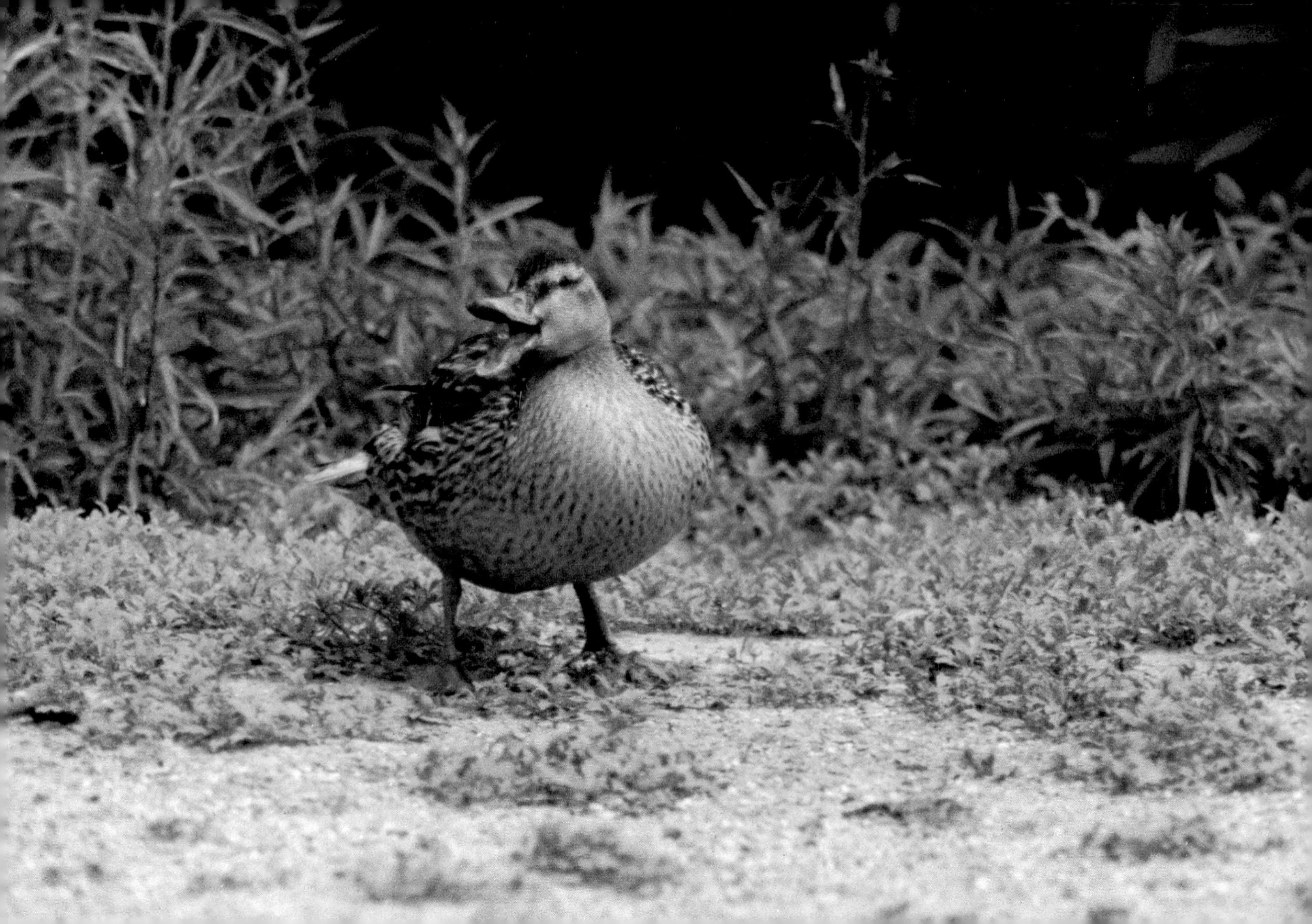

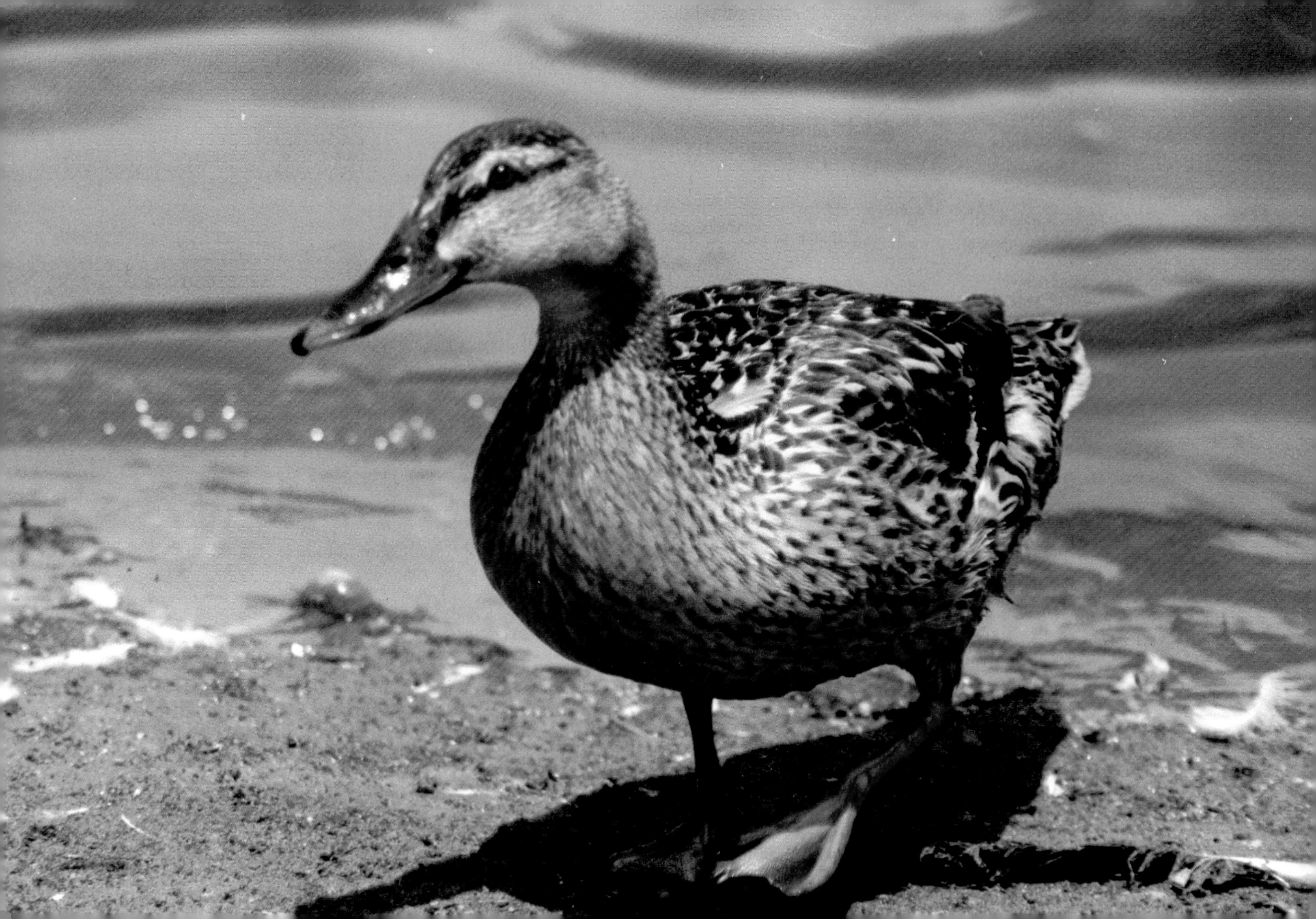

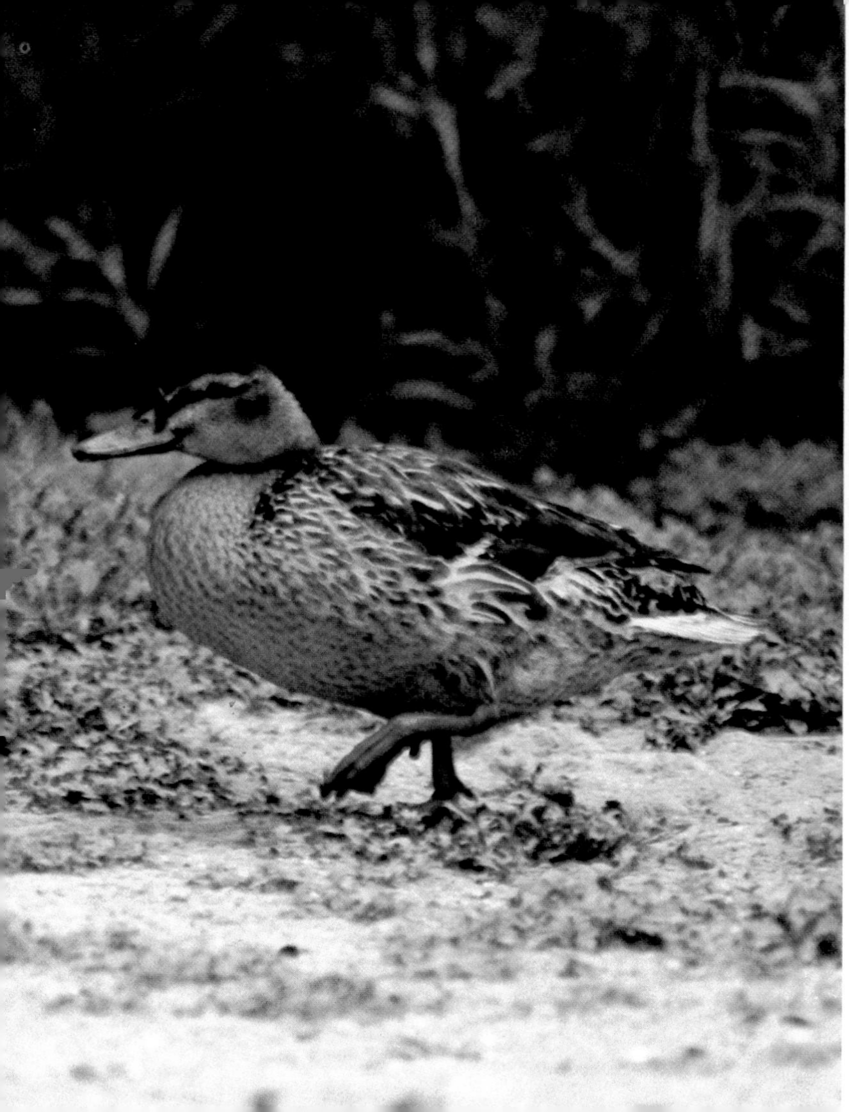

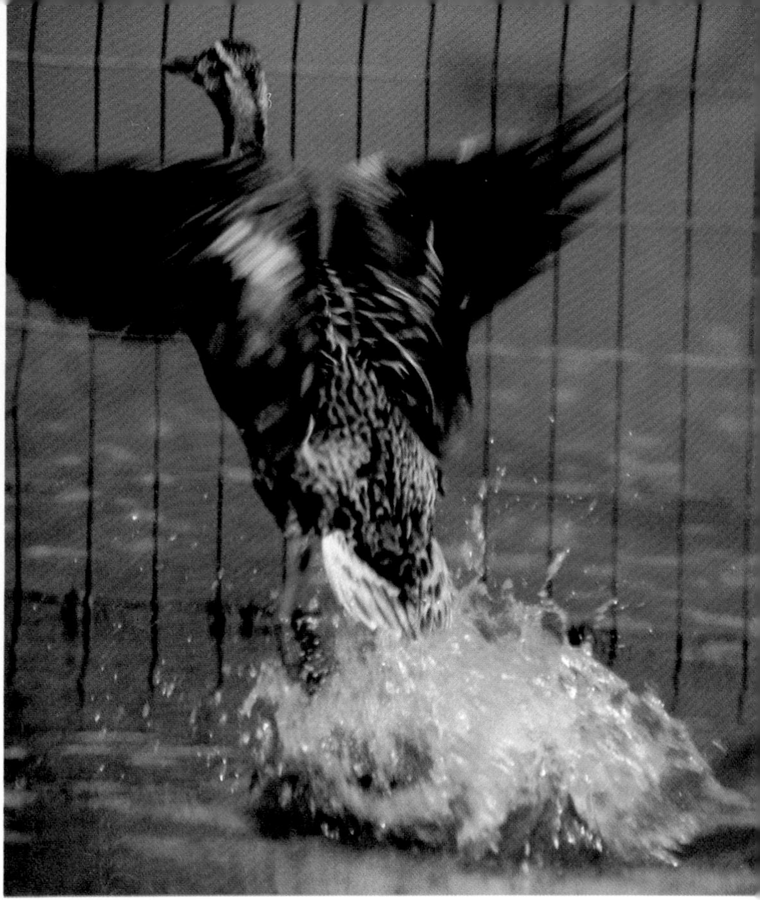

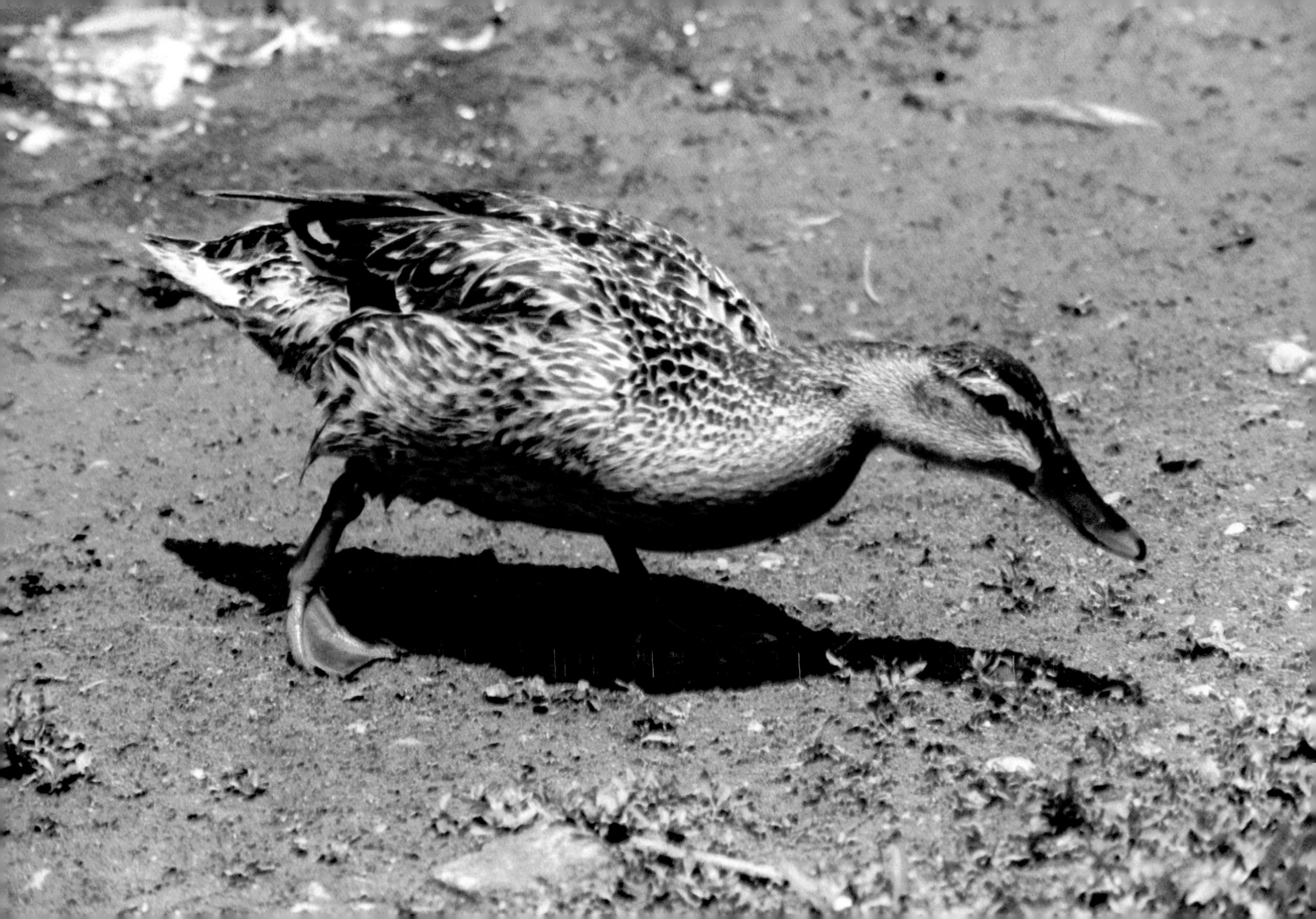

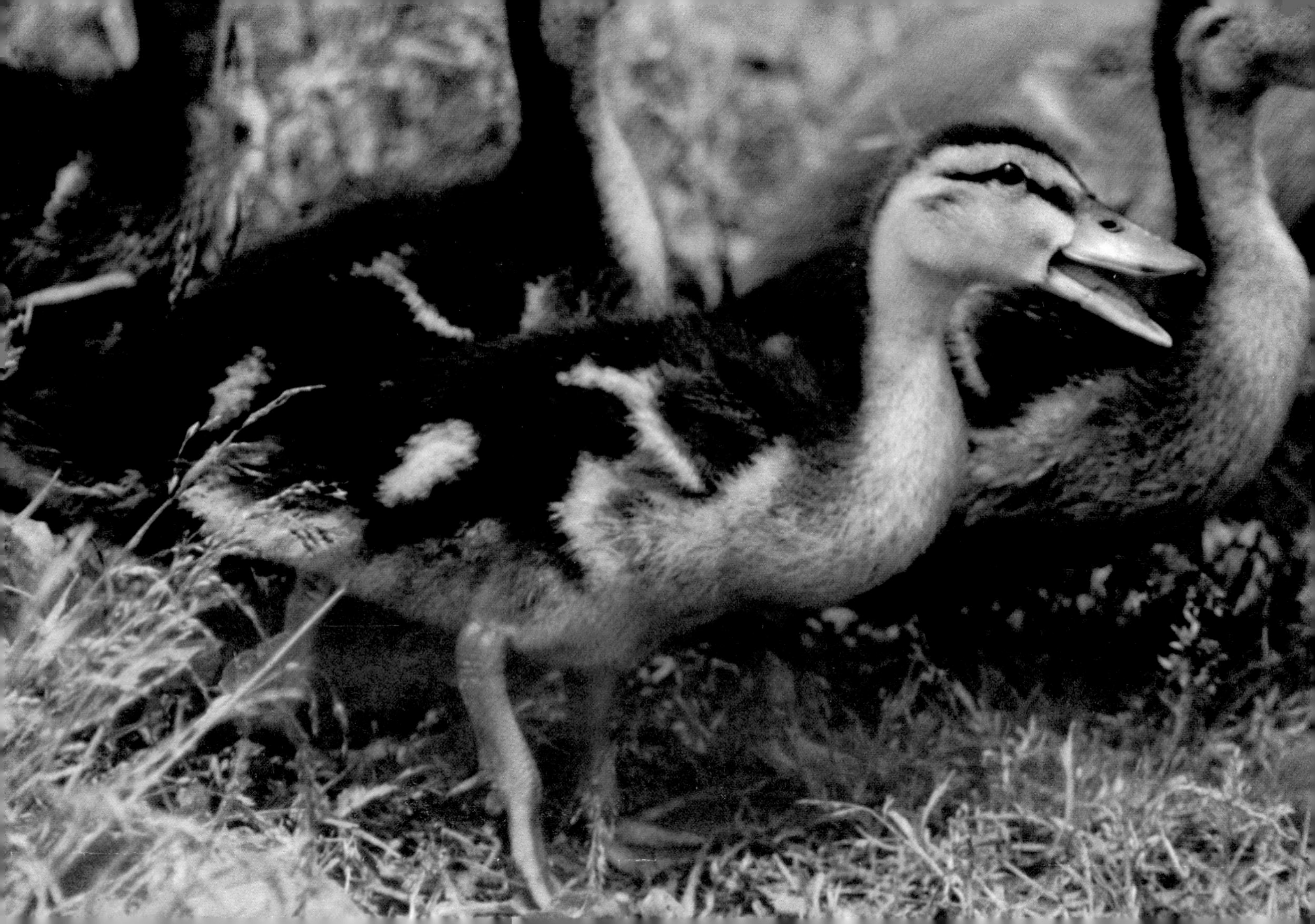

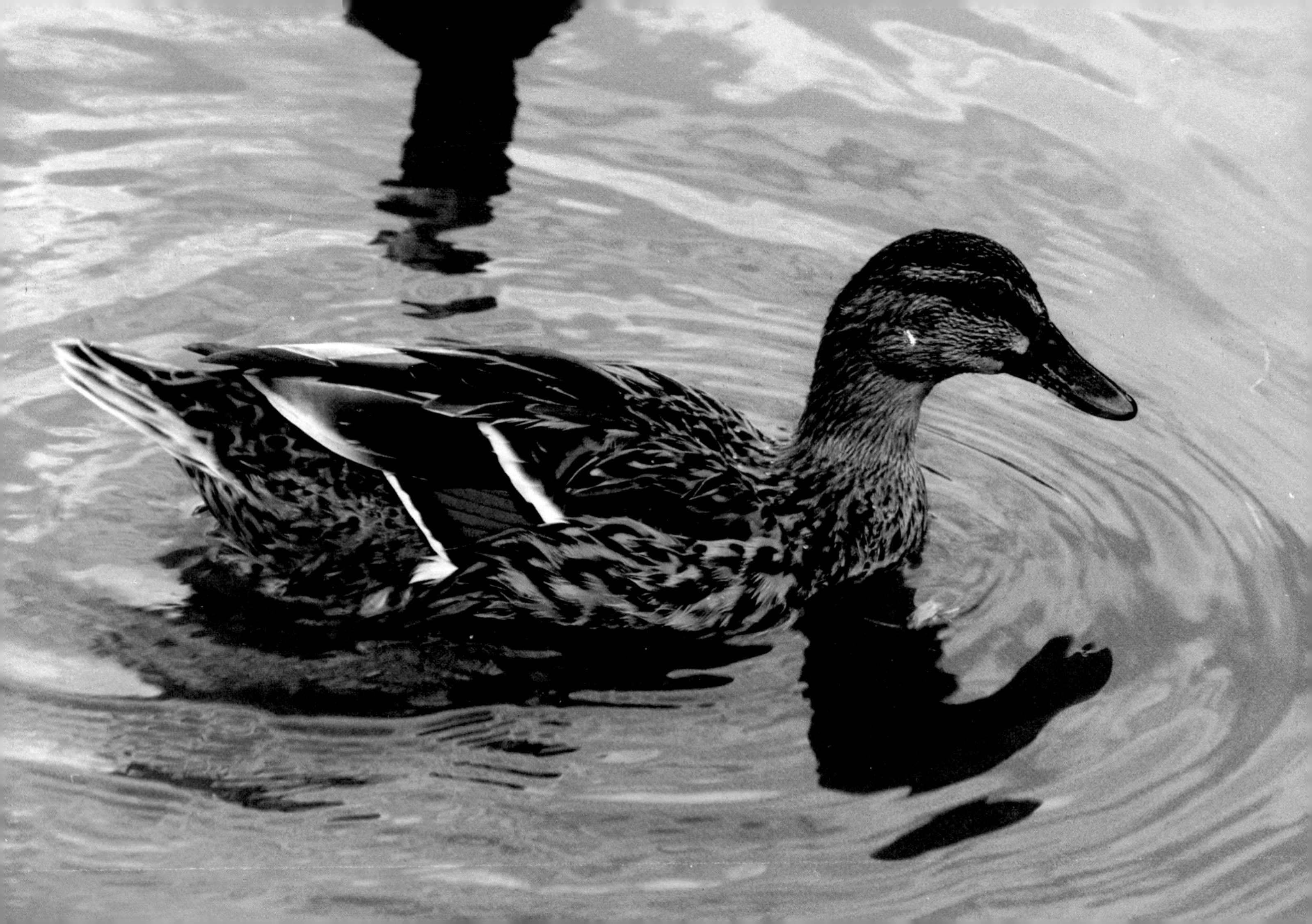

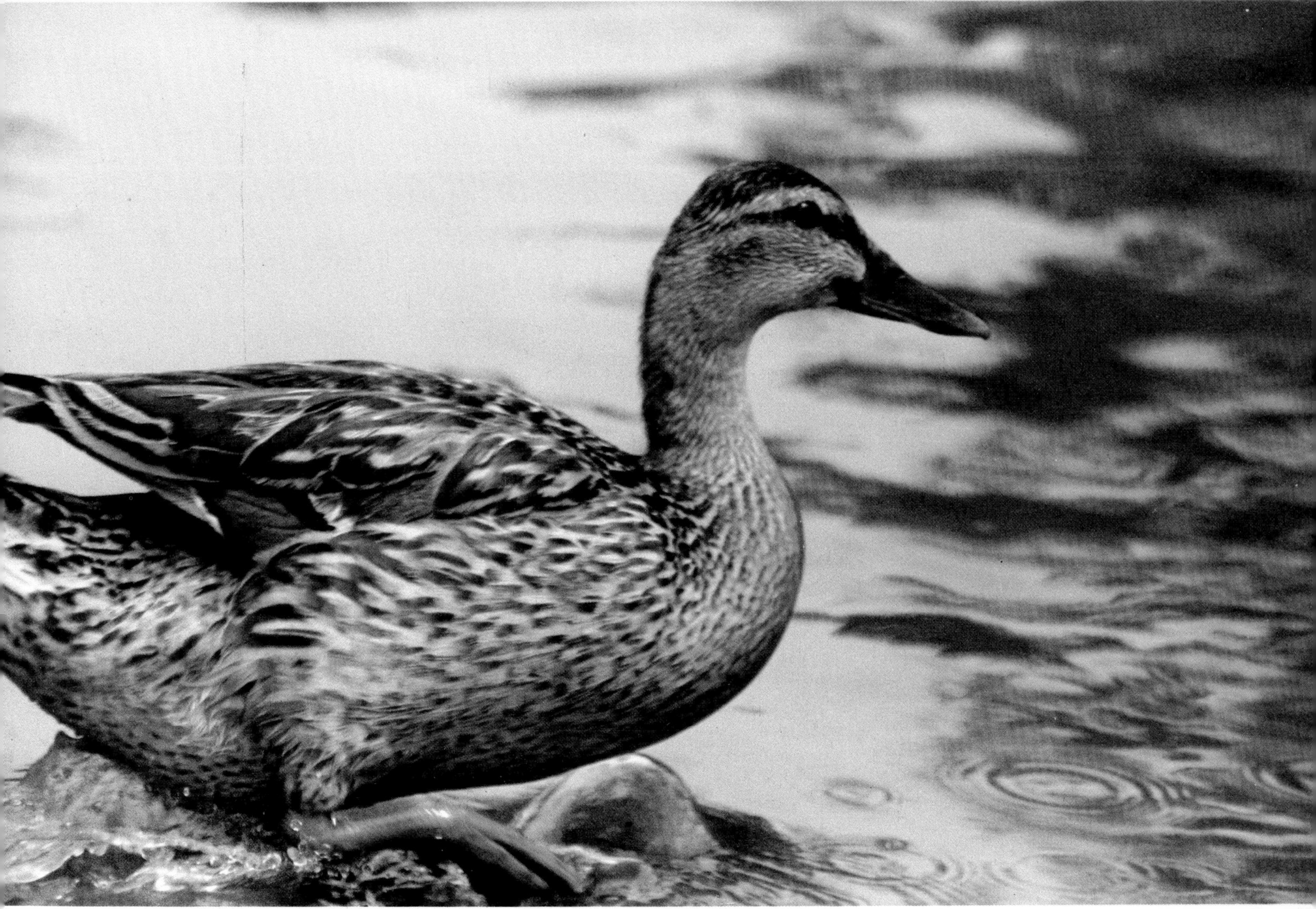

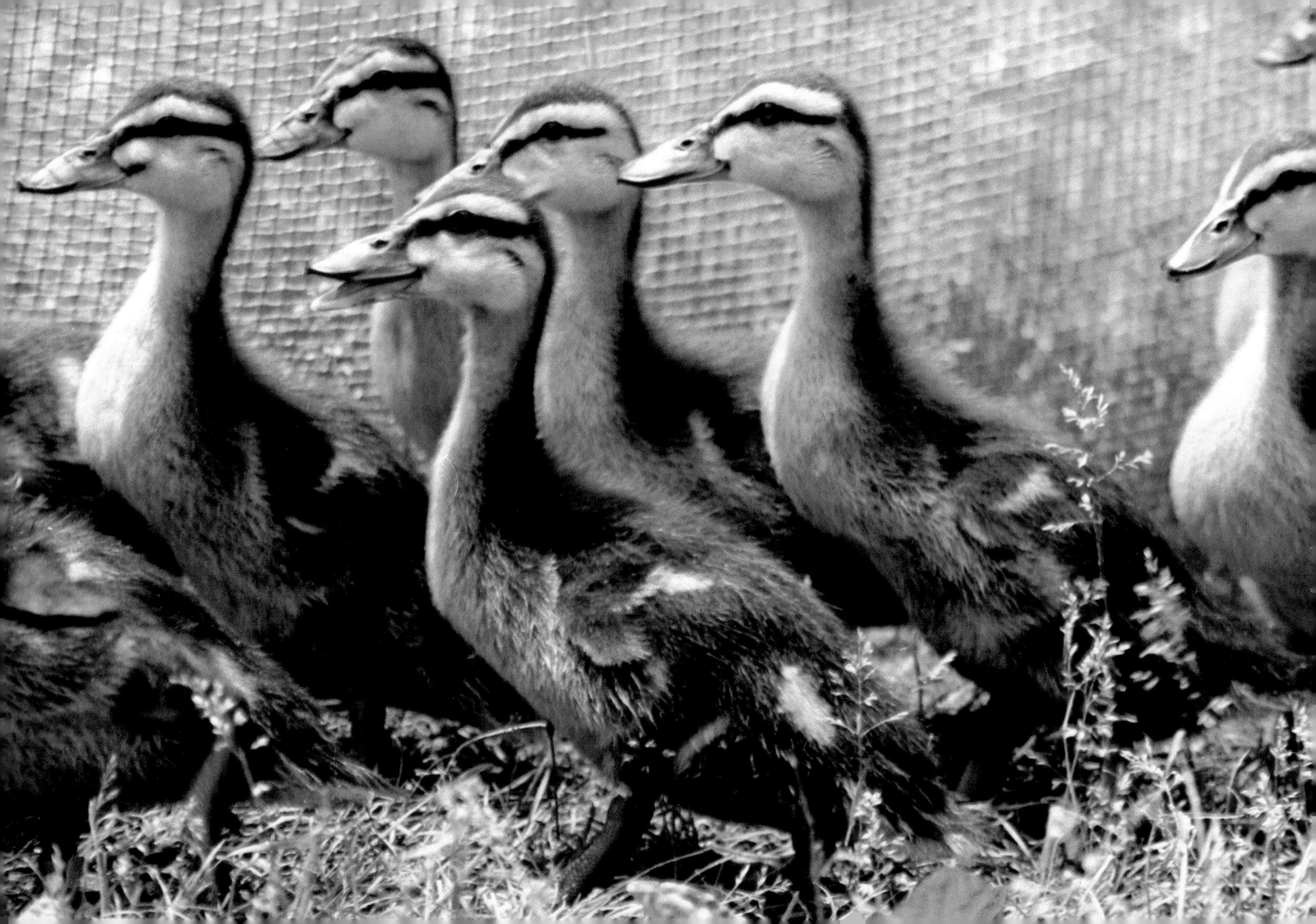

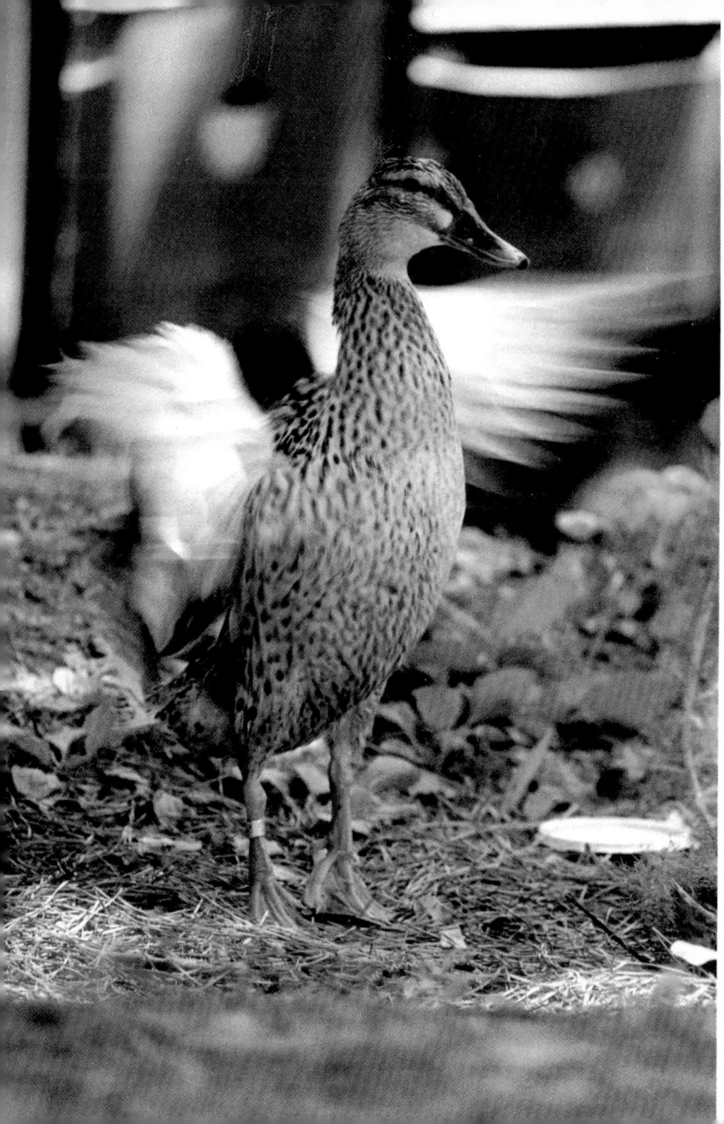
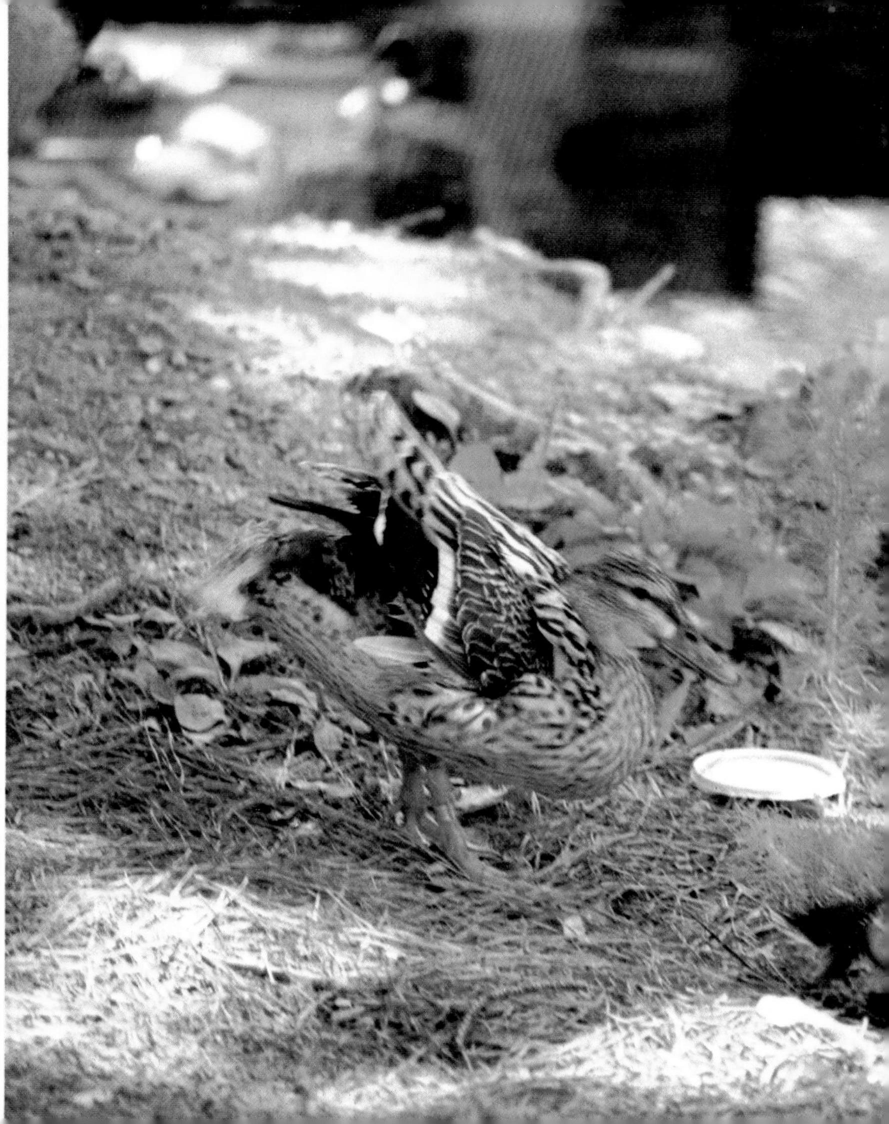

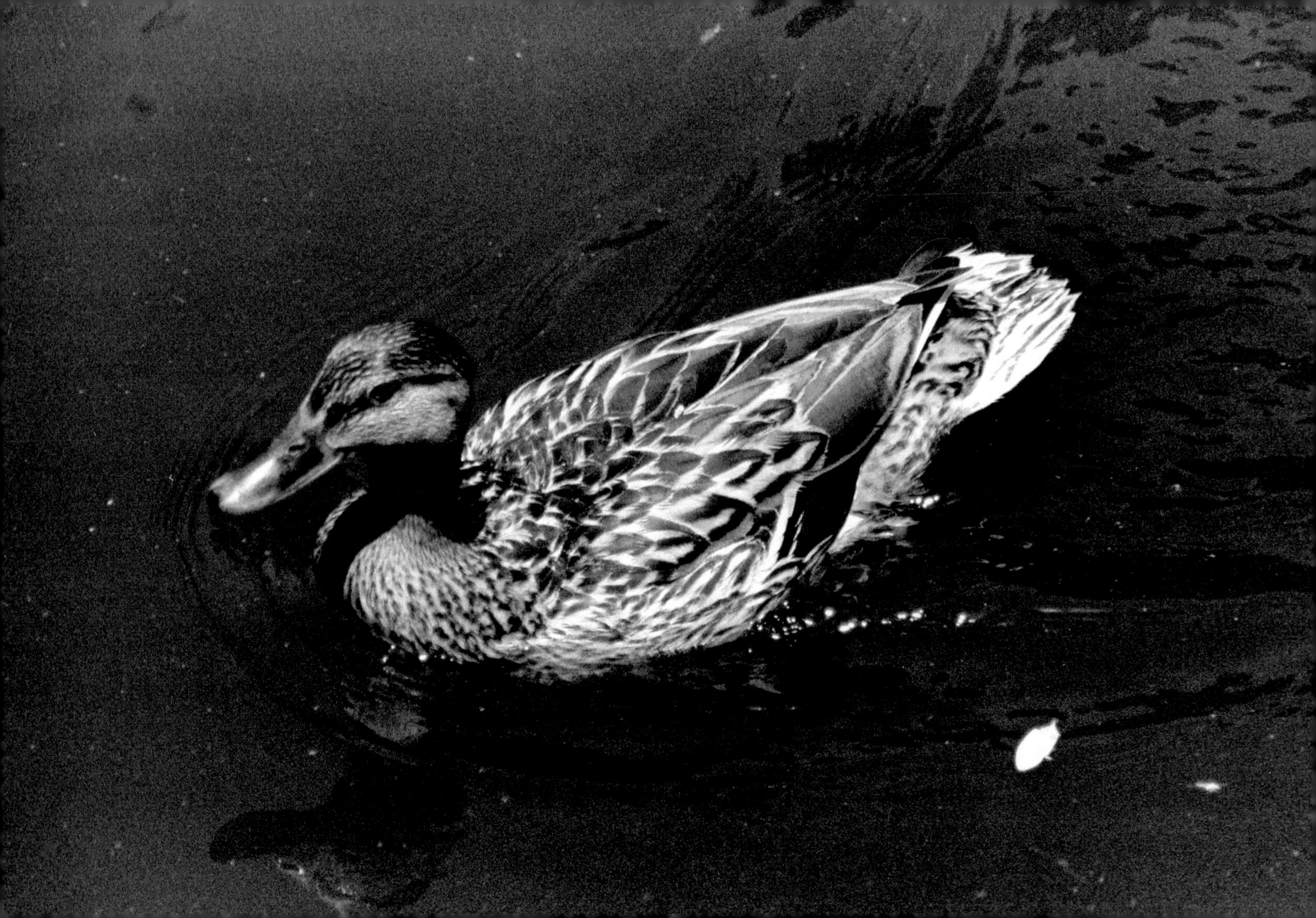

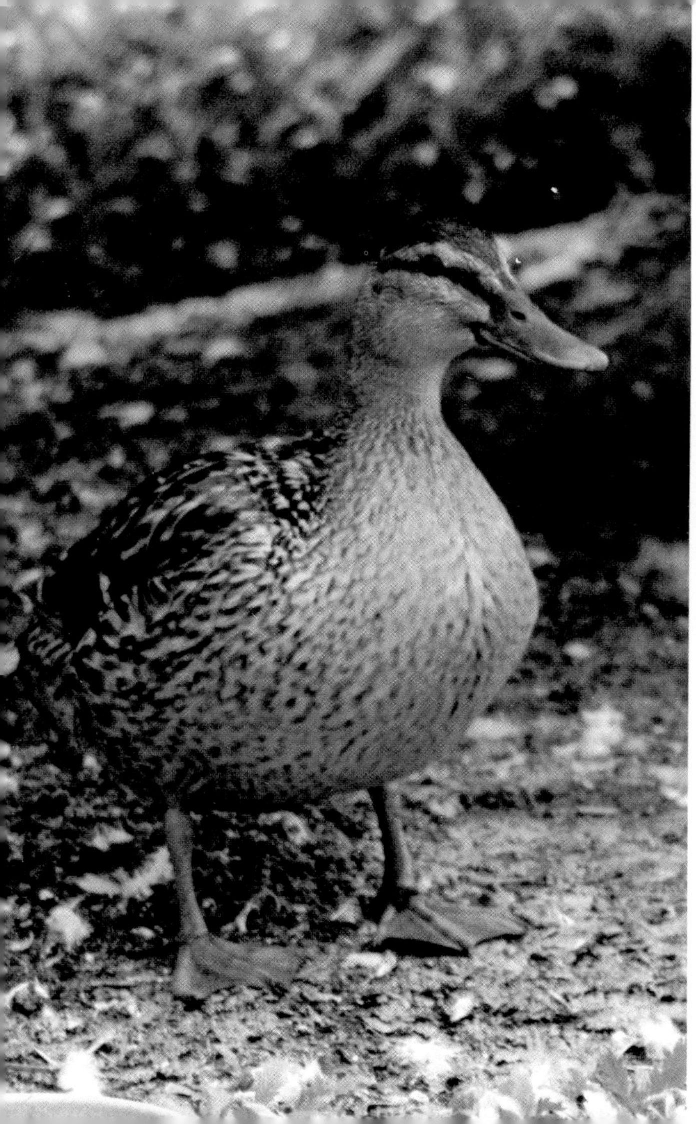
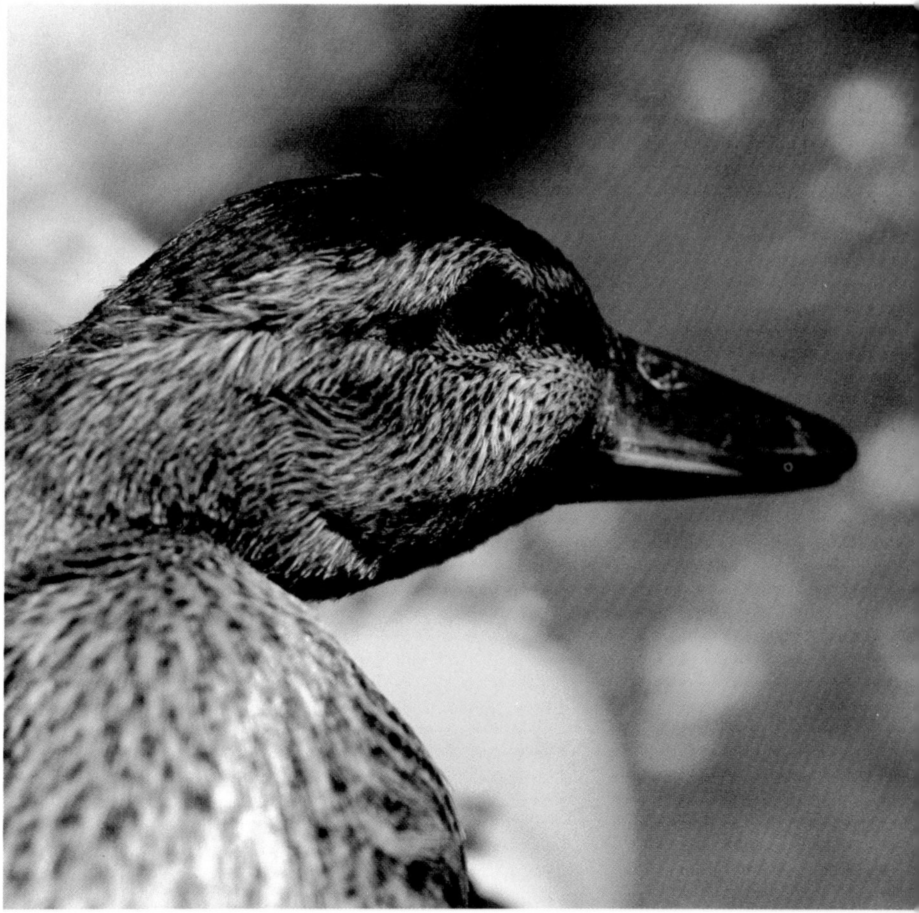

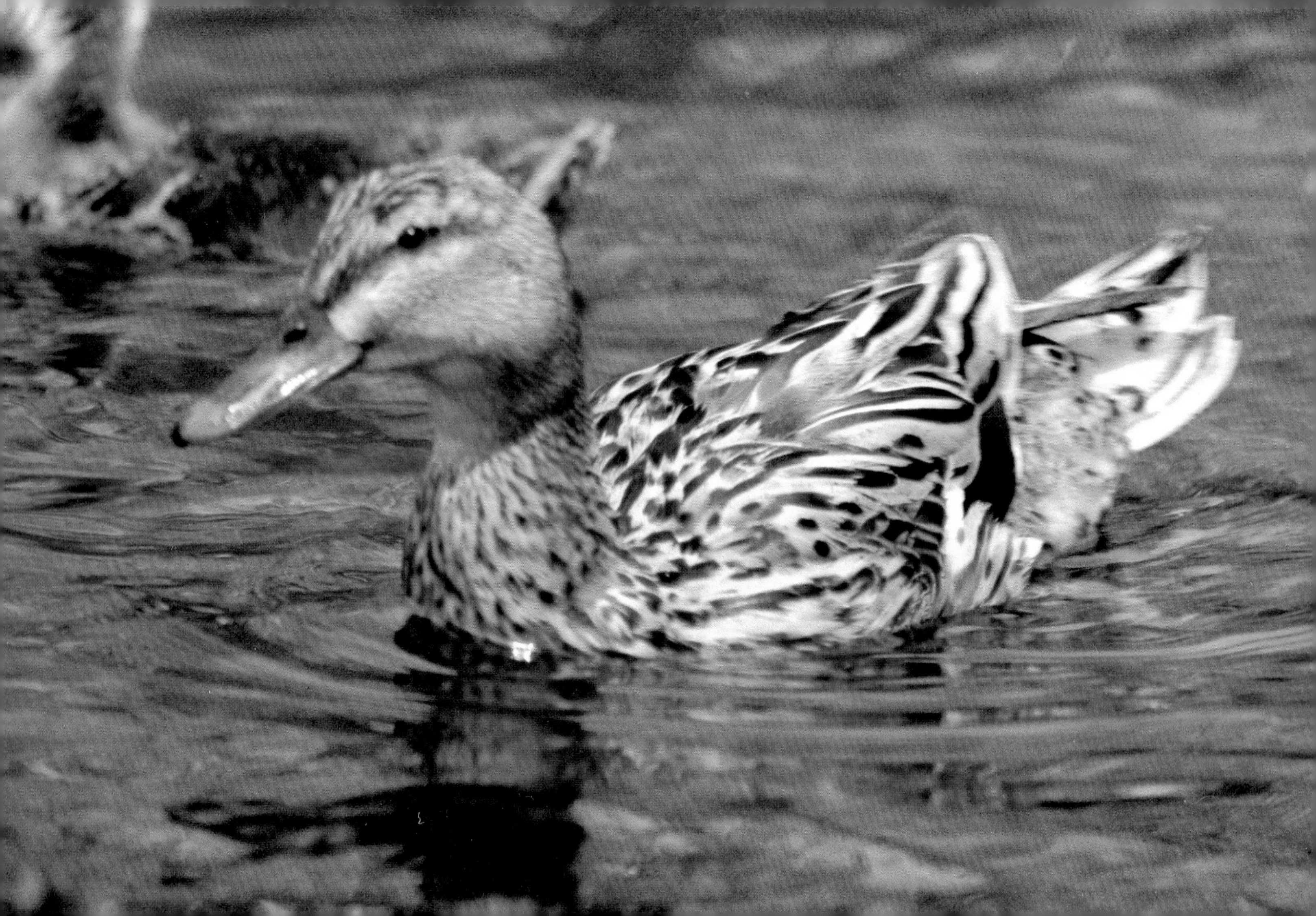

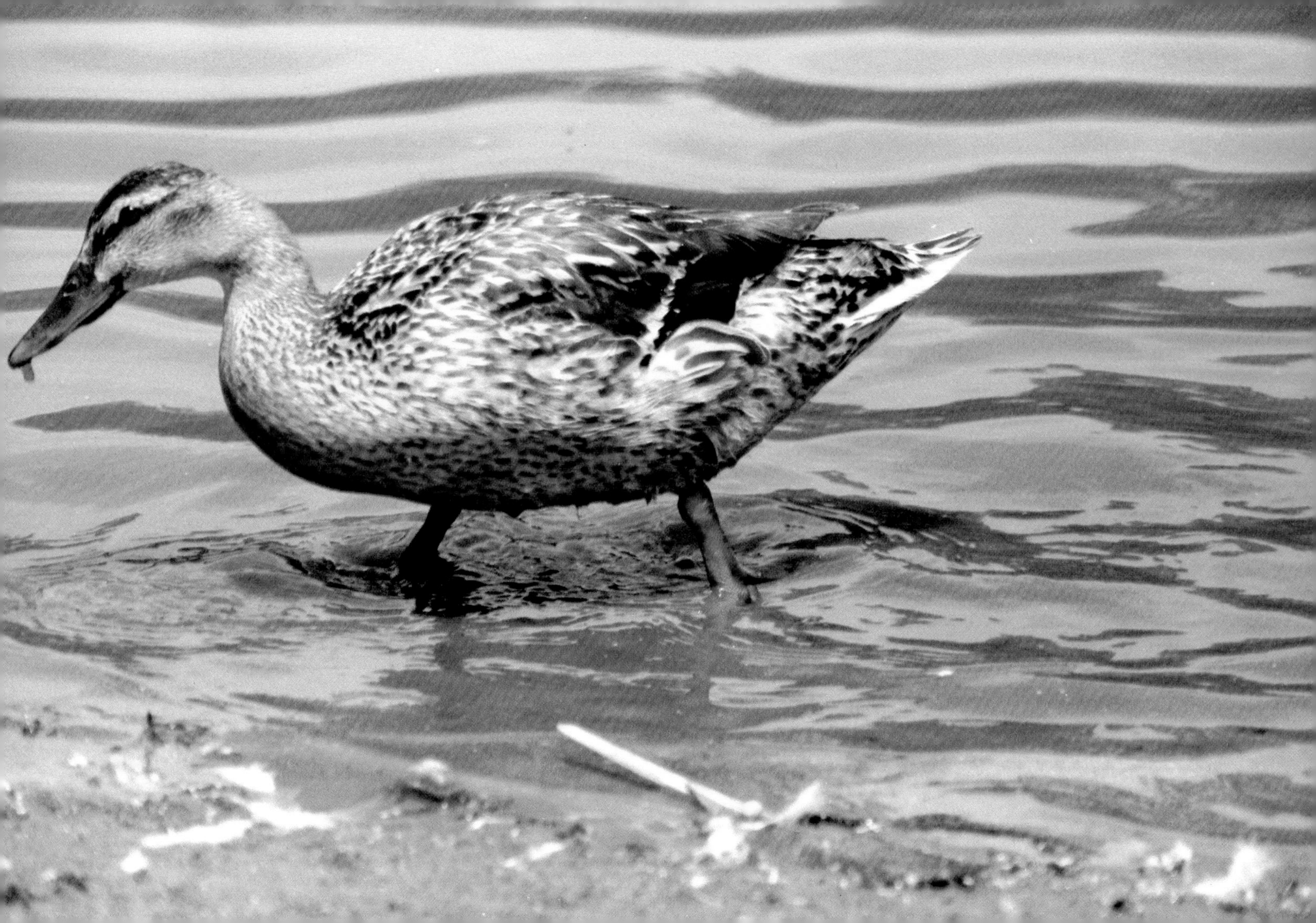

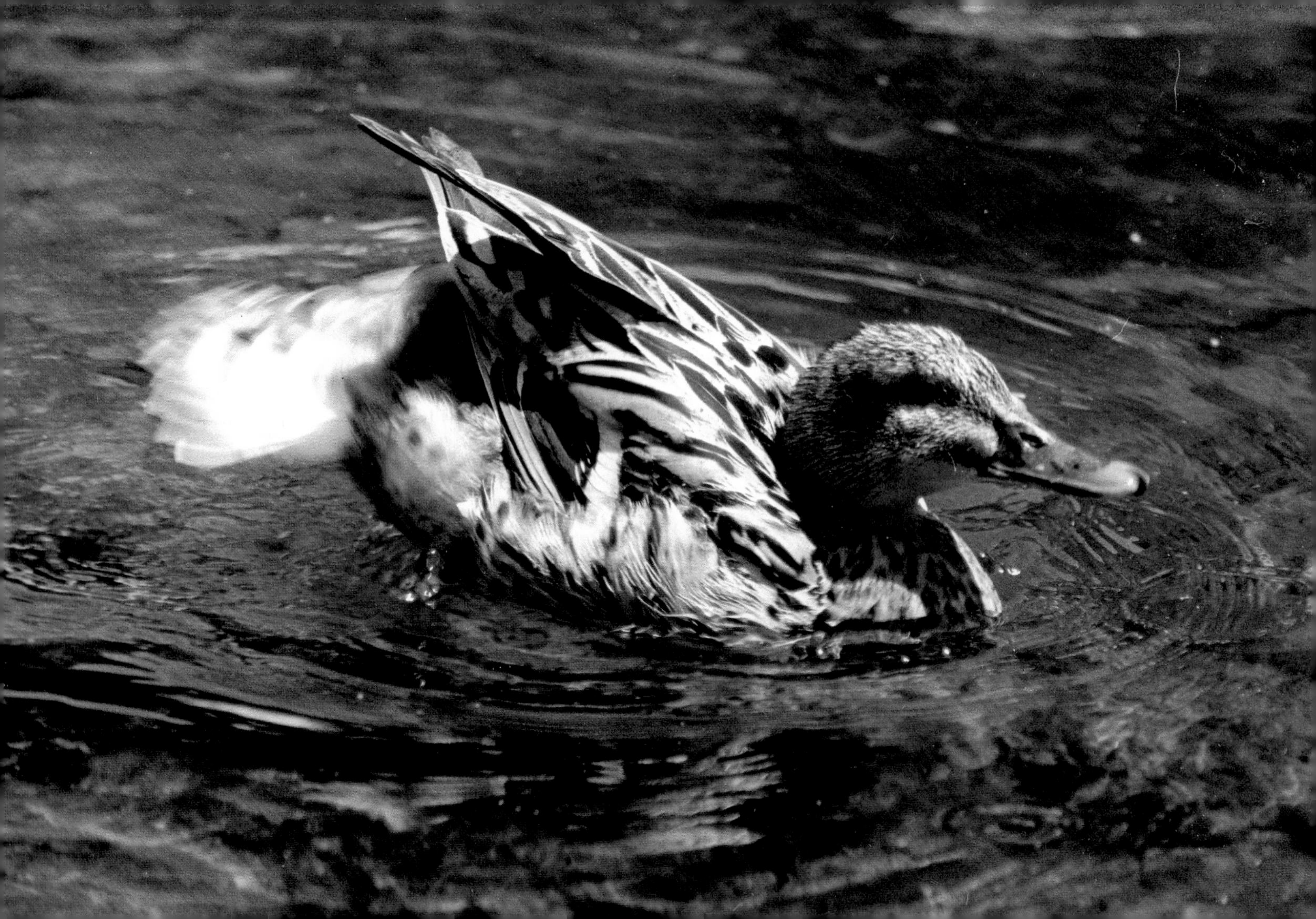

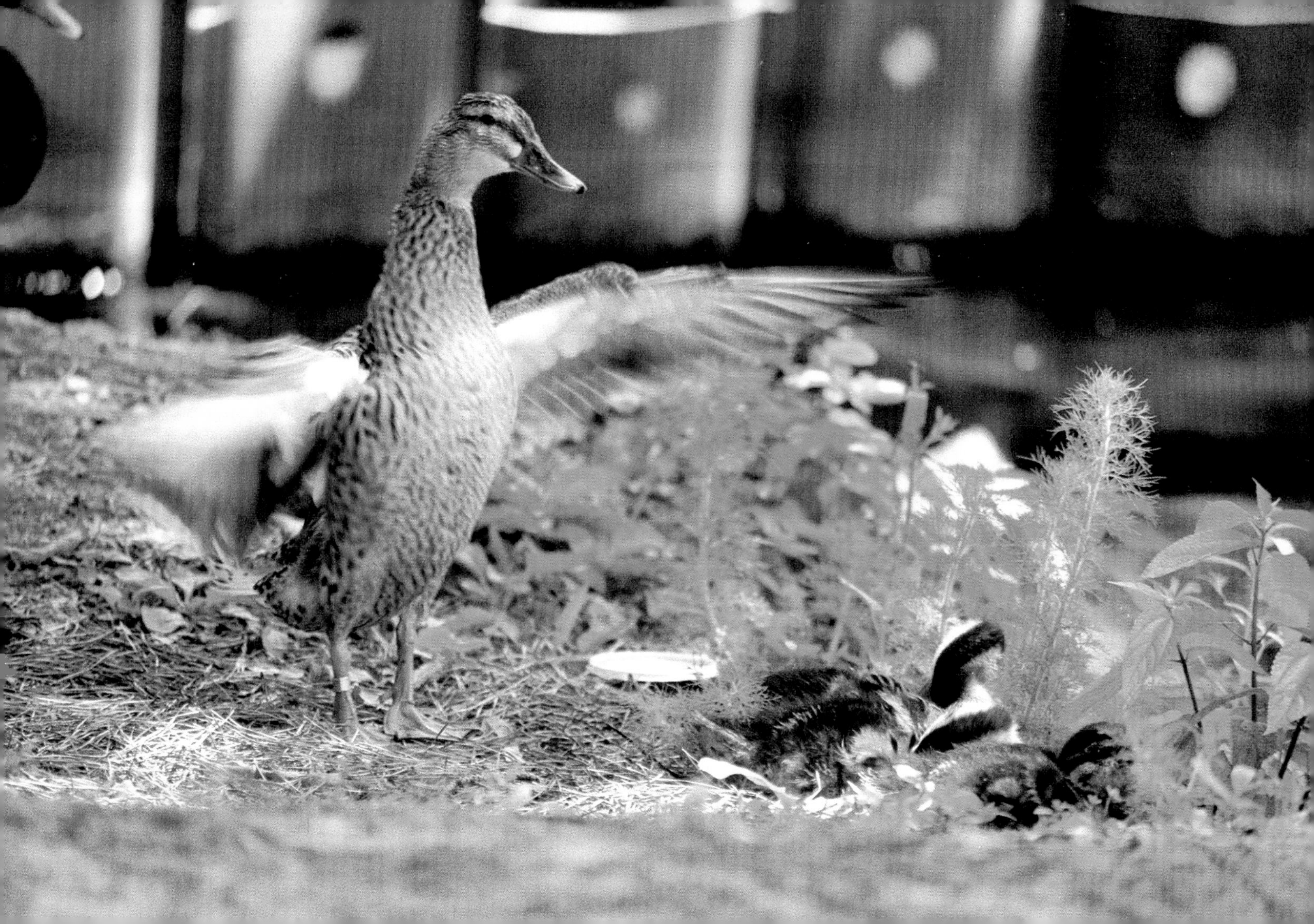

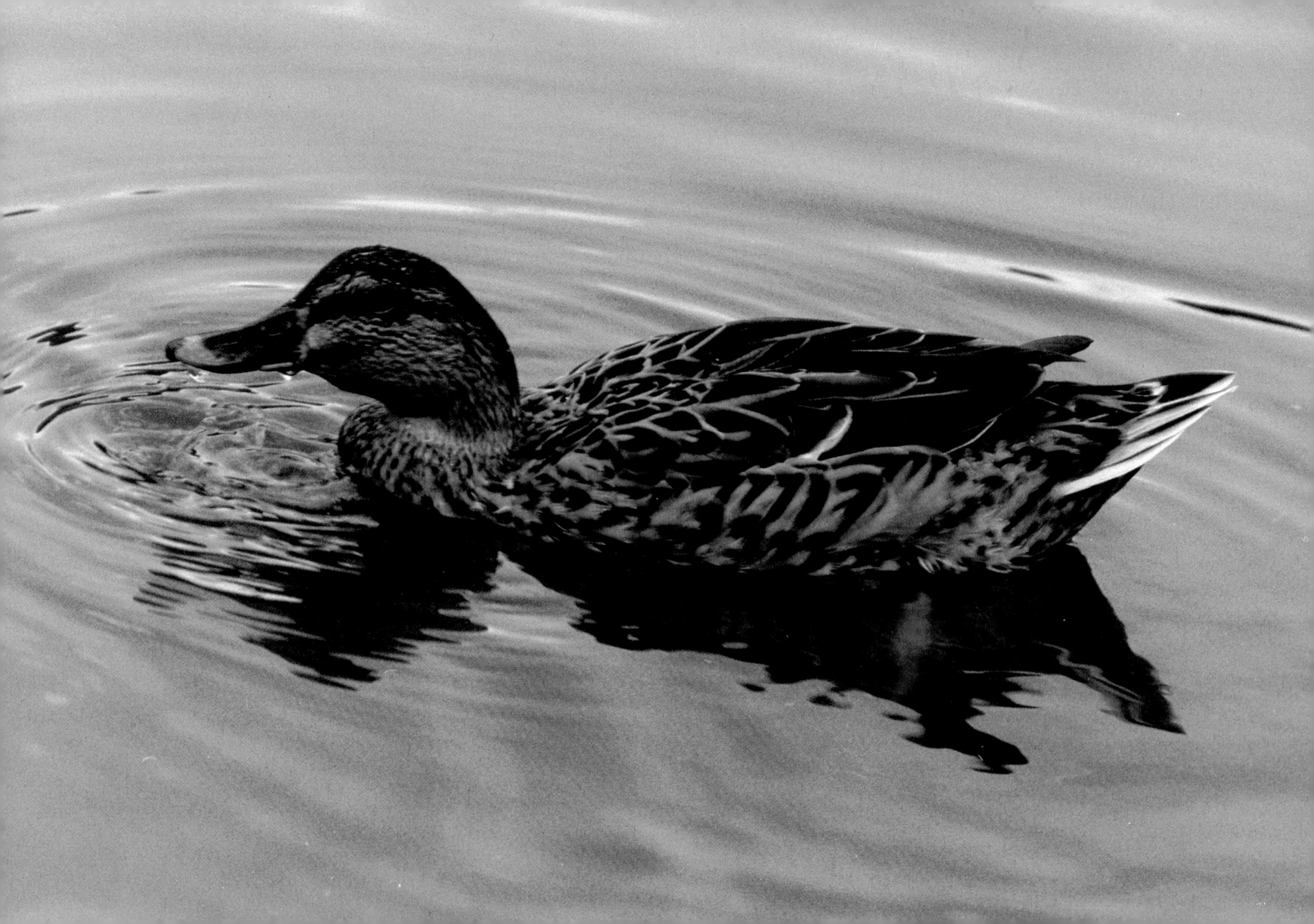

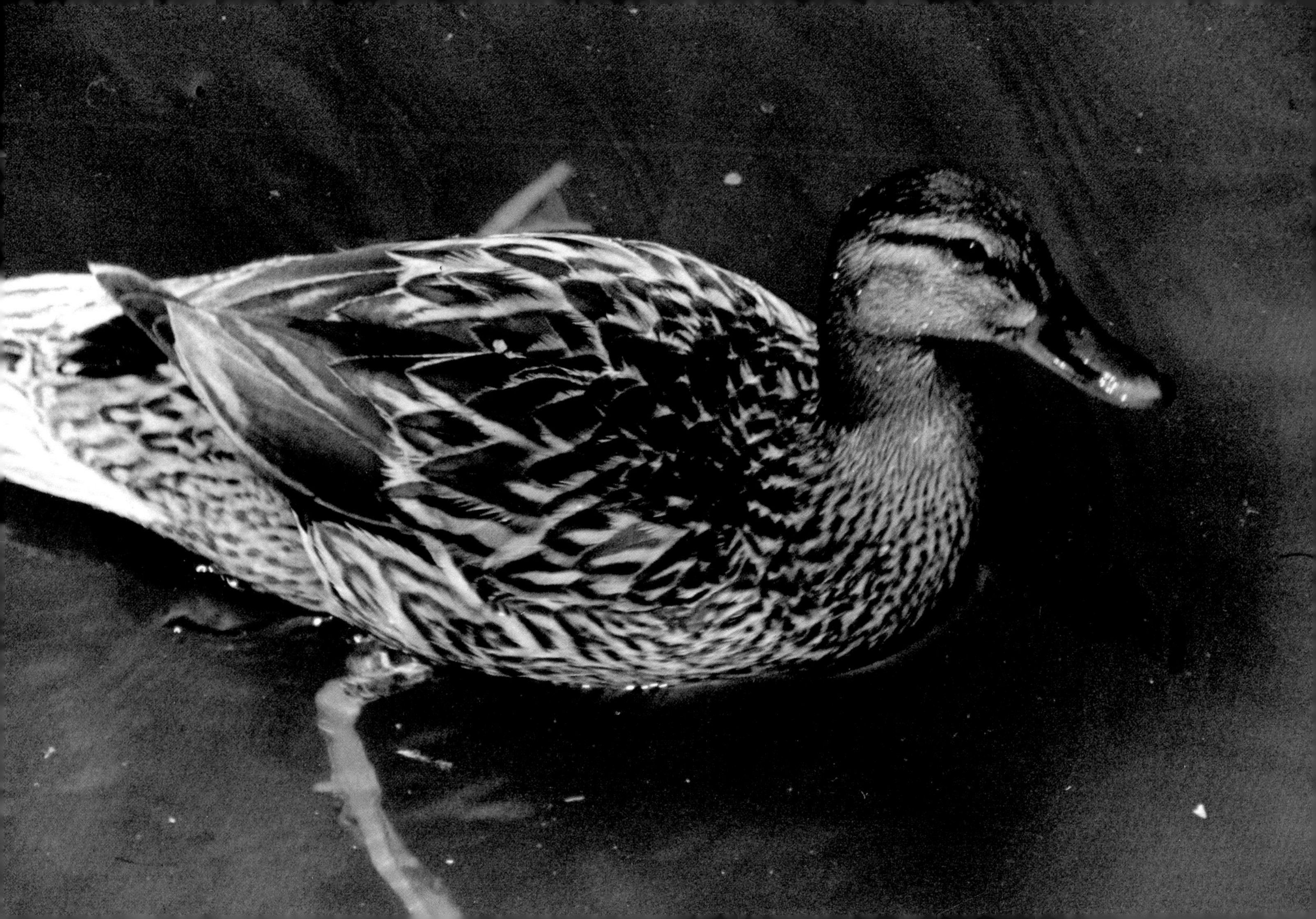

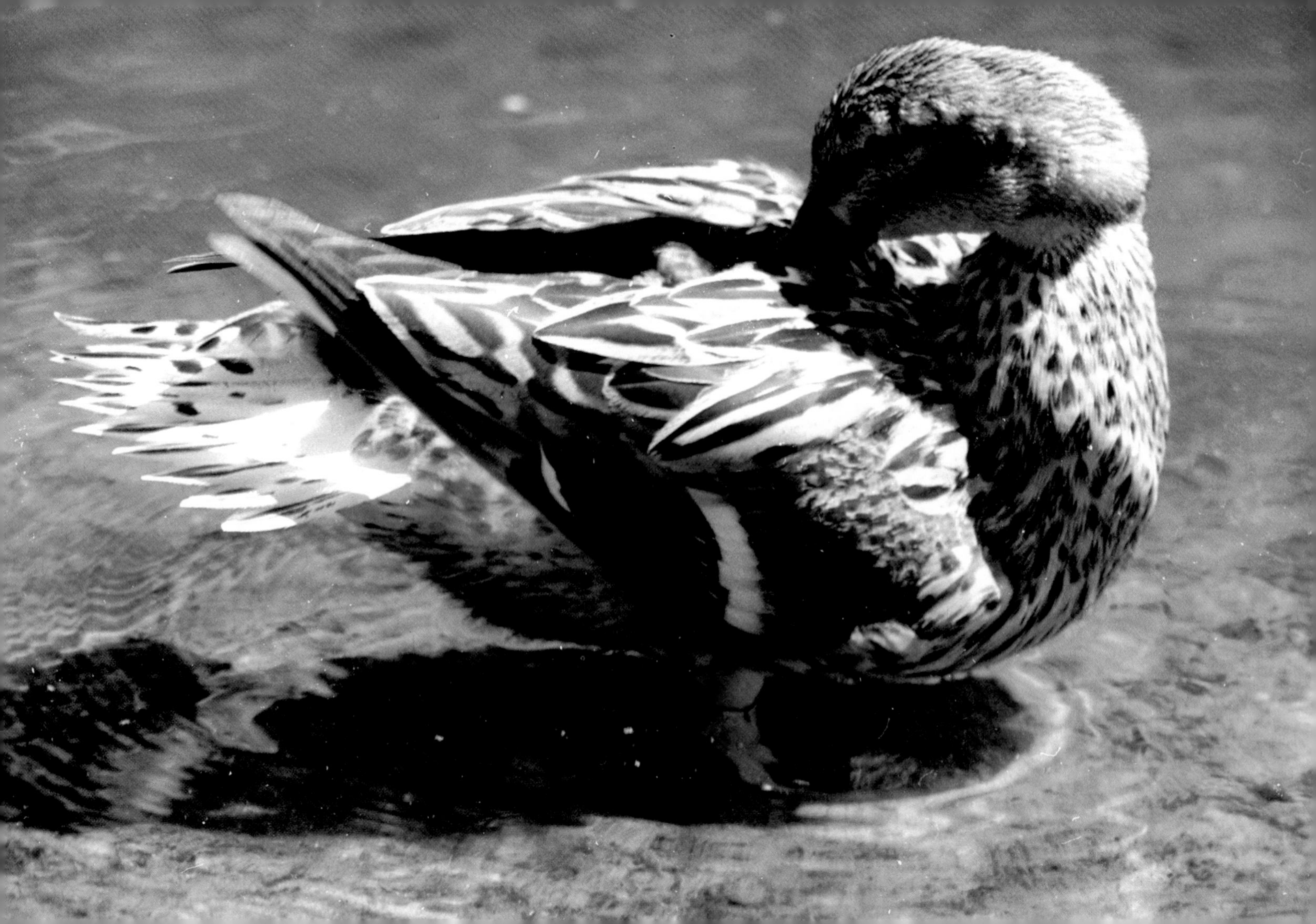

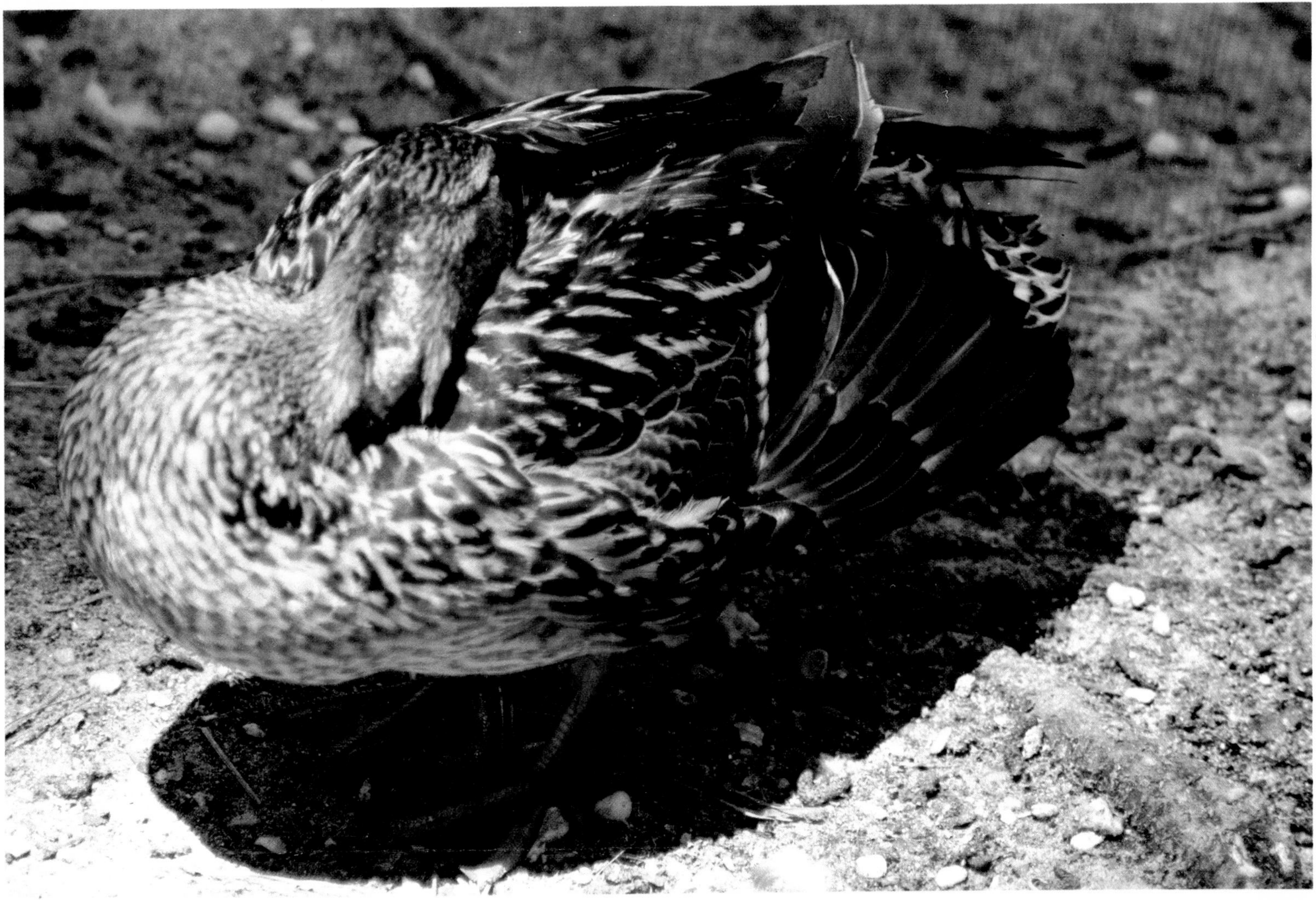

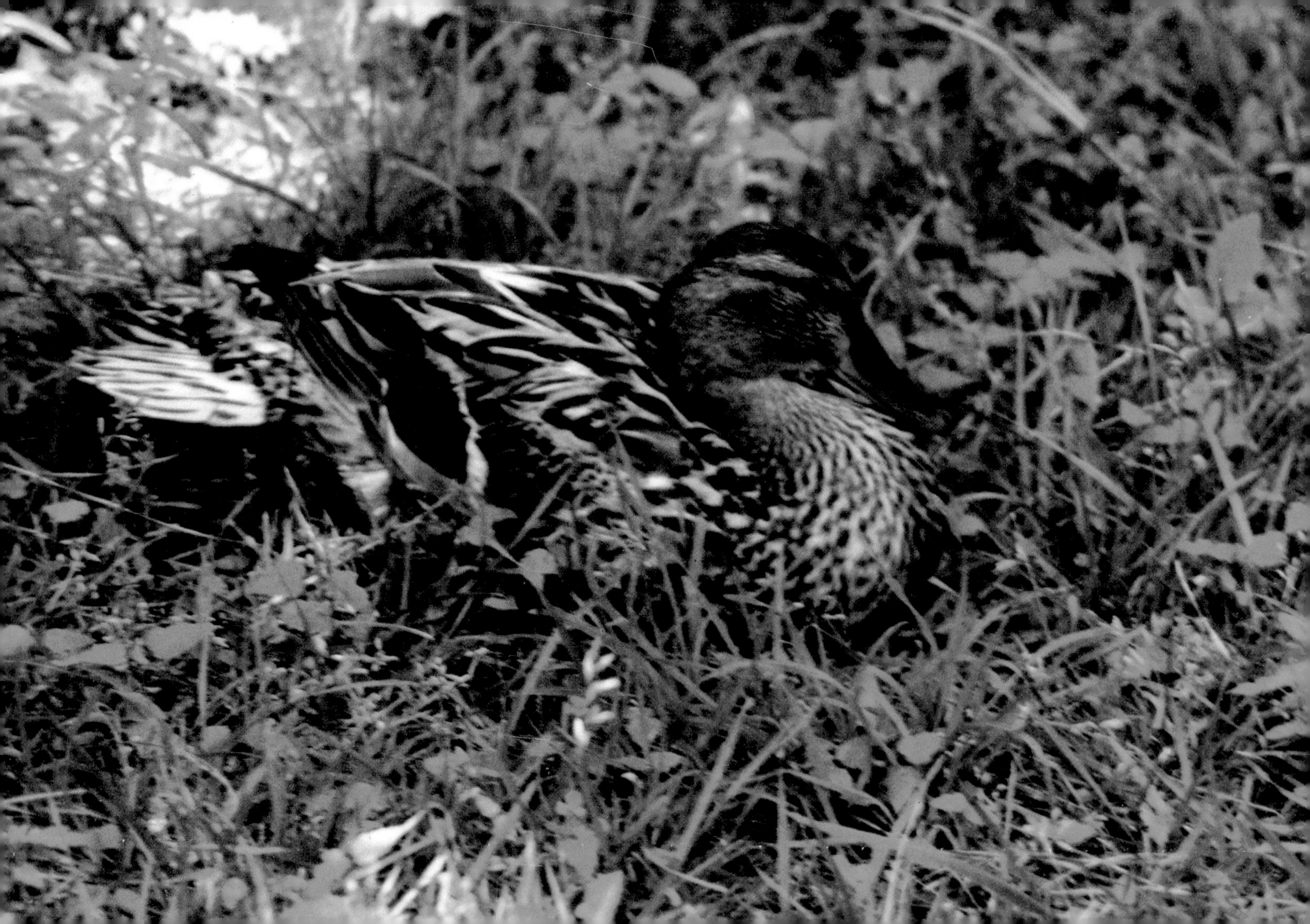